Object-Oriented Application Development with

VisualAge for C++ for OS/2

The VisualAge Series

Bitterer, Brassard, Nadal, and Wong
  VisualAge and Transaction Processing in a Client/Server Environment

Bitterer, Hamada, Oosthuizen, Porciello, and Rambek
  AS/400 Application Development with VisualAge for Smalltalk

Carrel-Billiard, Jakab, Mauny, and Vetter
  Object-Oriented Application Development with VisualAge for C++ for OS/2

Fang, Chu, and Weyerhauser
  VisualAge for Smalltalk SOMsupport: Developing Distributed Object Applications

Fang, Guyet, Haven, Vilmi, and Eckmann
  VisualAge for Smalltalk Distributed: Developing Distributed Object Applications

Object-Oriented Application Development with

VisualAge for C++ for OS/2

Marc Carrel-Billiard
Peter Jakab
Isabelle Mauny
Rainer Vetter

INTERNATIONAL TECHNICAL SUPPORT ORGANIZATION
SAN JOSE, CALIFORNIA 95120

PRENTICE HALL PTR
UPPER SADDLE RIVER, NEW JERSEY 07458

This edition applies to Version 3.0 of the VisualAge for C++ for OS/2 product set, and to all subsequent releases and modifications until otherwise indicated in new editions.

Comments about ITSO Technical Bulletins may be addressed to:
IBM Corporation ITSO, 471/80-E2, 650 Harry Road, San Jose, California 95120-6099

```
For information about redbooks:
http://www.redbooks.ibm.com/redbooks




Send comments to:
redbooks@vnet.ibm.com
```

Published by Prentice Hall PTR
Prentice-Hall, Inc.
A Simon & Schuster Company
Upper Saddle River, NJ 07458

Acquisitions Editor: Michael E. Meehan

Manufacturing Manager: Alexis R. Heydt

Cover Design: Andreas Bitterer, Marc Carrel-Billiard, Design Source

Copy Editors: Maggie Cutler, Mary Lou Nohr

Production Supervision:Patti Guerrieri

The publisher offers discounts on this book when ordered in bulk quantities. For more information, contact:
Corporate Sales Department, Prentice Hall PTR, One Lake Street, Upper Saddle River, NJ 07458
Phone: 800-382-3419; FAX: 201-236-7141; E-mail (Internet): corpsales@prenhall.com

```
For book and bookstore information




http://www.prenhall.com
```

Printed in the United States of America

10 9 8 7 6 5 4 3 2

ISBN   0-13-242447-9

Prentice-Hall International (UK) Limited, *London*
Prentice-Hall of Australia Pty. Limited, *Sydney*
Prentice-Hall Canada Inc., *Toronto*
Prentice-Hall Hispanoamericana, S.A., *Mexico*
Prentice-Hall of India Private Limited, *New Delhi*
Prentice-Hall of Japan, Inc., *Tokyo*
Simon & Schuster Asia Pte. Ltd., *Singapore*
Editora Prentice-Hall do Brasil, Ltda., *Rio de Janeiro*

To my wife, Dominique, for her unfailing support and understanding and to my children, Fanny and Thomas, for their patience and their cheerful smiles. To my parents for giving me a passion.

Marc

This book is dedicated to my wife Mabel and my children Jessie and Justin for their support during the summer of 1995 when I was absent from home for long periods of time. Their love and understanding made my participation in writing this book possible.

Peter

To teamwork and friendship that were our companions all along this writing adventure. I dedicate this book to my family and all those who can understand this little sentence: "A la Gaude!".

Isabelle

To my family and all with whom we are joined together in friendship.

Rainer

Contents

Contents

Figures

Tables

Special Notices

This publication is intended to help project leaders to better understand the VisualAge for C++ environment. The information in this publication is not intended as the specification of any programming interfaces that are provided by VisualAge for C++. See the PUBLICATIONS section of the IBM Programming Announcement for VisualAge for C++ for more information about what publications are considered to be product documentation.

References in this publication to IBM products, programs, or services do not imply that IBM intends to make these available in all countries in which IBM operates. Any reference to an IBM product, program, or service is not intended to state or imply that only IBM's product, program, or service may be used. Any functionally equivalent program that does not infringe any of IBM's intellectual property rights may be used instead of the IBM product, program, or service.

Information in this book was developed in conjunction with use of the equipment specified and is limited in application to those specific hardware and software products and levels.

IBM may have patents or pending patent applications covering subject matter in this document. The furnishing of this document does not give you any license to these patents. You can send license inquiries, in writing, to the IBM Director of Licensing, IBM Corporation, 500 Columbus Avenue, Thornwood, NY 10594 USA.

The information contained in this document has not been submitted to any formal IBM test and is distributed AS IS. The information about non-IBM (VENDOR) products in this manual has been supplied by the vendor and IBM assumes no responsibility for its accuracy or completeness. The use of this information or the implementation of any of these techniques is a customer responsibility and depends on the customer's ability to evaluate and integrate them into the customer's operational environment. While each item may have been reviewed by IBM for accuracy in a specific situation, there is no guarantee that the same or similar results will be obtained elsewhere. Customers attempting to adapt these techniques to their own environments do so at their own risk.

Any performance data contained in this document was determined in a controlled environment; therefore, the results that may be obtained in other operating environments may vary significantly. Users of this document should verify the applicable data for their specific environment.

The following document contains examples of data and reports used in daily business operations. To illustrate them as completely as possible, the examples contain the names of individuals, companies, brands, and products. All of these names are fictitious and any similarity to the names and addresses used by an actual business enterprise is entirely coincidental.

Reference to PTF numbers that have not been released through the normal distribution process does not imply general availability. The purpose of including these reference numbers is to alert IBM customers to specific information relative to the implementation of the PTF when it becomes available to each customer according to the normal IBM PTF distribution process.

The following terms are trademarks of the International Business Machines Corporation in the United States and/or other countries:

AIX®	Common User Acess
CSet ++™	DB2™
CUA™	DB2/2™
Presentation Manager™	IBM®
Multimedia Presentation Manager/2™	OS/2®
SOMobjects™	OS/2 Warp®
Workplace Shell™	VisualAge™
WebExplorer™	WorkFrame/2™

The following terms are trademarks of other companies:

Windows™ is a trademark of Microsoft® Corporation.

PC Direct™ is a trademark of Ziff Communications Company and is used by IBM Corporation under licence.

UNIX® is a registered trademark in the United States and other countries, licensed exclusively through X/Open Company Limited.

C-bus™ is a trademark of Collary, Inc.

i386™ and Pentium™ are trademarks of Intel Corporation.

Smalltalk™ is a trademark of Xerox Corporation.

Motif® is a registered trademark of Open Software Foundation.

Solaris® is registered trademark of Sun Microsystems.

Other trademarks are trademarks of their respective companies.

The icons used in this book are from the ClipArt Collection of the CorelDRAW! Version 3 CDROM.

Some videos provided with the sample application are extracted from the CDROM Nitro Explosive Animationen © 1994 Data Becker.

Preface

Welcome to the world of visual programming! With VisualAge for C++ for OS/2 you are ready to take the plunge into a radically new trend of programming. If you have just bought your IBM VisualAge for C++ and you are dying to build your first serious application, you are reading the right book. Indeed, learning VisualAge for C++ by example is all this book is about. With VisualAge for C++, application construction has never been easier. Even the most complex applications can be constructed from the large set of predefined parts from IBM Open class. This book will show you how you can employ IBM VisualAge for C++ for OS/2, Version 3.0 to implement software systems that have been analyzed and designed by use of object-oriented methods. It introduces the Visual Modeling Technique, a complementary approach of existing object-oriented development techniques and illustrates how this approach is applied to build a real application featuring relational database support, video and vivid sound capacity, and numerous graphical controls for a truly intuitive graphical user interface.

What Makes This Book Different

This book explains how to develop an application from the requirements specifications up to its coding with VisualAge for C++. Throughout the different chapters, you will be guided to develop your static and dynamic object models, using the Visual Modeling Technique. Then, you will translate your models visually in Visual Builder and generate their code automatically. This book is neither just a book on methodology nor just a book on programming: it is both of them!

For the first time, a book takes you by hand to roll out a complete application development cycle. So put on your cap of analyst-designer-developer and get ready for a trip to the visual programming world!

How This Book Is Organized

This book consists of three parts. The first part (chapters 1 and 2) introduces concepts and terms that go with visual programming and object-orientation and gives a first insight into the VisualAge for C++ development environment. In the second part (chapters 3 and 4), we present the sample application that you will build in the last part. This part is devoted to analyzing and designing the static and dynamic model of the application to ease its implementation with VisualAge for C++. The third part (chapters 5, 6, 7, 8, 9, and 10)

makes up the majority of the book, teaching you how to use VisualAge for C++ and its versatile tools to develop the sample application from the ground up.

❑ **Chapter 1, "VisualAge for C++ and Application Development," on page 3**

The first chapter welcomes you to the visual age of application development. You learn something about the new trends of software construction that have emerged during the past few years and how VisualAge for C++ meets these new challenges.

❑ **Chapter 2, "Getting Started in a VisualAge for C++ Environment," on page 19**

The second chapter provides an overview of all of the tools and features that are part of the VisualAge for C++ package. We do not intend to replace the user's guides, but we want to give you the keys that let you start off applying the tools.

❑ **Chapter 3, "Analysts at Work," on page 61**

This chapter and the next one invite you to play the role of a novelist. We compare the analysis and design phases that precede the implementation of a successful and neatly structured software system to the introductory work to be done before writing a bestseller. This chapter focuses on the analysis phase of our sample application.

❑ **Chapter 4, "Designers at Work," on page 83**

This chapter concentrates on the design phase.

❑ **Chapter 5, "Setting Up the Development Environment," on page 107**

This chapter describes the preparatory work that paves the way for well-organized software construction. You are advised how to favorably initialize your new project in the WorkFrame/2 environment.

❑ **Chapter 6, "Mapping Relational Tables Using Data Access Builder," on page 127**

This chapter and the next two feature the Visual Builder! During the development of this book, we enjoyed most dealing with this tool and assume that you also will get excited when you read how we succeeded in implementing the sample application. You will reap the best benefit if you duplicate the implementation process step by step following our instructions. In this chapter, you will use Data Access Builder to bring persistency to your application and enable your objects to be stored in a relational database.

❏ **Chapter 7, "Creating Visual Parts," on page 143**

This chapter will guide you in developing the graphical user interface of your application, using the visual parts provided with VisualAge for C++. Most of the parts are used in our sample application, and you will be shown hints and tips to make the best of them.

❏ **Chapter 8, "Creating Nonvisual Parts," on page 213**

Unlike other GUI development tools, Visual Builder allow you to develop your business object as nonvisual parts. In this chapter, we will show you how to develop the nonvisual parts that are used in the sample application.

❏ **Chapter 9, "Connecting the Parts," on page 227**

Once you have built your visual and nonvisual parts, you are ready to draw graphically the connections between them. In this chapter, we show you how to connect your different parts to trigger messages from one object to another to let your application perform. Then, you just need to generate automatically the C++ source code of your application and compile it! Throughout these last three chapters, we will focus on showing how to map your static and dynamic models from your detail phase to VisualAge for C++.

❏ **Chapter 10, "If You Want to Know More about Visual Builder...," on page 323**

If your curiosity is still not satisfied or if you want to take a closer look at some technical details, you should keep on reading. This chapter answers some questions that you did not ask before, such as: *What about the notification framework?* or *Can I reuse my legacy code?*

Related Publications

The publications listed in this section are considered particularly suitable for a more detailed discussion of the topics covered in this book.

❏ *Object-Oriented Software Engineering. A Use Case Driven Approach* by I. Jacobson, M. Christerson, P. Jonsson, and G. Övergaard. Addison-Wesley Publishing Company, 1992. ISBN 0-201-54435-0.

❏ *Object-Oriented Modeling and Design* by J. Rumbaugh, M. Blaha, W. Premerlani, F. Eddy, and W. Lorenson. Prentice Hall, 1991. ISBN 0-13-630054-5.

❏ *Designing Object-Oriented Software* by R. Wirfs-Brock, B. Wilkerson, and L. Wiener. Prentice Hall, 1990.

❏ *Modern Structured Analysis* by E. Yourdon. Yourdon Press, Englewood Cliffs, New Jersey, 1989.

❏ *Object-Oriented Analysis and Design with Applications* by G. Booch. The Benjamin/Cummings Publishing Company, 1994.

❏ *Object Technology in Application Development* by D. Tkach & R. Puttick. Benjamin/Cummings Publishing Company, 1994. ISBN 0-8053-2572-5.

❏ *Visual Modeling Technique—Object Technology Using Visual Programming* by D. Tkach, W. Fang, and A. So. Benjamin/Cummings Publishing Company, 1995. ISBN 0-8053-2574-3.

❏ *Effective C++: 50 Specific Ways to Improve Your Programs and Designs* by S. Meyers. Addison-Wesley, 1992.

❏ *OS/2 C++ Class Library, Power GUI Programming with C Set++* by K. Leong, W. Law, R. Love, H. Tsuji, and B. Olson. VNR Computer Library, 1993. ISBN 0-442-01795-2

❏ *C++ Programming Guide.*

❏ *C++ User's Guide.*

❏ *Open Class Library User's Guide.*

❏ *Visual Builder User's Guide.*

❏ *Building VisualAge for C++ parts for Fun and Profit.*

International Technical Support Organization Publications

❏ *Object Technology in Application Development*, GG24-4290.

❏ *Client/Server Computing: The Design and Coding of a Business Application*, GG24-3899.

A complete list of International Technical Support Organization publications, known as redbooks, with a brief description of each, can be found as follows:

To obtain a catalog of ITSO redbooks, VNET users should type:

```
TOOLS SENDTO WTSCPOK TOOLS REDBOOKS GET REDBOOKS CATALOG
```

A listing of all redbooks, sorted by category, can also be found on MKT-TOOLS as ITSOPUB LISTALLX. This package is updated monthly.

How to Order ITSO Redbooks ─────────────────

IBM employees in the USA may order ITSO books and CD-ROMs by using PUBORDER. Customers in the USA may order by calling 1-800-879-2755 or by faxing 1-800-445-9269. Visa and Master Card are accepted. Outside the USA, customers should contact their local IBM office.

Customers may order hardcopy ITSO books individually or in customized sets, called GBOFs, which relate to specific functions of interest. IBM employees and customers may also order ITSO books in online format on CD-ROM collections, which contain redbooks on a variety of products.

International Technical Support Organization on the World Wide Web (WWW)

Internet users can find information about redbooks on the ITSO World Wide Web home page. To access the ITSO Web pages, point your Web browser (such as WebExplorer™ from the OS/2 3.0 Warp BonusPak) to the following:

```
http://www.redbooks.ibm.com/redbooks
```

IBM internal users may also download redbooks or scan through red-book abstracts. Point your web browser to the internal IBM Redbooks home page:

```
http://w3.itso.ibm.com/redbooks/redbooks.html
```

International Technical Support Organization on the Internet

If you do not have World Wide Web access, you can obtain the list of all current redbooks through the Internet by anonymous FTP to:

```
ftp.almaden.ibm.com
cd redbooks
get itsopub.txt
```

The FTP server, *ftp.almaden.ibm.com*, also stores the sample from the accompanying CD. To retrieve the sample files, issue the following commands from the */redbooks* directory:

```
cd GG242593
binary
get GG242593.EXE
ascii
get READ.ME
```

All users of ITSO publications are encouraged to provide feedback to improve quality over time. Send questions about and feedback on redbooks to:

❏ REDBOOK at WTSCPOK
❏ REDBOOK@VNET.IBM.COM
❏ USIB5FWN at IBMMAIL

VisualAge for C++ Support

VisualAge for C++ Service and Support is staffed by developers who handle everything from how-to's to complex technical problems. The resolution may take the form of education, a workaround, or a fix to the product (Corrective Service Diskette, CSDs).

There are several ways to contact the VisualAge for C++ Service and Support department electronically:

❏ **CompuServe™ forums:** GO OS2DF1, library section 4

❏ **Internet**
  • anonymous logon to site ftp.software.ibm.com, directory: ps/products/visualagecpp/fixes/V30
  • sample URL: ftp://ftp.software.ibm.com/ps/products/visualagecpp/fixes/v30

❏ **Talklink (OS/2 Selected Fixes Area)**
  • 1-800-547-1283 for information (USA)
  • 1-800-465-7999 x228 for information (Canada)

❏ **Developer's Connection (DEVCON) CD**
  • Ordering information: 1-800-561-5293 (Canada) and 1-800-6DE-VCON (USA)
  • See also: http://www.austin.ibm.com/developer/programs/DevCon/OS2/faqAE.html for world-wide ordering information

❏ **IBM PC Co. BBS**
  • 1-919-517-0001 8,N,1
  • 1-800-772-2227 for information

About the Authors

Marc Carrel-Billiard, from IBM France, works at the IBM International Technical Support Organization in San Jose, California. You can reach him by e-mail at carrel@vnet.ibm.com.

Peter Jakab works for the IBM Software Solutions Laboratory in Toronto Canada. You can reach him by e-mail at pjakab@vnet.ibm.com.

Isabelle Mauny works in La Gaude (France) for the IBM EMEA Software Technical Support. You can reach her by e-mail at isamauny@vnet.ibm.com.

Rainer Vetter works in Stuttgart for the Developer Support Organization of IBM Germany. You can reach him by e-mail at rvetter@de.ibm.com.

Acknowledgments

This book would not have been possible without the help of the following people who contributed information, resources, and technical advice: Ueli Wahli and Walter Fang, IBM ITSO San Jose, Sergio Henrique Monteiro da Silva, IBM Brazil, Mike Polan, IBM Toronto, George DeCandio, Rich Kulp, Dale Nilsson, IBM Research Triangle Park.

Many thanks to Jens Tiedemann, ITSO San Jose Center Manager, Petter Sommerfelt, ITSO San Jose Center DM/ST Manager, and Barbara Isa, IBM Santa Teresa Lab, for getting this project started. Special thanks to everyone at the ITSO San Jose Center, in particular Elsa Barron, Mary Comianos, Stephanie Manning, Alan Tippett, and Guido De Simoni for their continuous support and to Andi Bitterer for designing the book cover and for speeding up the publishing process through his former experience. We are extremely grateful to Maggie Cuttler for meticulously editing our frenchy-germano interpretation of the Shakespeare language and whose patience and support continues to amaze us! Thanks also to Mike Meehan, and Patti Guerrieri at Prentice Hall for his support and to Lou Evart at Softline International Inc. for making this book look like a book.

Part 1

Introduction to the VisualAge for C++ Environment

We are condemned to live in interesting times.

-Chinese Proverb

Where are the good old days? Those days when computer vendors provided not only mainframes with appropriate operating systems but also matching software tools to extend the base equipment. When salesmen led happy lives supporting their two or three favorite customers. When application developers could focus on database transactions, concentrate their efforts on implementing the business logic, and forget about the user interface—because terminals behaved like typewriters, and the poor person who was allowed to give some piece of input felt like an external device, closely connected to the applications. Those days, when programmers as software gurus hacked thousands of lines of read-only code into their editors, are gone.

Look how times have changed! More people work out of their home offices, where they write at least a few lines of code in their preferred languages and fiddle with configuration files to tailor their individual environments. New technologies provide screens with brilliant graphical views of the user interface. Under constraints, programmers must build complex programs and be responsive to new requirements or changing environments. And most challenging of all, thousands of hardware and software suppliers freely offer their products but show little concern for connectivity.

Yes, those good old days have gone, and what we need right now are new tools and techniques to develop mission-critical applications that can run on various platforms and be easily adapted to new requirements. Otherwise, the software crisis will never end.

1

VisualAge for C++ and Application Development

When we look at the manufacturing industry, we find that many manufacturers use components to build their products. We discover that many standardized elements, such as bolts and nuts, can be purchased anywhere. We learn that companies use the same component for different products; for example, car manufacturers use the same rear-view mirror for all of their models or the same clutch for many of their models. We realize that, before going into actual production, engineers build a mock-up that reveals possible construction faults.

When we look at the software industry, we find that many new products are built from scratch, and for a number of reasons: A new programming language appears that is supposed to easily solve problems of a certain domain, an application requires a new database system that causes many changes in existing software, a new team member arrives with new and better ideas, or an old team member leaves the company, accompanied by all of his or her undocumented knowledge.

We discover that there are no standardized software modules on which programmers can rely. We learn that there are many function collections, so-called program libraries, that help deal with various software domains, such as databases, networks, communications, and graphical user interfaces (GUIs). If programmers want to use those libraries, however, they must laboriously look for each function and its parameters, leafing through multivolume manuals. Furthermore, if programmers mix libraries from different producers, they are often confronted with compatibility problems, such as duplicate names.

VisualAge for C++ does not do away with low-level function libraries and cannot prevent library producers from using the same names, but it supports the building of well-designed models and software parts that can be reused in multiple applications and on different hardware and software platforms.

Visual Programming

During the past 10 years, software designers have enriched the presentation of operating systems on personal computers and workstations, providing users with GUIs. At the same time, software developers have begun to accommodate their applications to this new environment.

The benefits of GUIs from the user's perspective are obvious:

❑ Users no longer have to type command lines with many arguments and cryptic options.

❑ Users can control applications more intuitively.

❑ Users can simultaneously look at different views.

❑ Applications look polished and provide a consistent interface.

Programmers, however, must deal with hundreds of new functions that exploit the capabilities of the GUI, and they must cope with a new programming approach: event-driven programming.

In the event-driven programming paradigm, programmers send messages to graphical elements, and, if an event occurs, the graphical system sends a message to a function that programmers must provide. So, from the developer's perspective, the disadvantages of a GUI also are obvious:

❑ New concepts must be learned quickly.

❑ Complexity increases.

❑ Thus, development time increases.

To shorten both the learning curve and development time, some large and small software companies alike offer tools that enable programmers to develop applications visually. Thus, programmers do not have to invoke their editors to start writing a new program; they can build the GUI by designing it on their screens. But, of course, there is more than the GUI—programmers must be able to add business logic and data access transactions. The trouble begins exactly at this point. With most existing tools, programmers can no longer develop visually; they must provide the code manually. Using VisualAge for C++, however, programmers can continue to work visually, because they have the components for building not only a GUI but also the entire application, including database access and multimedia features.

Before you can enjoy the powerful tools of VisualAge for C++, you should be acquainted with object-oriented application development, an approach that has begun to emerge as the software world becomes more and more complex. The GUI challenges us, as does the need for remote data access, with its underlying communication protocols, and the fact that we cannot quickly rewrite existing code to adapt it to a new hardware or software environment. We need methods and tools to help us comprehend and deal with this challenging complexity.

Instead of decomposing huge applications into procedures, today's software specialists understand problems as assemblies of objects. This approach simplifies their views of problems and helps translate those views into software. Object-oriented languages, in which the concept of objects is inherent, support programmers in their translation efforts.

Programmers do not necessarily have to use an object-oriented language; they could implement objects and their behavior by using a procedural language. Procedural languages, however, involve a certain degree of danger; namely, they do not hinder programmers from arbitrarily accessing objects. Programmers can directly modify an object's data during the execution of every module, so they must alter many modules whenever an object changes its behavior or data structure.

With object-oriented languages, programmers can access an object's data only within certain modules, so they know where to apply the changes. In addition, because the object-oriented approach includes an analysis and design phase that programmers must go through before they start writing programs, they are unlikely to write poorly structured code. In this book we explain all phases of the object-oriented approach and show you how to put the approach into practice with the help of VisualAge for C++.

Object Talk

In this section, we introduce some object-oriented terms and concepts that we use throughout this book. You will not find an in-depth discussion of the object-oriented approach to software development or the definition of every object-oriented term. If you are interested in an extensive explanation of object-orientation, we recommend that you consult the books listed in the Related Publications section.

Objects

In our real world, an object is, according to *Webster's Dictionary*:

Something perceptible, especially to the sense of touch or vision.

Indeed, according to this definition, we have a large assortment of objects! Let us take a car as an example. If you ask two people to describe a certain car, they will probably give two completely different answers, on the basis of their knowledge, their way of looking at and evaluating things, and their interests. A passionate driver will tell you about the car's motor and give you many other technical details about the internal workings of the car. A person who has never driven a car will tell you about the color of the car, its estimated length, width, and height, and anything else that is visible. No one, however, can give a "correct" description that encompasses all properties of a car. Even a car's manufacturer, who knows every element of the car, would fail to describe it correctly, because he or she would not know its current mileage or the amount of missing tire rubber. Objects in our real world have an infinite number of attributes and purposes. A car's purpose is as a driving machine, but it also can be (mis)used, as a dog house, for example.

In driving schools, instructors describe a car by emphasizing its function and explaining how to handle the steering wheel, gearshift, and pedals and how to interpret the indicators on the dashboard. In technical terms, we can say that instructors explain the interface of the car, how different input parameters influence the car's behavior, and how drivers can understand the car's output values.

So we see that real-life objects have various properties, namely:

❑ Attributes, such as color, length, width, height, weight, and mass

❑ Interfaces, such as steering wheels, pedals, and door handles

❑ Functions or actions, such as driving, braking, or sheltering dogs

By now we should have some idea of how we can realize the transition from our real world to the virtual world of computers. Of course, the object-oriented approach did not invent this transition, but it facilitates it in a neat and transparent manner. Procedural programming languages offer primitive data types, such as integers, floating-point numbers, characters, and pointers. Additionally, they offer compound data types, so-called structures or records, where several elements with primitive or compound data types can be stored. Object-oriented languages offer a particular data type that can store all properties of an object and guarantee that the object's attributes are manipulated only by its own functions or well-defined interfaces.

In the procedural approach, an object generally is divided into structures that contain its attributes and procedures that deliver its functions and operate with its data. The disadvantage of using procedural languages is that nothing (except rigid discipline) prevents programmers from directly manipulating the data of other objects. Although such manipulation was not originally intended, programmers are inclined to do so when there are time constraints. Therefore, the procedures and data structures of different objects often are heavily interdependent, which makes reusability almost impossible and complicates the process of extending the software system.

Objects in computer environments, once they are designed, are discrete, have a limited number of attributes, and behave as defined (but sometimes not as intended). Software objects represent real-life objects but are implemented in a manner that is appropriate for a particular problem. Again, let us take a car as an example of an object. For an application that supports car sellers, designers implement the car object with attributes that are important for marketing purposes, such as price, horsepower, color, and number of air bags. These attributes are rather high level, because customers usually are not interested in the amount of steel or aluminum that was used to produce the car. For an application that supports the car manufacturing process, however, designers must assign more attributes to the car object, because engineers are interested in details that are essential to the building of a car. In both applications, the car object adopts only some of its real-world attributes.

Classes

If we consult Webster's dictionary again, we find that a class is defined as:

A set or group whose members share at least one attribute.

This definition also offers unlimited possibilities. Let us take, for example, animals, as all members share the haveOrganism attribute. Biology teaches us that humans also share the haveOrganism attribute, so according to Webster's definition, humans belong to the same class. Sorry? Another example: car is a class, as all members have the fourWheels attribute. Rollerskates also share the fourWheels attribute, so they belong to the same class. Sorry again?

These examples show how difficult it sometimes is to find the correct level of abstraction. Here, of course, it is quite obvious that we chose the wrong level. Animals and humans do belong to the same class, but to a more generalized class, say, livingBeings. Rollerskates and cars can belong to the more generalized class, fourWheeled. We notice that we can describe classes in more abstract terms than we can describe objects.

We chose our first example of a class from science, not accidentally, as biologists actually group the world of living beings into classes, such as mammals, cold-blooded animals, and microbes. Chemists group substances into classes, for example, organic and inorganic substances, and physicists deal with solid, liquid, and gaseous substances. We see that in every domain scientists use classes to structure our complex world into comprehensive groups. Depending on the current focus of our interest, the classification may be very detailed.

Classes in computer environments are invented to structure a software problem and thus should be regarded as groups whose members share several (not just one) attributes or provide similar function. In our examples of both objects and classes, we look at cars. The Car class contains the set of all cars. Every car provides the same function and has similar attributes and interfaces. This fact is quite obvious because experienced drivers can operate every car entrusted to them, even if they have never seen a certain model before. The Car class describes the general functions that all cars have in common. A car object is a distinct instance of the Car class, such as your car or the car parked in your preferred space.

Inheritance

In real life we know the term "inheritance" very well, as we all dream of coming into a small fortune through inheritance. Its meaning in the object-oriented paradigm is completely different, however.

Strictly speaking, inheritance in the object-oriented world relates more to its biological meaning, because one class does not bequeath its properties to another class and pass away; the new class originally looks and behaves like its parent class, and the two classes coexist. The class designer specializes the new class by adding or changing the original attributes or functions, so that the class can fulfill its intended purpose. You can compare this work to that of a car design engineer who wants to create a new model. He or she probably does not begin from scratch but takes an existing car as a prototype, modifies it here and there, perhaps removing the roof to come up with a convertible version.

Note that the design engineer designs the new model by using drawings, or better, with the help of a computer-aided design (CAD) program. Consider also that the removal of the roof incurs many subsequent changes. We can assume that a car without a roof requires a different chassis, different front doors, and other parts that will differentiate it from a car with a roof. So, we do not recommend applying inheritance when the derived class undergoes this kind of change, because the main benefit of inheritance (and here we come back to computer science) should be reuse of existing classes.

Look at Figure 1. The Convertible class is a specialization of the Car class, and the Car class is a generalization of the Convertible class. A generalization of the Car class would be Vehicle. Inheritance means that the specialized class adopts all properties of its ancestor class; that is, the specialized class behaves exactly like the ancestor class and owns the same attributes. In fact, if you derive from an existing class, you work on its copy. But, you can add new attributes and functions to the derived (specialized) class or change existing functions. For example, the openSunRoof function is no longer valid for the Convertible class, whereas the rollbar attribute is not present in the Car class.

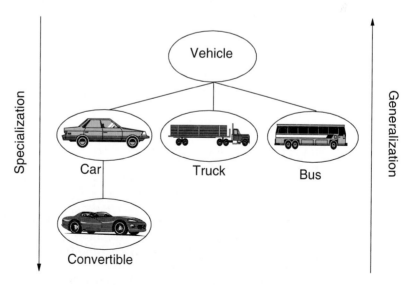

Figure 1. Inheritance

The ability of the descendants of a class to inherit all functions of their ancestor provides the means of reusing code. Modification of common behavior need be implemented only once, namely, inside the functions of the ancestor class.

Encapsulation

The implementation details of a car's functions are hidden from drivers, who must know only how to handle the interfaces.

Car drivers should treat their engines with care and shift the gears appropriately. For beginners, the procedure of depressing the clutch, shifting gears, letting out the clutch, and letting in the clutch again is most challenging during the first few lessons at a driving school. In cars equipped with automatic transmissions, drivers can shift gears without having to use any additional pedals or shifts. The gear change is encapsulated inside the acceleration process, so that drivers need only operate the gas pedal. Drivers also know that as soon as they apply the brakes, the car slows down, but they do not know (and do not care) whether the brake pedal activates a disk brake or a drum brake.

Object-oriented programming languages as well offer encapsulation. Objects reveal only their interfaces, not their internal implementation. Callers of the functions do not care how the underlying algorithms are implemented, but they rely on the promised behavior of the function.

Polymorphism

The term *polymorphism* looks so strange that we consult Webster's again and find it defined as:

Genetic variation that produces differing characteristics in individuals of the same population or species.

Well, this definition in itself looks strange. So let us try to understand the meaning of polymorphism by looking at its Greek root and constructing a noun phrase from the result: *poly* means many or multiple, *morph* means shape or form. So, we define polymorphism as:

Ability of a thing or organism to exist in multiple forms.

In the real world, we can find such examples as wax or amoebas. When you visit wax museums you can see that wax really exists in many different forms. And if you happen to have access to a microscope and a culture of microorganisms, you can see that amoebas constantly change shape as they move and engulf food.

Polymorphism in an object-oriented sense differs slightly from wax and amoebas. The characteristic of having different forms can also be interpreted as providing flexible, that is, nondetermined, behavior. Let us take a crisp example from real life: When you step on the tail of a dog, it barks, whereas when you step on the tail of a cat, it meows. With all apologies to the pet world, this is polymorphism in action! The same action executed on different species (understand type of object) provokes different reactions. Let us look at how polymorphism applies in your everyday life as a programmer.

Generally, when you invoke a function, you expect a determined flow of execution, because the function is designed and implemented to carry out a particular task. In pure object-oriented languages, however, a function is always coupled to a class. At coding time, the exact class that is coupled to the function when it executes need not (and often cannot) be known. Then, during run time, when the function is called, the class that actually executes the invoked function can be the specified class or a descendant of that class.

Say, for example, that we want to call the draw function of the Figure class, and we expect that the actual object should draw itself on the screen. We do not care, however, whether during run time the actual object will be an instance of the Circle or Square class, both of which are descendants of the Figure class. Obviously, the draw function behaves differently according to the actual class. In future releases of the application, one or more new descendants of figure might exist, for example, the Triangle class, which also provides its draw function. The good thing is that the caller of the draw function does not have to know about the existence of the new class.

Developers cope with many classes and objects. Some classes and objects directly represent the image of real-life objects; others are metaphors for services that are required to implement the business logic or communicate with either the user of the application or external devices. In large software applications, the associations and interactions among all objects are both difficult to describe and complex, so we must have methods to shed light on that complexity. Without such methods, developers would soon see themselves as "object-disoriented"!

Object-Oriented Methods

Webster's defines the term *method* as:

Orderly or systematic arrangement, sequence, or the like.

In fact, we need a systematically arranged model to define, refine, implement, maintain, and document complex software constructions. It is important that all participants of a project know the terminology of the problem domain. Generally, when you begin a new software project, you are given some ambiguous text or informal specifications. Your customers cannot express precisely what they want, and, if you do not know everything about their specific problem domain, you cannot ask the correct questions to fill in the gaps. As soon as development starts, the requirements for the product change, because some gaps now become obvious, and you can hardly estimate how long you will work on the implementation. In most cases, development goes on indefinitely, because users always find something that is worth changing or adding. Object-oriented methods cannot prevent your customer from having additional requirements, but it can decrease the effort you expend to integrate the extensions into your design and implementation.

Several analysts, such as Rumbaugh, Jacobson, and Wirfs-Brock, have published techniques for translating real-life problems into different models that offer a view of the problem domain and facilitate system implementation. Because object-orientation is a rather new subject, some of the methods are likely to be refined in future publications. One common thread among the methods that is not likely to change, however, is the recommendation to develop applications iteratively. The visual modeling technique (VMT), which we introduce next, has adopted the object-oriented methods of Rumbaugh, Wirfs-Brock, and Jacobson.

James Rumbaugh's object modeling technique (OMT) is popular because of its simple notation. Basically, OMT consists of three models: the static model, which captures the relations among objects; the dynamic model, which captures the run-time behavior of objects; and the functional model, which sketches the flow of operations.

Rebecca Wirfs-Brock's responsibility-driven design (RDD) reflects the responsibilities, that is, the tasks, that a class must accomplish. Ms. Wirfs-Brock introduces collaborators, which are classes that help a class fulfill its responsibility. She suggests creating one class-responsibility-collaborator (CRC) card per class; each card indicates the class, lists all of its responsibilities, and for each responsibility gives the related collaborators.

In Ivar Jacobson's object-oriented software engineering (OOSE) technique, objects and classes are found with the help of use cases. A use case is an external view describing an interaction between a user and a system. The technique essentially draws a border around the problem domain and defines user roles.

Rumbaugh, Jacobson, and Wirfs-Brock state that there are static and dynamic models. The static model, also known as object models, focuses on the hierarchy and associations of objects. The dynamic model emphasizes the interdependencies and run-time behavior of objects.

Visual Modeling Technique

In *Webster's* we find the term *technique* defined as:

The systematic procedure by which a complex or scientific task is accomplished.

Software development is actually a complex task. Although several attempts have been made to approach the task scientifically, with the goal of automating software development, the inherent complexity is (still) a big obstacle. We need heuristic and iterative techniques to master the problem.

If we look at the methodologies of Rumbaugh, Wirfs-Brock, and Jacobson, we notice that they thoroughly explain their respective systematic procedures, but none of them address the new programming technique that has become important for modern application development, namely, visual programming. The authors mention the importance of developing an analysis prototype that customers can use to verify the correctness and completeness of the user interfaces, and they demand the development of a design prototype that reflects the current state of the design model and evolves toward the final implementation. But, they do not explain how to implement the prototypes.

VMT fills the prototype implementation gap and, by using the following methods or techniques, serves as a roadmap for developing applications with GUIs:

❑ OOSE: VMT uses the use case model to find potential objects and classes in the problem domain that form the object model. The use case model also serves as a starting point for the development of dynamic models.

❑ OMT: VMT uses the static model (object model) and the dynamic model (event-trace diagram and state-transition diagram) to illustrate the relationships among objects and the run-time behavior of the objects.

❑ RDD: VMT uses the CRC card technique to identify an object's responsibilities and collaborators.

VMT is a complementary approach to object-oriented application development (Figure 2). It uses OMT notation to illustrate the static and dynamic models, and it divides the development process into three phases: analysis, design, and implementation.

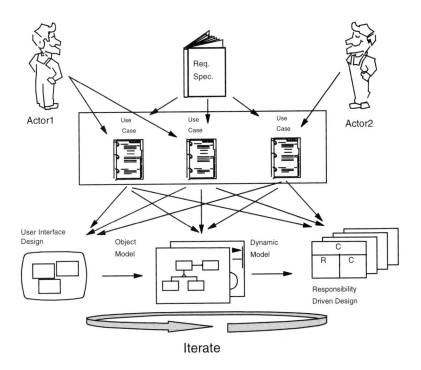

Iterate

Figure 2. VMT: A Complementary Approach to Object-Orientation

Furthermore, VMT proposes that you not draw strict boundaries between the phases; rather, you should analyze a little, design a little, implement a little, verify your results, and iterate. With VMT, you can check whether the resulting models are complete and consistent and thus provide a stable and verified system.

Analysis

The goal of analysis is to understand the problem domain, that is, to clarify *what* the system should provide. So, the first step is to separate the problem domain from the real world. In most cases, you would carry out this first step together with your users and define problem statements that are based on the requirements specification. Then you would arrange these problem statements to form use cases (*Object-Oriented Software Engineering. A Use Case Driven Approach by I. Jacobson et al.*). At this stage, the use cases are rather high level. You do not consider any implementation constraints, except that the system should be affordable and implemented within a reasonable time frame. You simply describe the essentials of the system's functions, regarding the functions as black boxes. Consequently, you take only those objects that directly represent their real-life counterparts; you can find these objects by analyzing the use cases (the process of finding objects is discussed in Chapter 3, "Analysts at Work," on page 61).

You develop an analysis prototype and show it to your users, so that they can verify that the use cases are complete and correct. If the use cases are not complete and correct, seize the opportunity: extend existing use cases or add new problem statements and formulate new use cases that were not obvious at the very beginning. Then, refine the prototype and go back to your users.

When you have finished developing the use cases and the corresponding user interfaces, determine whether you can group some of the objects in classes. Once you have found all classes, you can establish their relationships (especially inheritance and aggregation), attributes, and behaviors. The dynamic model describes how the objects interact. As the objects of the analysis model are derived directly from the problem statements and therefore represent real-life objects, they are also called *semantic objects*.

We discuss the analysis phase in detail in Chapter 3, "Analysts at Work," on page 61.

Design

The main goal of the design phase is to devise a solution, that is, answer the *how* question. As input you use the models that you developed during the analysis phase. VMT divides design into system design and object design. In system design, you determine the hardware and software components that are relevant for the application, such as the operating system, programming language, development tools, database system, and communication protocol. You also chart a high-level structure for the application functions. In object design, you refine the models from analysis, considering the constraints that the hardware and software components impose on the system. You then use these refined models for the design prototype.

We explain the design phase in detail in Chapter 4, "Designers at Work," on page 83.

Implementation

The goal of the implementation phase is to translate the design model into the implementation model, that is, the actual application construction. The design and implementation phases are closely coupled as the design prototype gradually evolves toward the final implementation model.

We explain the implementation phase in detail in Part 3, "Building the Visual Realty Application" on page 105.

Visual Programming with VisualAge for C++

VisualAge for C++ takes advantage of the visual programming construction technology of IBM's VisualAge Smalltalk™ product. VisualAge for C++, a follow-on product of the former CSet++™ product, includes the development tools from the CSet++ product. This powerful, object-oriented combination lets you build parts visually and then combine the parts to construct sophisticated applications. The key concept of VisualAge for C++ is that all existing or built parts are designed for reusability.

Using VisualAge for C++, even inexperienced programmers can build partial or complete applications because they do not have to write any code, provided that all components already exist. These components consist of graphical elements, the so-called visual parts, and the classes that handle business logic and data access, the so-called non-visual parts.

In truth, only in rare cases will you develop an application without having to add a piece of code! If you must add some code manually, however, VisualAge for C++ supports you in adhering to the object-oriented paradigm, that is, building reusable parts. It provides a library of prefabricated, ready-to-use components that you can use "as is" or enhance. You decide whether you write the missing code yourself or buy additional libraries with parts that meet your needs.

Once you start using VisualAge for C++, you gradually learn the concepts of object-orientation. At first, you might take advantage of the GUI creation capability only, while still calling your existing code. Then, you take the plunge into visual programming, reusing your GUI. Finally, having improved your skills in object-orientation and C++, you explore the advanced features of the product that enable you to create your own parts.

When you program visually with VisualAge for C++ you develop your applications by using a graphical, not a textual, tool. The Visual Builder tool provides a powerful framework for developing not only simple GUIs but a complete application. You choose the visual parts that your application requires and, using the mouse, lay out the application interface by dragging and dropping the parts on a free-form surface. In this way, you and the end user of the application can look at the GUI before you have included the business logic and invoked the compiler.

Before we show you how to build an entire application by using an object-oriented approach, let us describe the complete set of VisualAge for C++ tools.

2

Getting Started in a VisualAge for C++ Environment

We recommend that you read this overview of the VisualAge for C++ environment if you want to learn the basic concepts and develop a broad understanding of the VisualAge for C++ tools.

Tip!

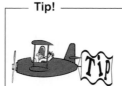
If you are familiar with the C Set ++ Version 2.1 environment, you can step through the **What's New and Nifty** boxes to discover what has changed and has been added in Version 3.0.

VisualAge for C++ provides you with all of the tools you need, from developing a prototype with the Visual Builder to tuning application performance with the Performance Analyzer. VisualAge for C++ lets you manage your project, build your application with the Visual Builder and Data Access Builder, edit the code, compile it, and finally link it. The Debugger eases the task of fixing problems. The Browser and Performance Analyzer, respectively, help you understand the structure of your code and the behavior of your application at run time. Of course, if you do not want to use Visual Builder to build your application, you can still type in your source code and take advantage of the powerful VisualAge for C++ compiler and linker.

Within VisualAge for C++, tools can interact through the Work-Frame/2 services. An environment with this capability is called an *integrated development environment* (IDE). Unlike most IDEs, Work-Frame/2 seamlessly integrates OS/2, Windows™, and DOS programs, enabling them to cooperate without actually knowing each other.

Managing Your Project

Good programming discipline suggest that you do not start coding as soon as you have a rough idea of what your application should do. Rather, you should plan your development and organize files on your system. WorkFrame/2 is a highly customizable application development environment that can help you with these planning and organization tasks.

WorkFrame/2 Concepts

What's New and Nifty?

• Full integration with the OS/2 Workplace Shell™ • Project hierarchies instead of separate concepts for base and composite projects • Common container for project files and project monitor window • New Build and MakeMake facilities • Fast and easy generation of skeletal applications with Project Smarts • Ability to customize projects with OS/2, DOS, or Windows tools

When building an application, you deal with many different pieces of data, such as C++ source files, resource files, and help files—the project elements. All project elements that make up an application or a subsystem are grouped inside a project, which is the core of the WorkFrame/2 environment. Each project has a single target, for example, an executable file or a library.

Each project element has a type. WorkFrame/2 uses this type to choose which action to apply to a project part. For example, if you define a C++ SourceFile type as all files matching the `*.cpp` file mask and a SystemEditor action that takes the C++SourceFile type as input and corresponds to the enhanced editor for OS/2 Presentation Manager™ (EPM OS/2), all project elements with the `.cpp` extension can be edited through the EPM editor.

An action can correspond to any file that can be run, such as an executable file or a command file written in the REXX language. For each action, an entry point is associated into a specific support dynamic link library (DLL). This DLL defines the action default options and provides the GUI to easily alter them. For example, all VisualAge for C++ compiler options can be accessed through the interface shown in Figure 3.

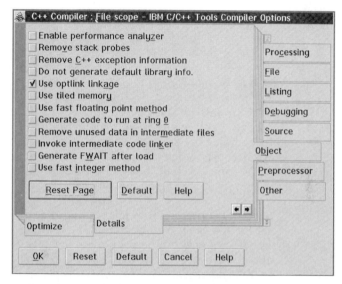

Figure 3.   Interface to Alter Options for the VisualAge for C++ Compiler

Actions must belong to a class, such as Edit or Compile. Classes allow you to use the same action name for different types. For example, when you apply the Edit action class to either a bitmap or a C++ SourceFile, you obviously call different actions that start different tools, but this is hidden from the user through the WorkFrame/2 interface. Figure 4 shows the list of actions defined in the default VisualAge for C++ project for the Edit class.

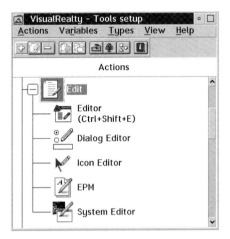

Figure 4. Actions for the Edit Class

An action can be file or project scoped. File-scoped actions can be invoked only from the project elements defined as their source types. For example, the IconEditor action is available only from icon files. Project-scoped actions apply to the project entity and can generally be invoked from any tool that has been started within the project. A typical example of a project-scoped action is the Make action

Types can be grouped into more general entities: for example, *editable* could be a way of grouping the C++ SourceFile and C++ IncludeFile types. If you now define an action that takes *editable* as input, that action applies to all files that match all types grouped in the *editable* type. Editable is called a *logical OR* type.

Warning!

Actions that define both source and target types are eligible to the MakeMake utility when generating a make file for your application. The choice of source and target types deeply influences the behavior of the MakeMake tool. If the choice is incorrect, the generated make file will be unusable.

Actions and types are configured for each project through the tools setup feature. A project's tools setup can be inherited by several projects and then modified locally.

Creating a Project with WorkFrame/2

To take full advantage of the integration facilities of WorkFrame/2, you must create a project for your application or subsystem, either from a predefined template or by using the Project Smarts facility.

Using Templates

The Workframe/2 Version 3 project template is created in your system at installation time. With the template, you can create a new, "empty" project; that is, you must configure some types and actions in the tools setup before you actually start using the project.

To help you begin, VisualAge for C++ is shipped with a default Visual-Age for C++ project template, fully configured with the VisualAge for C++ tools and the most common types. Even if you reuse this template, you can still add your own actions and types to reflect your needs and preferences. Any OS/2, DOS, or Windows application can be added as an action to the project's tools setup.

Using Project Smarts

Project Smarts is a new facility that offers a catalog of skeletal applications to use as a quick start for your project. With Project Smarts, you can create a project configured according to an application category, such as:

❑ Visual Builder application
❑ Presentation Manager application
❑ Resource Dynamic Link library
❑ C++ Dynamic Link library
❑ Data Access Builder application

Any application created from Project Smarts inherits from the Visual-Age for C++ default project.

Choosing a certain catalog entry starts a REXX installation script. The script lets you specify the project settings, such as its working directory and name, and then creates a project configured with the tools setup appropriate to the application. Each skeletal application consists of some project parts that you can use as a basis for your own application development. Figure 5 shows the description of the Presentation Manager skeletal application.

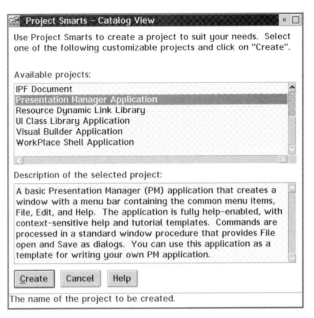

Figure 5. Project Smarts Catalog View: Presentation Manager Application

You can add your own skeletal applications to the Project Smarts catalog. Project Smarts provides REXX utilities to use for writing the installation script of your application. For example, you can create file templates according to your own corporate standards and define them as basic project parts for a standard project. Building file templates is discussed in more detail in Chapter 5, "Setting Up the Development Environment," on page 107. You can also create your own catalog of applications, as Projects Smarts is not an executable file but an OS/2 Workplace Shell object template.

Inheritance or Templates?

What is the difference between creating a project:

- ❏ by inheritance? You cannot modify existing actions, types, or variables in the base project, but you can add your own. Any change to the base project, however, is automatically reflected in all child projects.

- ❏ by copy (or using templates)? You can modify any actions, types, and variables. You must use this solution if, for example, you want to add a new type and use it as input for an existing action. This solution provides more flexibility for updating the tools setup, but it implies that you update projects one by one if any feature must be changed.

In both cases, you can modify the project settings, such as the target name or the project location. You also have to specify action options, such as compilation flags or the libraries required for linking.

Creating Composite Projects

Most applications, unless they are truly simple, consist of a hierarchy of projects. The way in which you organize your projects reflects their dependencies. Defining a project as composite is equivalent to creating other projects as project parts of that project. Typically, an application can be divided into several subsystems. For each subsystem there is a corresponding library, which you must build before building the application itself. You could manage such an application, as depicted in Figure 6, where the main project depends on its nested projects; that is, it cannot be built if the subproject targets have not been completed.

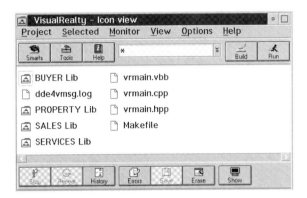

Figure 6. Example of Composite Project

WorkFrame/2 handles composite projects in such a way that the Build and MakeMake facilities recursively build the project hierarchy.

The MakeMake and Build Facilities

Used together, the MakeMake and Build facilities let you build your application without having to create and maintain make files. The MakeMake facility creates a make file for a project by examining the tools setup actions and types and determining the correct sequence of commands to build the project target.

The Build facility uses the MakeMake facility to build the make file for your application and to start a make utility such as nmake against the generated make file. The Build facility understands project organization and thus builds subprojects first in a project hierarchy

Customizing a Project with Build Smarts

With the Build Smarts facility, you can temporarily modify the requested compiling flags and linking options for the most common build options, such as debug, browse, or optimize. Build Smarts overrides the current options for the compile and link actions as defined in the project's tools setup.

When you are working with composite projects, Build Smarts lets you specify whether you want to build subprojects first. This specification prevents the Build facility from trying to recursively build all projects in the project hierarchy. You can also specify preprocessor macro values to be added or removed at the development or production stages.

Migrating Existing Projects

 If you are a C Set ++ customer, you must migrate your existing Work-Frame/2 projects to WorkFrame/2 Version 3. The migration utility scans the drives on your system to search for WorkFrame/2 Version 1 and Version 2 projects and provides you with a list of those projects. You can choose among several options:

❑ Migrate the Project only
❑ Migrate Projects and Actions profiles
❑ Migrate Actions Parameters

We suggest that you refer to the *C/C++ User's Guide* for more information about project migration.

Generating Your Code

In this section we introduce Visual Builder, a tool for visual programming; the IBM Open Class Library, which provides building blocks for your application; and the Data Access Builder, which maps relational database tables to C++ classes.

Using Visual Builder

 Traditional GUI builders let you create the interface of your application and generate the code for that interface. They do not provide a visual way of generating the behavior of your application, such as the piece of code executed when you click on a push button.

Visual Builder is not a traditional GUI builder. It lets you create a complete application visually by reusing parts, connecting them, and generating the code for the entire application. The generated code uses the IBM Open Class Library and therefore is portable across the platforms where the library is available. See "Building from Blocks" on page 37 for more information about the IBM Open Class Library.

Visual Builder Concepts

Just as you would use building blocks to build a wall, Visual Builder uses parts to build applications. You can think about parts as reusable components that you can tailor to fit your needs, just as you would cut a building block to fill a gap in your wall.

Any application made from parts is a part itself: Assembling primitive parts results in a composite part. A primitive part can be a window or an entry field—it is also called "control" to refer to the PM controls; a composite part can be a complete panel for a database information update (Figure 7). The composite part can be reused as a building block in another application.

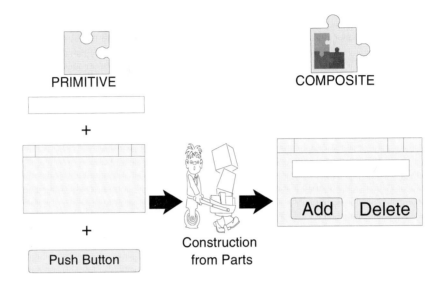

PRIMITIVE

COMPOSITE

+

Push Button

Construction
from Parts

Add   Delete

Figure 7. Primitive and Composite Parts

Parts are either visual or nonvisual; an entry field and a frame window are examples of visual parts; a list of customers is an example of a nonvisual part.

Parts Interface. Parts communicate through their interface. A part interface consists of three features: *attributes, actions*, and *events*. These features correspond to a natural way of viewing parts in terms of the properties they have (attributes), the services they can provide (actions), and the notifications they can send (events). Figure 8 shows a sample part interface for a nonvisual part called SmartHouse.

Technical Information!

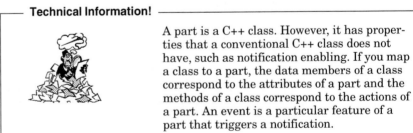

A part is a C++ class. However, it has properties that a conventional C++ class does not have, such as notification enabling. If you map a class to a part, the data members of a class correspond to the attributes of a part and the methods of a class correspond to the actions of a part. An event is a particular feature of a part that triggers a notification.

The SmartHouse nonvisual part manages an "intelligent" house that can detect when someone enters the house and monitor a smoke detection system. SmartHouse has been designed to send events if it detects anything unusual (doorOpened and smokeDetected events) and start actions, such as activating the alarm or automatically switching on the lights.

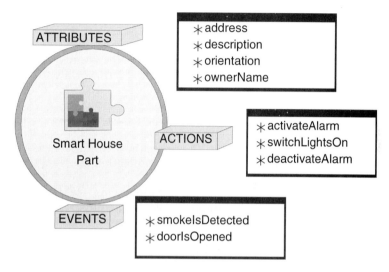

Figure 8. Sample Part Interface: SmartHouse

Connecting Parts. Connections define how parts interact through their interface. A connection is a one-to-one visual relationship between two parts (visual or nonvisual). Connections are categorized as:

Attribute-to-attribute

> Whenever the value of the first attribute is changed, the value of the second attribute is updated, so the attribute values are always the same.

Event-to-attribute

> Whenever an event occurs, the attribute is updated.

Event-to-action

> Whenever an event occurs, the action is performed. A variation of this, the attribute-event-to-action connection, starts an action when a certain attribute event (for example, attribute changes value) occurs.

Event-to-custom logic

An event-to-custom logic connection lets you call some user code when the event occurs. The customized code is encapsulated in a codeSnippet() function. A variation of this connection is the attribute-to-custom logic connection.

Event-to-member

Whenever an event occurs, a member function of the currently edited part is called. This connection lets you call any member function, even if it has not been added to the part interface. A variation of this connection is the attribute-to-member connection.

In Visual Builder, the origin of a connection is called the *source* part and the destination of the connection is called the *target* part.

Figure 9 shows several connections for the SmartHouse nonvisual part. In this example, we create a simple GUI to monitor the state of a SmartHouse. We first build an entry field (Owner Name) to reflect the value of the ownerName attribute from the SmartHouseControl part. Then we use two radio buttons to reflect the alarm status: The alarm is either on or off. Whenever the door is opened, the Smart House self-activates the alarm. To monitor the lights in the different rooms of the house, we use the Light Control button, and we can specify in which room (represented here by a number) the lights must be turned on

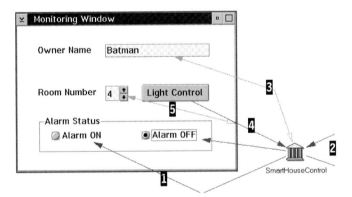

Figure 9. Sample Connections: SmartHouse Monitoring System

Table 1 explains in more detail connections we have to create for the SmartHouse monitoring system in Figure 9.

Table 1. SmartHouse Connections

Key	Source	Target	Description
1	doorOpenedEvent	enable	This event-to-action connection enables the Alarm ON radio button whenever the doorOpenedEvent event occurs.
2	doorOpenedEvent	activateAlarm	This connection illustrates that a part can be both the source and target of a connection. In this case, the house self-activates the house alarm if the doorOpenedEvent event occurs.
3	ownerName	text	With this attribute-to-attribute connection, you ensure that the text attribute (that is, the value of the entry field) always reflects the value of the SmartHouseControl's ownerName data member.
4	buttonClickEvent	switchLightsOn	Because the switchLightsOn action requires a room number parameter, this event-to-action connection is not complete without connection **5**.
5	value	roomNumber	This connection passes the value of the numeric spin button as a parameter to connection **4**.

Visual Builder Editors

Visual Builder provides three editors that you can use to build your parts.

The Composition Editor. With the Composition Editor (Figure 10), you can design the graphical interface of your application, add the nonvisual parts you need for the logic of your application, and make the appropriate connections.

Visual Builder comes with a set of nonvisual and visual parts classified by categories in the parts palette **1**. The base parts are mainly mapped from the User Interface Class Library and the Collection Class Library. The palette can be extended by adding your own categories and primitive or composite parts.

The toolbar **2** provides direct access to a set of tools that you can use to arrange the parts layout on the free-form surface **3**.

To create a new application, just pick up the visual and nonvisual parts you need from the parts palette and drop them onto the free-form surface. Then make the appropriate connections and generate the code.

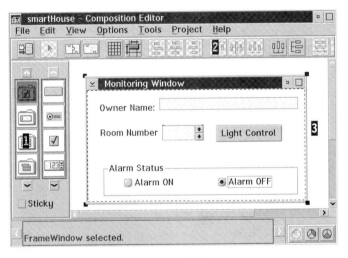

Figure 10. Visual Builder: Composition Editor

Visual Builder can generate the following code:

- ❏ Part source, that is, the code for creating the parts and the logic derived from the connections
- ❏ Main source file, that is, a file containing a main() entry point, if you want to test your part
- ❏ Make file for building the application (if you are not using WorkFrame/2 and the MakeMake facility)
- ❏ Application resource file (for national language support (NLS)

The Part Interface Editor. You can use the Part Interface Editor to create or modify the interface of your parts. With the Part Interface Editor, you can create the attributes, actions, and events related to your part, promote features, and select your preferred features.

Creating attributes

You create an attribute by entering its name and type. The Part Interface Editor automatically generates the declarations for the attribute accessors (set and get member functions) you need as well as the identification of the event corresponding to the attribute. Visual Builder uses this event to signal any changes to the attribute value. You enter a short description for the attribute. Figure 11 shows an example of using the part interface to create a Boolean attribute.

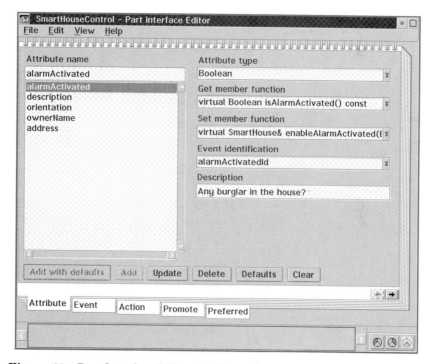

Figure 11. Part Interface Editor: Attribute Creation

Creating actions

The Part Interface Editor generates a default member function declaration from the action name provided. The tool automatically reflects any changes to the returned type or any addition of parameters to the function call.

Creating events

The Part Interface Editor generates a unique event identification from the event name you provide. Visual Builder uses the identification to notify other parts when this event occurs.

An event can have parameters that indicate the name and type of some data corresponding to that event. For example, if your part must read a queue element when receiving an event, the event parameters contain the element address and its type, such as IString, so that you can directly access the data with any subsequent query.

Promoting features

With the promote feature facility, you can provide access to part features when the part is embedded as a subpart within another part. Say you define a default-ButtonsPanel composite part from a simple canvas to which you add three push buttons (*OK, Cancel, Help*) as shown in Figure 12. If you then reuse the default-ButtonsPanel part in another application, only the attributes, events, and actions of the defaultButtons-Panel base part, that is, the canvas, are available.

Because you no longer have access to the default-ButtonsPanel subparts, such as the three push buttons, you cannot directly create a connection that would start a specific action when clicking on the *OK* push button. You must *promote* any feature that you want to access from another part that reuses the part.

Figure 12. defaultButtonsPanel Composite Part

The Part Interface Editor lets you select a subpart name (such as OKPushButton), the feature type (for example, event) and name (for example, buttonClickEvent). Visual Builder generates a name for the promoted feature (OKPushButtonButtonClickEvent). This name is now added to the list of features for the defaultButtonsPanel composite part.

Selecting preferred features

You can select preferred features to customize the list of features in the connection menu for each part. The list typically contains the features that you use most often.

The Class Editor. With the Class Editor (Figure 13), you can customize code generation parameters. For example, you can change the source and include file names where the generated code is saved **1** or modify the default constructor and destructor code **2**. You can also attach a specific icon **3** to the part. The icon is displayed when you reuse the part in the Composition Editor.

By default, all graphical resources, such as the label of a push button, are hardcoded in the generated code. If you want those resources to be generated in a separate resource file, you must specify such from the Class Editor, **4**, by selecting the *Starting resource id* check box and providing the entry field with a resource identifier. This feature lets you create applications that are enabled for NLS.

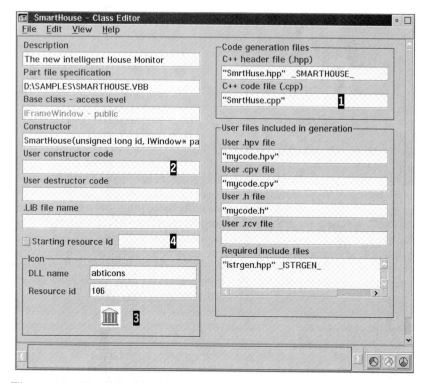

Figure 13. Visual Builder: Class Editor

Whenever you create or modify the interface of a part, such as adding an action or attribute definition, the code is generated in user-defined files (with extensions .hpv, .cpv, and .rcv). This code is referred to as the *part features source code*. Unlike other files that Visual Builder generates, user-defined files are not overwritten whenever you generate the part features source code. Rather, the new code is *appended* to the files. Thus, you can modify the generated code without fearing that those changes will be lost at next code generation.

Accessing DB2 Tables with Data Access Builder

With Data Access Builder, you can graphically map your existing relational database tables to an object interface. In a simple case, a relational database table maps to a class, and a column of the table maps to an attribute of that class. Once you have defined your mapping, Data Access Builder generates nonvisual parts to be used in Visual Builder. Moreover, you can take full advantage of the IBM System Object Model (SOM) technology by generating the code in the SOM interface definition language (IDL). (For an introduction to SOM technology refer to "Direct-to-SOM Support" on page 43.)

Let us take a simple example: We create a car table with four attributes, color, license, make, and model, as depicted in Figure 14. If we map this table to a class and generate the code, Data Access Builder creates two classes:

❏ **Car**

An instance of the Car class maps to a single row of the car table. The Car class provides the member functions for adding, updating, retrieving, and deleting a row of the car table.

❏ **CarManager**

The CarManager class provides the services for manipulating a set of car instances. You can use a Car Manager instance to select some rows of your table through an SQL query (select method) or display the complete set of rows (refresh method).

The generated code uses static SQL for efficient data access. Data Access Builder also comes with a library of classes and parts for database management (connect and disconnect) and transaction management (commit and rollback).

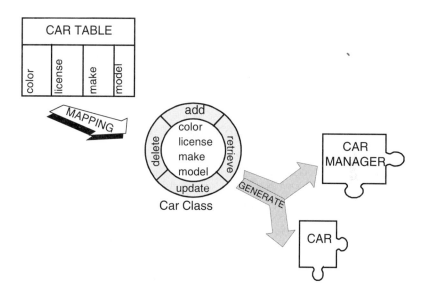

Figure 14. Database Access: From Mapping to Parts Generation

Building from Blocks

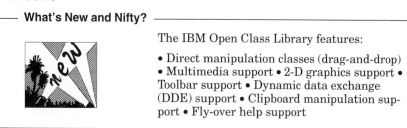

┌─ **What's New and Nifty?** ─────────────────────┐

The IBM Open Class Library features:

• Direct manipulation classes (drag-and-drop)
• Multimedia support • 2-D graphics support •
Toolbar support • Dynamic data exchange
(DDE) support • Clipboard manipulation sup-
port • Fly-over help support

└──┘

Without doubt, one of the greatest advantages of object-oriented programming is class reusability. The IBM Open Class Library provides a
comprehensive range of reusable classes from which you can create
and manipulate objects. It is supported across many IBM and non-
IBM platforms to provide maximum portability of your C++ programs.
Most of the VisualAge for C++ tools have been developed by use of the
IBM Open Class Library.

The IBM Open Class Library provides you with more than 500 classes,
grouped in the following libraries:

❑ User Interface Class Library

❑ Collection Class Library

❑ Data Access Builder Class Library

❑ Application Support Class Library

❑ Standard Class Libraries

User Interface Class Library

The user interface class library facilitates the development of *portable* applications that have a GUI. It is built as a layer on top of the native window presentation system (OS/2 Presentation Manager (PM)) and encapsulates its concepts in C++ classes (Figure 15).

With a common interface across platforms, you can recompile your code without worrying about the low-level changes of the native operating system. However, some PM features might not be available in another graphical environment such as Motif®, so you must follow some rules to guarantee that your code is fully portable. The documentation precisely identifies portability issues for each class across the available platforms.

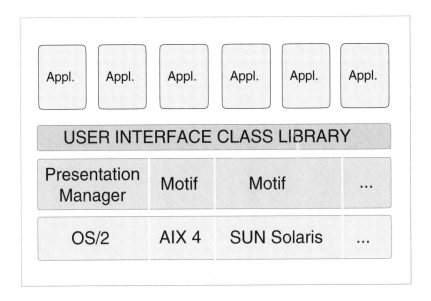

Figure 15. User Interface Class Library Architecture

The User Interface Class Library includes the following elements:

❑ Base windows, menus, handlers, events, and help files (display help, define contextual help, and fly-over help)

❑ Base controls, such as entry fields, static texts, buttons, and boxes

- Advanced controls, such as containers, canvases, sliders, notebooks, toolbars, and font and file dialogs
- Application control classes to manipulate threads, timers, resources, profiles, and the OS/2 clipboard
- Dynamic data exchange (DDE) classes for communication between applications on the same machine
- Direct manipulation classes (drag-and-drop support)
- 2-D graphics classes for drawing primitives (lines and arcs) as well as support for reading and displaying various graphical formats (available only in OS/2)
- Multimedia classes for control of multimedia devices (available only in OS/2)

Collection Class Library

The Collection Class Library includes a complete set of abstract data types to manipulate such objects as:

- Bags and sets: unordered collections of elements
- Sequences: ordered collection of elements
- Queues and dequeues (double queues)
- Heaps
- Stacks
- Trees

Bags and sets can inherit from various properties such as indexing and sort. As a result, you can use sorted bags or key sets. You can alter queue properties to assign an access priority to added elements.

Data Access Builder Class Library

The Data Access Builder Class Library provides classes that you can use to manage the connection to a database (authentication, connect, disconnect) as well as transactions (commit, rollback) on the database. It also contains the abstract classes that Data Access Builder uses to generate the C++ classes issued from the mapping of DB2/2® tables (refer to "Accessing DB2 Tables with Data Access Builder" on page 36).

Application Support Class Library

The Application Support Class Library provides the classes used most often while developing C++ applications:

- String manipulation classes: provide member functions to edit, compare, convert, format, and test strings

- ❏ Date and time classes: provide member functions to test and compare dates or times, convert date and time formats

- ❏ Exception classes: provide the framework for throwing exceptions within the class libraries

- ❏ Trace classes: provide trace facilities to help debugging code

Standard Class Libraries

The Standard Class Libraries consist of the standard I/O stream library for C++ input and output handling and the complex mathematics library for manipulating complex numbers.

The UNIX System Laboratories introduced the standard class libraries in the C++ Language System Version 3.0. Since then, the libraries have become a de facto standard and are shipped with all C++ compilers. The set of standard class libraries usually includes the task library. However, as the OS/2 operating system natively supports multitasking, the task library is not provided on the OS/2 platform.

Building Your Application

In this section, we introduce you to the VisualAge for C++ editor and present the main features of the compiler and linker.

Editing Your Code

The VisualAge editor, also known as the live parsing extensible (LPEX) editor, is a language-sensitive editor. It reacts to the type of the edited file and uses live parsers for keyword highlighting and code formatting, such as automatic indenting. The LPEX editor dynamically detects errors in your file and does "stupid error checking"; for example, it finds missing closing brackets and detects nested comments. Figure 16 shows an example of C++ source code formatting and dynamic error detection. The LPEX editor is shipped with live parsers for C, C++, FORTRAN, Pascal, COBOL, REXX, and BASIC.

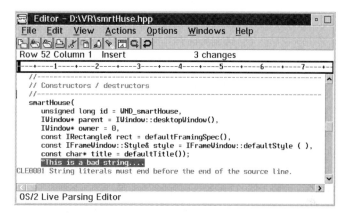

Figure 16. LPEX: Source Formatting and Dynamic Error Detection

The LPEX editor provides selective views of your code, such as a class definition list, function list, and error list. You can also choose to show only the lines containing a given string. The LPEX editor features all of the functions you would expect from any editor, such as block manipulation, a search facility, a toolbar for fast access to common commands, and multiple views of the same file.

The LPEX editor is fully customizable. With it you can easily change key assignments, parameters, menus, the toolbar, fonts, and colors and write your own parser or modify existing parsers. You can extend the capabilities of the LPEX editor if you have some REXX and C programming knowledge.

Compiling

What's New and Nifty?

• Direct generation of SOM classes from C++ source code through Direct-to-SOM support • Improved memory management component • Facilities to trace heap of memory usage (together with the Debugger) • Locales support • Generation of reduced debugging information (line numbers only)

The VisualAge for C++ compiler generates highly optimized code for any Intel® architecture from the i386™ to the Pentium™ and conforms to the major industry standards (ANSI C, ANSI C++ Draft X3J16) to allow you to write portable C and C++ code. It supports the key features of the C++ programming language, including templates and exception handling.

Precompiled Headers

With precompiled headers, the compiler does not have to recompile header files each time you change a source file that uses the header files. Precompiled headers improve compile time. The VisualAge for C++ compiler groups precompiled headers in a single file.

Memory Management

The entire memory component has been redesigned. New features and functions are now available:

❑ Overhead reduction of allocated objects
❑ Extensive checks on entire heap with descriptive error messages
❑ Optimal page tuning
❑ Additional migration routines: _heapchk, _heapset, _heap_walk
❑ Support for user heap and shared memory
❑ Transparent user heap allocations using malloc
❑ Support for debug tiled memory

The /Tm+ compiler option lets you generate additional code for all functions, so that you can debug memory management functions such as new, calloc, or malloc. Used together with the Debugger, this option enables automatic heap checking each time your program stops on a breakpoint.

Support for Locales

Locales help you define "internationalized" applications. They provide a way of changing the behavior of your application according to language and cultural differences, such as character sets and date formats. The VisualAge for C++ compiler provides the facilities to create and manipulate locales in your code. Such facilities include LOCAL-DEF, to create a locale object, and ICONV, to convert a file from one code set encoding to another. You can either reuse the locale objects supplied with the VisualAge for C++ compiler or create your own.

Support of locales is based on the IEEE POSIX P1003.2 and X/Open Portability Guide standards. For a detailed description of locales support, refer to the *C/C++ Programming Guide*.

Code Optimization

You can optimize your program by improving its execution speed or decreasing its size. All optimizations that the VisualAge for C++ compiler performs are safe. The VisualAge for C++ compiler uses advanced technologies for code optimization, such as:

Intermediate code linking

The intermediate code linker combines the intermediate code from several compile units into one compile unit. Thus, because the optimizer does not have to optimize each compilation unit separately, it performs more efficiently for function inlining and global optimizations. The intermediate code linker might also detect errors that would cause unexpected run-time behavior or linker errors such as:

- Redefinition of variables or functions
- Inconsistent declarations or definitions of functions
- Type mismatch between definitions or declarations of the same variable
- Conflicting compiler options

Global optimizations

The VisualAge for C++ compiler performs loop analysis, dead code removal, and advanced switch analysis.

Interprocedural optimizations

The VisualAge for C++ compiler reorganizes your code for function calls, uses registers for variables storage, and performs instruction scheduling. The built-in functions are optimized according to the processor type.

See the *C/C++ Programming Guide* for more details on optimization techniques.

Direct-to-SOM Support

Code reusability is one of the great promises of object-oriented programming. The reality, however, is that if you deliver a library of C++ classes in an OS/2 environment, it will not work in an AIX™ environment unless you recompile and relink the library. Moreover, if you make changes in the library, it is likely that the applications using that library will have to be recompiled. Obviously, delivering the same library in a different programming language such as Smalltalk is not a straightforward operation.

SOM addresses these issues and provides an environment where reuse is a reality. SOM clearly separates the interface of a class from its implementation to provide language independence (see Figure 17). With SOM, you can define classes in one programming language and use them in another. You can also update a SOM library without having to recompile the client code (provided that you do not delete any library member).

SOM objects can be shared across processes through the Distributed SOM (DSOM) framework. Processes can be in the same or different systems. They also can run on different platforms. The interprocess communication is totally hidden from the programmer.

Both SOM and DSOM conform to the Common Object Request Broker Architecture (CORBA) specification of the Object Management Group (OMG).

Previously, to create a SOM object, you had to go through the time-consuming process of writing its interface in a neutral language (IDL), generating C++ bindings with the SOM compiler, and compiling the generated C++ source code.

With the Direct-to-SOM (DTS) technology, you can generate a SOM class from a C++ class definition. The compiler also generates the corresponding IDL whenever you want to access that SOM class from another language or use DSOM. Because you are writing C++ directly, you can benefit from the C++ features such as templates, operators, and static members.

Although SOM imposes some restrictions on the C++ syntax, you should be able to convert most of your C++ programs with minimal effort.

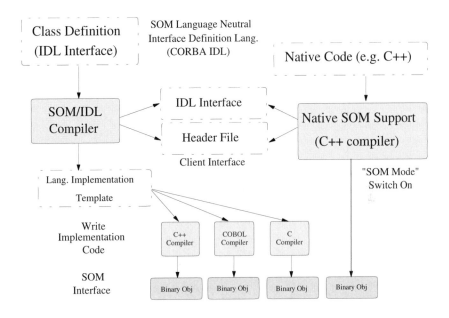

Figure 17. Language-Independent Implementation with SOM

Linking

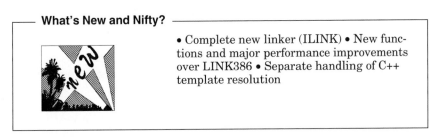

ILINK replaces LINK386 in the VisualAge for C++ development environment. ILINK has been designed to work closely with the compiler and provides better performance and optimization techniques than link386. Although ILINK has new options and syntax, you can invoke it with the LINK386 syntax by using the /NOFREE option. ILINK can produce either an executable file, a DLL, or a device driver (DRV,VDD).

ILINK has the following improved optimization techniques, which you might want to use when your program is tested and stable:

Unreachable functions removal

The unreachable functions removal technique, also referred to as *smart linking*, lets you remove the unreferenced functions in your code or in the libraries with which you are linking. An unreferenced function is any function that you do not call directly in your program or that is not called by one of the functions you call. This optimization technique can significantly reduce the size of your program, and thereby improve its performance.

> **Technical Information!**
>
>
>
> If you are linking with a DLL, the unreachable functions removal technique will not remove the functions that are exported from that DLL.

Executable packing

With ILINK, you can slightly reduce the size and enhance the speed of your executable file by packing the code or data segments that have similar attributes. ILINK also provides a new option (/EXEPACK) to compress your executable file according to the target operating system (OS/2 2.11 or Warp).

At the development stage, you can use the debugging information packing option to generate a smaller and therefore faster executable file.

Unlike LINK386, which required the compiler to correctly resolve C++ templates, ILINK can be invoked independently to handle C++ template resolution.

Understanding Your Code

VisualAge for C++ has features that help you understand your code. The class browser graphically displays the structure and hierarchy of your C++ classes. The Debugger helps you understand why your application fails. You can use the Performance Analyzer together with the Debugger for thread interaction analysis, deadlock detection, and performance tuning.

Browsing Your C++ Hierarchy

— **What's New and Nifty?** —

• New user interface for enhanced usability •
Smaller database files for faster load • Fully
customizable interface, including fonts and
colors • Ability to browse C++ source code
without compiling it (QuickBrowse facility) •
Ability to browse projects, executable files, and
libraries • Support for SOM classes generated
through Direct-to-SOM

Inheritance and therefore reuse are two of the keys to object-oriented
programming, but they come with the cost of increased complexity.
Finding the right class among the thousands available is often a tricky
task.

Browsing helps you analyze and understand which class and its associated member functions can provide the service for which you are
looking. With the VisualAge for C++ Browser, you can navigate
through the class hierarchy, obtain the interface available to you,
locate a function, edit the source files, and access the online help for
the IBM Open Class Library classes.

The Browser is particularly useful when you develop a large project
with a team of developers. Typically, developers reuse the classes
defined in another subsystem and have to know how they can use a
particular class and the services offered by that class. Developers also
might want to check the impact of changing the prototype of one of
their functions that other developers are using.

The VisualAge for C++ Browser creates an internal representation of
your program in a so-called browser database. The database contains
full information about your program if you specified certain compile
and link options. However, for those cases when you cannot compile or
would like to browse your code before you compile, you can use the
QuickBrowse facility. With QuickBrowse, you can generate the minimum amount of information the browser requires to analyze your
code. (Some information that would be known only at compile time is
not available, such as viewing call chains.) The QuickBrowse facility is
typically useful where the project design phase has ended; that is, the
definition files (header files) have been completed, but the project has
not been implemented.

Browser Windows

The Browser can display information either as lists or graphs. When
you start the Browser, the initial window displays a list of all classes
that are defined in your executable file or library, that is, all classes
that are defined in the header files you included in your program.

For each class displayed in the initial window, you can access:

❑ List of members with inheritance. This option displays an incremental list of all members (that is, constructors, destructors, functions, and variables) of the class, as shown in Figure 18. With this list, you develop a good understanding of the complete class interface and have access to all relevant information, such as the online documentation or the header file where these members are implemented. A special notation is used for members that have been generated by the compiler.

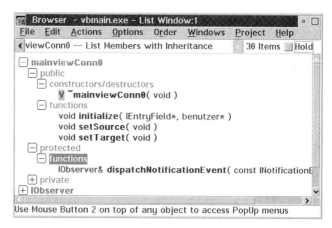

Figure 18. Browser List Window: List Members with Inheritance

Class members are usually classified according to the class name, but you can categorize the list by either access (public, protected, private) or type (functions, variables).

For each member function, you can display either the list or graph of caller and callee functions, as well as the list of exceptions that can be thrown from that member function. With the callers and callees graph, you can develop a better understanding of the execution flow of your program, as shown in Figure 19. You can also use this information to measure the impact on the entire application of modifying a function.

A graph window is divided in two parts: The left side of the window shows the graph itself, and the right side of the window displays the list of objects in the graph. The list of objects can be used to retrieve an object in a graph. It generally displays more information about the object than is displayed on the graph itself, such as the complete definition of a function (Figure 19). The slider on the left side of the graph (**1**) is used to zoom in on and zoom out from the graph.

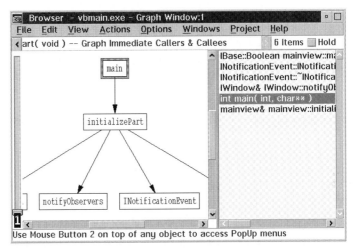

Figure 19. Browser Graph Window: Graph All Callers and Callees

❑ List of friends or friendships, that is, the answer to such questions as Whom do I declare to be my friend? and Who declared me as being its friend?

❑ List of implementing files, that is, a list of header files where the class is declared. With this list you can find the correct header file name to include in your code when you want to use the class.

❑ Graph of all base and/or derived classes.

```
┌─ Tip! ─────────────────────────────────────────────┐
│                  The Browser provides a graph overview window    │
│     for large graphs. From the overview window, you │
│                  can select which part of the graph you want to  │
│                  display and zoom in on or out from an area of the│
│                  graph.                                           │
└──────────────────────────────────────────────────────┘
```

From the initial window, you can also display the list of all files that your executable file or library uses. For each file, you can access the following information:

❑ List of defined objects. This option displays the list of classes, functions, variables, and types that are defined in the corresponding file.

❑ Graph of all includers and includees (Figure 20.). This option is useful for measuring the impact of modifying a header file in your files hierarchy.

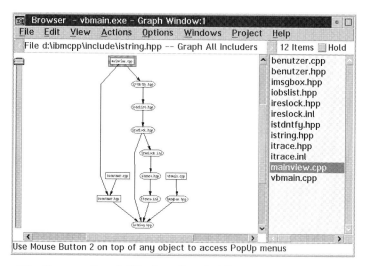

Figure 20. Browser Graph Window: Graph All Includers

If you are dealing with a large library, use the search facility for fast access to information. It lets you scan the loaded database and find objects according to simple criteria such as object type, access type, class type, and function type.

Visual Builder and Browser Interaction

Visual Builder interprets and uses the data stored in a browser database file. From Visual Builder, you can either read a database file or call the QuickBrowse facility (provided that you started Visual Builder from a WorkFrame/2 project).

You can use the browser information to:

❑ Create event-to-member function or attribute-to-member function connections. Event-to-member function or attribute-to-member function connections enable you to call a member function of a part whenever the corresponding event occurs (see "Connecting Parts" on page 29).

❑ Incorporate existing code with the Part Interface Editor (see Chapter 8, "Creating Nonvisual Parts," on page 213.)

In both cases, Visual Builder loads the list of function definitions, which you can then reuse. You can directly access those definitions from the various Visual Builder editors. Figure 21 shows the GUI for creating an event-to-member connection after the browser data is loaded.

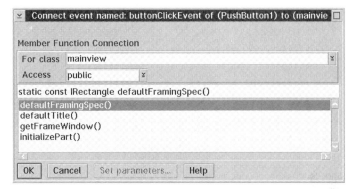

Figure 21. Visual Builder: Creating an Event-to-Member Connection

Debugging Your Code

┌─ **What's New and Nifty?** ─────────────────────────────┐

  • Support for SOM objects • Debugging of child processes • Support for deferred breakpoints • Exceptions filtering • Automatic heap check

└──┘

The VisualAge for C++ Debugger lets you debug your 32-bit C or C++ code at the source level. You can also use it to debug child processes and SOM objects generated through DTS or the SOM compiler.

The Debugger provides advanced features for breakpoint management, memory management, and functions monitoring.

Breakpoint Management

You can set a breakpoint at any place in your program where you want to stop execution. The Debugger supports simple breakpoints, such as stopping when a certain line number in a source file is reached. It also supports more complex breakpoints, such as stopping program execution when a certain address in memory is modified or putting conditional breakpoints on variables. (For example, you can stop execution whenever a variable in a loop reaches a given value.)

The Debugger supports the following breakpoint types:

Line   Stops program execution at a specific line number

Function   Stops program execution when the first instruction of the corresponding function is called

Address   Stops program execution when a specific address is reached

Change address   Stops program execution when the contents at a specific address are changed; you can specify either an address or a variable name to set such a breakpoint.

Load occurrence Stops program execution when the program loads the specified DLL.

When working with DLLs, you can defer breakpoints so that they are activated only when the corresponding module is actually loaded. This option is supported for line and function breakpoints.

You can manage all active breakpoints from the Breakpoint List window shown in Figure 22.

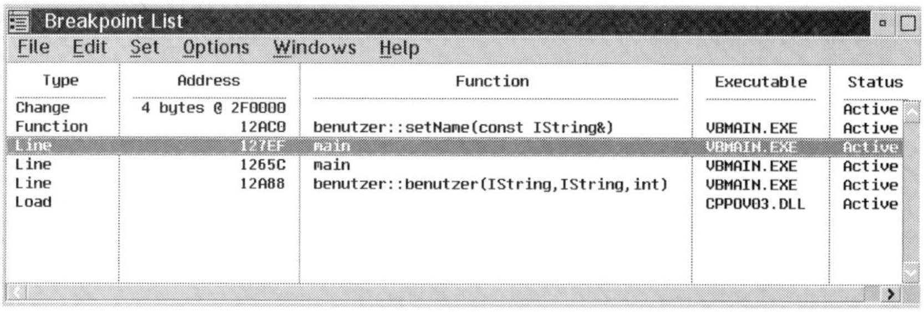

Figure 22. Breakpoint List Window

Memory Management

With the *check heap when stopping* option, you can perform memory checks each time the program stops executing, for example, when a breakpoint is reached. The check heap facility detects memory block allocation problems such as writing data outside a block segment or freeing the same memory block twice. When the Debugger detects a problem, the program stops executing and displays the exact line where the problem occurred.

Functions Monitoring

Advanced monitoring functions let you get a complete view of your program's behavior. You can simultaneously track the call stack, storage status, and registers value as well as analyze the graphical windows if you are debugging a PM application:

Call Stack window

> The Call Stack window dynamically lists all active functions for a particular thread in the order in which they are called.

Storage window

> The Storage window dynamically displays the storage contents and storage address.

Registers window

> In the Registers window, you can display and alter the contents of registers.

Windows Analysis window

> With the Windows analysis window, you can graphically display the relationship among the graphical windows that are created when you run a PM application.

Debugging Session Management

For each application that you debug, you can choose to save the current debugging session. The next time you debug that application, the Debugger tries to restore the saved session, including breakpoints and the various windows that were active when you stopped your previous debugging session.

Performance Analysis

The Performance Analyzer provides you with facilities to improve application performance or to detect problems at run time that are difficult to find with a traditional Debugger.

When compiling and linking your program with the correct options, you create hooks in your program. The Performance Analyzer uses those hooks to create a trace file. The hooks cause a small monitoring function to be called inside every program's callee function. The monitoring function stamps the event, dumps it into a trace file, and then actually calls the function. Because the monitoring function is called in the program's address space, the trace overhead is minimal. Moreover, all chronological diagrams take the trace overhead into account and are therefore accurate. The Performance Analyzer uses a high-resolution clock (provided by the CPPO3PA.SYS device driver), which is loaded at boot time in your CONFIG.SYS file. The DEVICE statement is added to your CONFIG.SYS file at installation time.

Customizing Trace Generation

The Performance Analyzer views applications as a set of components. A component can be the executable file itself, a DLL, an object file, or even functions. You can influence the size of a trace file by enabling components to be analyzed inside an application.

In you have a multithread program, you can exclude threads that you do not want to trace and select the call depth for those threads. The maximum number of threads you can trace simultaneously is 64.

If you need better trace granularity, you can modify your program source. The Performance Analyzer provides two functions calls: PerfStart() and PerfStop(). You place the calls anywhere in your code to start and stop trace generation.

The PERF(string) macro lets you create user events in the trace file. The string you pass as a parameter is dumped into the trace file during program execution. User events in the call nesting, statistics, and time line diagrams appear as diamonds. You also can trace system call events by linking with specific libraries, such as _doscall.lib or _pmgpi.lib.

Performance Analyzer Diagrams

From the trace file that it creates, the Performance Analyzer provides several diagrams that you can use to time and tune applications, trace thread interactions, find where a program hangs, and detect deadlocks. Filters allow you to temporarily reduce the amount of data displayed in a diagram or graph. The filtering options may vary from one diagram to another but are essentially based on thread numbers and function names.

Call Nesting Diagram. The call nesting diagram shows the trace file as a vertical series of function calls and returns. Each thread has its own starting column of functions. Use this diagram to build an understanding of thread interaction in your program—each context switch between threads is represented by a dotted line—and follow the flow of function calls in your application.

To reduce the amount of data displayed by the call nesting diagram, use the pattern recognition option, which looks at a single thread and finds patterns of calls and returns. The patterns are displayed as curved arcs, and the number of repetitions is indicated on the right-hand side of the corresponding arc, as shown in Figure 23. The pattern recognition view helps you isolate patterns of code that you reuse frequently. Then, for better performance, you can group instructions belonging to a pattern into the same code segment.

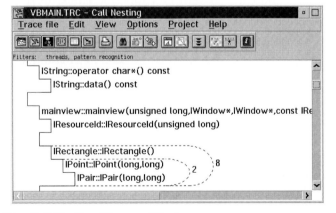

Figure 23. Call Nesting Diagram Window

Dynamic Call Graph. The dynamic call graph is a graphical view of the application execution, where functions and functions calls are represented, respectively, by nodes and arcs. Selecting a graph node gives you access to execution statistics for the corresponding function and filtering capabilities such as "Who calls me?" or "Whom do I call?" (See Figure 24.) The dynamic call graph uses color to represent the time spent in each node and the number of calls in an arc. For example, a red-colored node indicates that more than one-half of the total execution time was spent in that node.

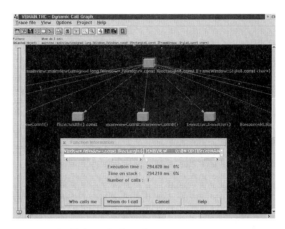

Figure 24. Dynamic Call Graph Window

Execution Density Diagram. The execution density diagram displays execution time divided into fixed horizontal time slices. If you compare this graph to a table, you can see that each row is a time slice and each column is a function called during the time slice. Color is used to indicate the percentage of the time slice that the function uses.

Statistics Diagram. The statistics diagram summarizes all data about functions or executables. Functions can be sorted according to execution time, time on stack, and minimum and maximum time for a call (Figure 25). The trace overhead time is also listed.

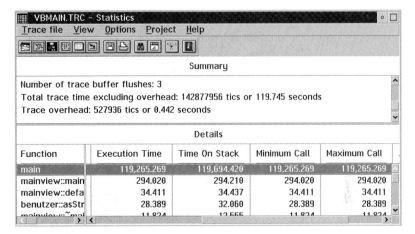

Figure 25. Statistics Window

Time Line Diagram. The time line diagram displays the sequence of nested function calls and returns. It is similar to the call nesting diagram, with the exception that time is represented on the diagram. Time is divided into horizontal time slices, and function names appear on the right-hand side of the diagram.

Windows Correlation. All chronologically scaled diagrams (time line, call nesting, and execution density) can be correlated according to a particular event or specific point in time. Thus, you can select a time period in the time line diagram and use correlation to get a different view of it in the call nesting diagram.

Part 2

Developing with
VisualAge for C++

If you only have a hammer, all your problems look like a nail. (Proverb)

In the rest of this book you will learn how to build a real-life application, the Visual Realty application, that supports real estate agents who manage properties and customers. A customer of a real estate agency is either a seller who wants to sell property and asks the agency for assistance or a buyer who wants to be the proud owner of new property. So, an agency must keep track of properties that are available for potential buyers and mediate between sellers and buyers. Potential buyers have particular notions of the kind of property they want, so an agent must be able to search for property that matches their notions.

Our goal is not to build a complete application that would solve all of the problems of real estate agents. Rather, we want to illustrate how to apply VMT and use VisualAge for C++ tools to build a good object-oriented software system.

In Part 2 we analyze and design the Visual Realty application to develop static and dynamic models that you will implement with VisualAge for C++ in Part 3.

3

Analysts at Work

Analysis lets you stay ignorant, but with much more detail.

- (The Financial Procedures Handbook, Apocrypha)

To illustrate the process of object-oriented application development we can compare it to the process of writing a novel, because there are as many potential domains to describe in a novel as there are different software domains. We focus on novels that entertain (but not dime novels) because with more complex literature we might lose sight of our actual goal. We do not want to teach dramaturgy or style. Rather, we want to show what the art of writing novels and the art of developing software have in common (from the distorted points of view of computer specialists).

Without playing down the complexity inherent in software development, we want to demonstrate that you can intuitively learn how to apply object-oriented methods. You should not expect, however, to derive benefits from using this approach at the very beginning. It is obvious that the reuse of code in your first project is not of as great importance as it will be in future projects. As usual, you must gather experience yourself or hire someone who has experience. Likewise, you cannot expect to write a successful novel if you start writing now.

In the sections that follow you play the role of a novelist, and we are assigned to be the software developers applying the approach suggested by VMT. We assume that, as a novelist, you do not write as a hobby but want to sell your book in bulk, just as we want to sell our applications to become rich and famous. If you were to write novels just for your private fun, you could write whatever you want without obeying any rules. The same would be valid for us: If we created applications to satisfy our own needs, nobody would blame us if we wrote our code in the old-fashioned, poorly documented, spaghetti-like freestyle.

Before we proceed, let us state the big difference between writing novels and developing software applications: Writing novels is an art; developing software is applied science. Therefore, although object-orientation aims to "industrialize" software development some day, assembly-line production is not desirable for the process of writing novels (but we notice such a trend when we look at light fiction). We want to be able to enjoy future novels and admire an author's particular style of writing that fills his or her characters with life and unleashes our imagination. Nevertheless, we want to compare the two processes because software development undeniably involves the developer's creativity and imagination.

Although we cannot partition the preparatory work of an author into analysis and design phases, we discover that preparing to write a novel and the preliminaries of software development have a great deal in common. For example, the preparations take considerably more time than the actual writing or coding. In this chapter we deal with the analysis phase, and in Chapter 4, "Designers at Work," on page 83, we focus on the design phase.

Collecting the Material

If you put yourself in an author's place, how would you proceed? First of all, you would define your subject, answering the following questions: Would you like to write a historical, contemporary, or science fiction novel? Which contexts should your novel cover? (Contexts include the historical period, the location, and the culture.) Should your novel be a romance, a crime story, a biography, or a drama? If you do not know what you are going to write about, you simply cannot begin, and, if you have only a vague idea of the contents of your book, you should not begin, unless you want to rival some intractable software developers.

The decision that has the greatest impact on your novel concerns the subject of the main story. This decision influences your style as well as the selection of the participating characters. You might combine several

subjects; for example, if you write a biography, your protagonist proba-
bly experiences the vicissitudes of life, which include love, jealousy, pas-
sion, grief, comedy, and despair, to name a few.

First, you certainly want to create an outline of the main story, that is,
the thread of the entire novel. Your publisher probably wants to look at
your abstract to decide whether your story is promising or a reject. You
should formulate your outline clearly, so that your publisher can follow
it. Surely, you will not succeed in formulating your outline on first try.
You probably will read it, delete some sentences, rearrange it, or even
start all over again. Your final epitome reveals what your novel essen-
tially is about and serves as a guide, as you further develop your novel.

Let us consider what you should include in your outline of the main
story: You should define certain "constants" before you start writing,
namely, the location of the action, the historical period, the principal
characteristics of the leading roles, and the thread of the plot. To create
a successful story you should research the characters of your novel and,
if possible, inspect the locations where the events take place.

Problem Domain

When we start developing a software application, our first task is to
analyze the specific problem domain, distinguish it clearly from the
real world, but not worry about any constraints that the implementation environment would impose; in object-oriented application development we call it object-oriented analysis (OOA). The result of our
analysis can be directly compared to the outline for your novel, as it
answers the "what?" question. In other words, we define the complete
function of the application and the system boundaries. Initially, we are
probably better off than you are, because our customers tell us what to
do; that is, they give us their requirements for the application.

After we have collected all material that is relevant to the system, we
must arrange and put the finishing touches on our customer's requirements. Generally, the specifications lack completeness or exactness
and show redundancy. To complete the requirements, we must learn
about our customer's business domain and its terminology. On our
first try seldom (between you and me, never) do we succeed in correctly defining what we should develop. Through ongoing communication with our users, however, we gradually acquire both the knowledge
and understanding that are essential to fulfilling our task.

The deliverables of the analysis phase help us understand the problem
domain as they provide different but complementary views or descriptions of the system that we develop. The deliverables are the complete
and exact requirements specifications, the use case model, the
sketches or prototypes of the user interfaces for each use case, the

class dictionary, the CRC cards for all classes, the static object model, and the dynamic model (refer to *Visual Modeling Technique–Object Technology Using Visual Programming* by D. Tkach et al.).

Requirement Specifications

We developed seven problem statements when we first thought about the daily work of a real estate agent:

1. Manage buyers
2. Manage sellers
3. Manage properties
4. Manage sale transactions
5. Track earnings
6. Document activities
7. Exchange data with the agency's computer

To keep the implementation simple, we established the following constraints:

❑ The application would not cover

➢ Seller management
➢ Sale contracts
➢ Documentation of agent activities

❑ The commission for an agent and the down payment for a property would be fixed values computed from commission and down payment rates.

❑ Agents and buyers would negotiate directly concerning the sale.

We know that our seven problem statements will not drive us to seize the closest keyboard and start hacking the code, because they are rather vague. So, we must define more precisely what we mean. Preferably, we formulate the definitions together with our customers, because they know best what they want.

In fact, we visited a real estate agency and interviewed two of the agents to learn how they do their job and how computers might help them. Our interview with the agents led us to refine the seven problem statements, as you can see in the 12 requirement specifications listed below. Twelve requirements specifications can in no way handle the real estate business. If, however, we had to describe everything that a real estate agency requires, this book would be a multivolume encyclopedia, and you would have to read a huge amount of analysis and design scribblings before you could learn VisualAge for C++.

You also can see, in the requirement specifications listed below, the transition from the rather simple, initial problem statements to the elaborate, precisely defined requirement specifications (for example, we explode the first statement into three specifications).

1. **Record, update, and delete buyer information and preferences.**

   Here, the terms *buyer information* and *buyer preferences* must be further defined. As you know from Chapter 1 ("Objects" on page 6), real-world objects have a tremendous number of attributes, but our application must concentrate on those that are most important for the problem domain. (The process whereby one tends to concentrate only on the relevant information for the problem domain is also known as *abstraction*.) So, we decide that buyer information includes the buyer's name, identification (social security number or driver's license number), telephone, address, and household income. Buyer preferences, which describe a buyer's particular notion of a property, include price range, size range (in square feet), number of bedrooms, number of bathrooms, number of stories, type of cooling, and type of heating.

2. **Search buyers by name.**

   It should be possible to search buyers by last name. It should also be possible to do a "pattern" search; for example, look for all buyers whose last names start with "Que."

3. **Show the buyers who are interested in a selected property.**

   From a list of properties, the agent can select one and retrieve the buyers whose preferences match the property characteristics. The buyers should be listed so that the agent can select one to retrieve the detailed information.

4. **Record and update property information.**

   Here, registration number, address, area, number of bedrooms, number of bathrooms, number of stories, size (in square feet), type of cooling and type of heating are of interest. Further, a second category of information is relevant for a property, namely, marketing information, such as price, price per square foot, commission for the agent, commission rate, number of days the property has been on the market, down payment rate, down payment value, and status (available, sale pending, or sold). Note that some attributes of the property information match the attributes of the buyer's preferences. Additional features or information about other categories that do not fit with the preceding attributes can be entered as textual description. A video that features the property completes the property information.

5. Show available properties of interest.

List the properties that have the "available" status and match some specific criteria, such as area, price range, size range, number of bedrooms, and number of bathrooms. These properties should be listed so that the agent can select one to retrieve the detailed information

6. Show affordable properties.

List the properties that have the "available" status and that a selected buyer can afford according to his or her income. The mortgage calculation should remain simple.

7. Display description or video of a selected property.

This feature provides potential buyers with a first impression of the property. On the basis of this first impression, they can either take a closer look at the property or avoid visiting it in vain.

8. Show the properties in which a selected buyer is interested (based on his or her preferences).

From a list of buyers, the agent can select one and retrieve the properties whose characteristics match the buyer's preferences. These properties should be listed so that the agent can select one to retrieve the detailed information or show the video.

9. Initiate, confirm, or cancel a sale transaction.

The agent initiates a sale transaction when a buyer decides to buy a desired (and affordable) property. The agency must go through several processes until the buyer is finally the owner of the property. For example, it must determine whether the buyer has liquid assets or is creditworthy, but the Visual Realty application does not cover these processes. Instead it creates an agreement form, which states that the property is reserved for the buyer for 10 days from the date of signature. During that period the property is marked as "sale pending." The agreement also states that the buyer has provided a down payment as proof of good faith. If the transaction is canceled, the agency returns the down payment, marks the property as "available," and destroys the agreement form. If the transaction is confirmed, the property is marked as "sold," and the agent's account is credited with the proper commission.

The agreement form contains the property's registration number, area, address, and price; the buyer's identification, name, and address; the amount of the down payment; and the date of the agreement.

10. Search agreement forms by date.

This function enables the agent to list all properties marked "sale pending" and to examine the associated sale transactions.

11. **Show how much commission the agent earned during the current month.**

We assume that there is a one-to-one relationship between agent and computer, so the application shows the sum of the commissions for the sold properties.

12. **Receive from the agency's computer or send to the agency's computer properties, customers, and sale transaction data that is relevant for the agent.**

The agency should be aware of its agent's activities, track the status of each property, and acquire information on new prospects.

All information about properties, buyers, and agreement forms is transferred to and from the agency's database. We must consider that a real estate agency usually employs more than one agent. The agency is responsible for maintaining the database, keeping it synchronized, and assigning properties and buyers to agents.

Just as your publisher should agree with your abstract, our customers should understand what we write down and fully agree with the functions of the system. If they do not agree, we must add other specifications or redefine them. At this stage of analysis, we iterate the refinement of the specifications to ensure that the problem definition is accurate.

Thread and Subplots

Your first cut must be appealing enough to convince your publisher of the potential success of the book. Before you deliver your work, you should consult with some reviewers, perhaps a friend or your spouse who can assess whether the flow of the story is comprehensible. Note that at first you create the skeleton of the story, and only later do you embellish it.

In your novel you not only tell the main story, you also delineate several subplots that run concurrently or sequentially. Subplots make the story more interesting, create tension, and make your readers stick to the book. While you sketch the thread of your story, you focus on the plots in which your protagonist is involved. If you wanted to summarize Michael Ende's book, The Neverending Story, *you could do so very concisely: a boy is absorbed by a book and seeks out a new environment. When he learns that his world is going to vanish, he tries to rescue it with his imagination. (Do not go to your publisher with only two sentences!) Michael Ende used several hundred pages to embroider and embellish his story; that is the actual art of writing.*

We software developers, however, must ensure that our project does not turn out to be a never-ending story. We have already collected and completed the customer requirements. At this stage, we must discuss with our users all services of the system, because our first model must capture all of their functional requirements. We group the requirements into use cases, which are ...*behaviorally related sequences of transactions in a dialogue with the system (Object-Oriented Software Engineering. A Use Case Driven Approach* by Jacobson et. al, p. 127).

Use Case Model

We write down use cases in the form of a dialog with complete sentences and assign a unique title to each. The dialog represents an interaction between the application that performs the function and the user of the system. According to Jacobson, a use case does not contain conditional branches, that is, each use case describes one distinct sequence of functions. If a function of the use case depends on the successful completion of a preceding function, we must define a second (alternative) use case that covers the event when the preceding function fails. In this case, an "extend" relationship represents the extension between the two use cases. In addition, a use case behavior can be embedded in other use cases, leading to a "use" relationship (Figure 26). Actually, to write the use cases we present the requirements specifications from the different users' points of view. In our case we only have one user: the agent.

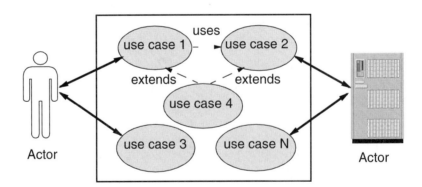

Figure 26. Use Case Representation

Throughout this book we focus on realizing problem statement 3, that is, *Manage properties*, so the following examples of use cases relate to requirement specifications 4 and 5.

Record Property Case
```
Agent:  Call the Record property function.
System: Present a form that the agent must fill in to specify all of the
        required information for a property.
Agent:  Fill in the form and click on an OK button or the like.
System: Verify the information and store it if it is correct.
```

Property Search Case
```
Agent:  Call the Search property function.
System: Present a form that the agent must fill in to specify the
        items of interest.
Agent:  Fill in the form and start a search.
System: Present the properties that match the specifications.
```

Jacobson also designates users of the system as actors to emphasize that users play roles. (*Object-Oriented Software Engineering. A Use Case Driven Approach* by Jacobson et. al, p. 171). A certain role, or type of user, is assigned to an actor. Usually, our application supports several actors: the "normal" actor, supervisors, and system administrators. The normal actor of the Visual Realty application would be the agent (Figure 27). The supervisor would be the manager of the agency, and the system administrator would be an office worker who cares about the consistency of the property database. Consequently, one person can play several roles. For example, John is a real estate agent who calls functions of the property management and, as he sometimes works in the office, of the system administrator, but he is one single user of the system. On the other hand, Mary and Denise, the general managers of the agency, are only interested in calling the supervisor functions to control John; they are two users playing one role. Generally, the use cases that normal actors activate make up the system's principal functions, which we focus on during the analysis phase. That is why we interviewed real estate agents and not their managers.

Actors are not necessarily humans; they can be external devices or other computer systems (Figure 27). Each use case is related to at least one actor. The set of all use cases describes the entire function of the system. Together with the set of all actors, it constitutes the use case model. Every actor must be connected to at least one use case, and vice versa; an unconnected actor or use case would be superfluous. In addition, an actor is outside the system; that is, it does not belong to the problem domain, so we do not describe its function in detail.

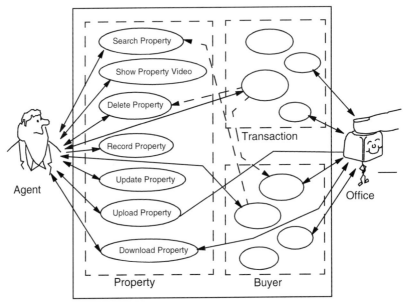

Figure 27. Visual Realty Use Cases

The use case model is fundamental, as it is the collection of all requirements and serves as input for all subsequent models that will be developed, including the final model—the source code. The system's overall function is reflected in the use case model, and we take the use cases to develop the analysis model, the design model, and the source code. Every model can be tested against the use case model for completeness and consistency. If we must change or enhance the application, we do so by first adding or changing one or more use cases and then changing the other models accordingly.

The use case model also helps to maintain the traceability of the system because we know from which use case each component of the later models derives. Remember that traceability is the most important characteristic of our system, as it enables us to make corrections and modifications in a straightforward manner.

User Interface Prototype

Because we have described the system's functions in the form of use cases, we can envision the user interface of the application prototype. We know which function each actor can invoke, so we can illustrate for potential users what the screen might look like (Figure 28). We can sketch the interface on white paper and then (if we are skilled enough and well equipped), start Visual Builder and paint the screens right before our customer's eyes. Sometimes, a prototype of the user interface makes the customers bubble over with a wealth of ideas, because they finally see what they can do with computers. In this case, we should stay cool and not promise too much....

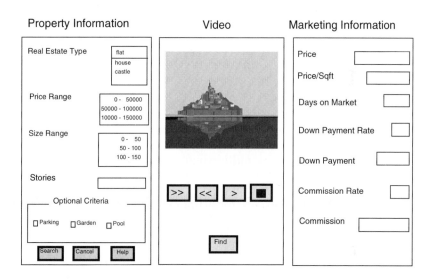

Figure 28. User Interface Samples

We suggest starting with the most important use case and developing the interface with a top-down approach; that is, begin with the main screen and then define the secondary windows, dialog boxes, and pop-up menus. Again, we come to the best solution after some iteration.

Defining Roles

Before you start writing, one of your important decisions is the selection of the characters of your novel. Initially, you only rough out their traits; you refine them later. Barry Morrow, who wrote the screenplay for the movie Rain Man, *says: "Creating a character is like shaping a lump of clay, or like whittling a stick." First, the character is rather amorphous; that is, you have only a vague idea of his or her being. Then, the first broad strokes begin to define the character, and you add emotions, values, and attitudes to provide depth. You also can infuse your character with conflicting behaviors to increase the interest and tension of your readers (for example, your character is a tough broker who sentimentally loves his or her children).*

To create a novel, you can select from several patterns, and the pattern chosen determines the traits of your characters. If you decide to write a romantic novel, you will deal with love, fidelity, affection, sacrifice, and yearning on the one hand, and infidelity, indifference, and heartlessness on the other hand. If you decide to write a crime novel, you will deal with cruelty, loneliness, revenge, as well as heroism, justice, and readiness. You can mix several patterns within your novel to make it more interesting, but the main thread follows one distinct motif.

Patterns and Types

The patterns for software systems as well are numerous and varied. The *machine control* pattern provides a modest user interface that consists only of some switches, sensors, and digital or analog indicators but must react very quickly to changing process states; sometimes a delay of 1 millisecond can have fatal consequences. The *business graphic* pattern must provide a highly elaborate user interface, but the response time is not so crucial. The *compiler* pattern must hold a lot of information during run time, whereas its user interface is poor, and the response time is of (almost) no importance.

The pattern of the application that we develop determines which object type we must primarily use in our system. Jacobson defines three object types: interface objects, which are responsible for communicating with the world outside our system; entity objects, which mainly store information; and service objects, which control the flow of operation. Highly dialog-oriented applications primarily use interface objects, data-oriented systems primarily use entity objects, and service objects prevail in function-oriented applications.

Do you recognize the correspondence between your characters and our objects, and your characters' traits and our objects' types? As our computer environment is rather unemotional, we deal with only a few object types but many objects. We notice that for each actor (remember that an actor is a user or device outside the system) there must exist at least one interface object, as an actor communicates with our system. Our system also contains at least one entity object, which holds the current state of the process that is running. Service objects are necessary only if we cannot clearly assign a certain function to an entity or interface object or want to guide our user through a sequence of operations.

Finding Objects

To find the objects of our system as well as their attributes and functions, we must analyze the requirements specifications syntactically and semantically. As a rule of thumb, we can say that nouns in a formulated sentence represent objects, adjectives represent attributes, and verbs represent functions.

So, let us have a look at requirement specification 1: *Record, update, and delete buyer information and preferences*. This specification tells us that we must deal with buyers who have information and preferences, and the user should be able to record, update, and delete that data. If we obey our rule, we would come up with three objects (Buyer, Information, and Preference), but we already have found the famous exception to the rule, because some nouns can represent attributes. And a Buyer object with information and preference attributes sounds reasonable because information and preference are tightly coupled to the buyer, as we can see from the context of the requirement specification.

Another exception to the rule: synonyms. Often, we encounter synonyms for an object because we interview different people, or we pick up information here and there and write it down, each of us in our own terms. Thus, during the search for candidate objects and their properties, we must homogenize and structure the requirement specifications and agree on common terms.

Requirement specification 2, *Search buyers by name*, confirms that *name* is an important attribute of the Buyer object and introduces the search function that must be applied for a set of buyers.

Specification 3, *Show the buyers who are interested in a selected property*, reveals a new candidate object, namely Property. As the business of real estate agencies is about properties, there is no doubt that property is a real object. In addition, this specification hints that there is a link between the Buyer object and the Property object. The link is based on the property characteristics. We come back to links between objects in "Defining Interactions and Relations" on page 76.

Specifications 4 through 7, *Record and update property information*, *Show available properties of interest*, *Show affordable properties*, and *Display description or video of a selected property,* tell us which attributes are necessary for the Property object and provide information on a second link between buyer and property based on the buyer's income. Specification 8, *Show the properties in which a selected buyer is interested*, also indicates a link between buyer and property. The link is based on the buyer's preferences.

Specifications 9 and 10, *Initiate, confirm, or cancel a sale transaction* and *Search agreement forms by date,* introduce the Sale Transaction object with the agreement form and date attributes. Specification 9 states that the agent initiates a sale transaction when a buyer decides to buy an affordable property. It introduces the Agent object and reveals a link among buyer, property, and agent. The agent manages information on buyers and properties. This leads us to consider two other links among these objects.

Finally, specifications 11 and 12, *Receive from the agency's computer or send to the agency's computer properties, customers, and sale transaction data that is relevant for the agent* and *Show how much commission the agent earned during the current month,* describe three additional service functions.

So, through this syntactical analysis we discover the following objects: Buyer, Property, Sale Transaction, Agent. The next step is to group the objects into classes. If the problem domain is small, as it is in the Visual Realty application, every object typically maps to a class. If we include the management of sellers in the problem domain, we could group the Seller and the Buyer objects into the Customer class.

Class Dictionary and CRC Cards

The traits of the characters in your novel are unveiled in the way they think, talk, and behave. It would be worthwhile to establish a fact file for every character in your novel. The fact file would include, for example, the particular behaviors, dreams, and appearance of each character. If you have a talent for drawing, you might even sketch your characters. The goal is to create vivid characters who have consistent traits and with whom your readers can identify. For the most part, the characters impel the action; sometimes, however, some fateful events or coincidences give a fresh impetus to the course of the story.

As we mentioned earlier, we software analysts must deal with actors who are outside the system; they are users of the system and the main initiators of the flow of the system's functions, but they do not execute the functions themselves. The object-oriented approach assigns the responsibility of executing functions to objects.

Class Dictionary

As software analysts we also must set up a fact file. Ours is a class dictionary that contains an entry for every class. As you can read in "Classes" on page 7, classes describe the attributes and functions for a certain group of objects. Thus, the entry in the dictionary describes the class responsibilities and the attributes that the class must have. The class dictionary helps us correctly define and develop the classes and serves as a means of communication with our customers. The definitions and responsibilities must be formulated in complete sentences to create a stable base for our object model. We must avoid "woolly" dictionary entries from the beginning, so that we can rely on our classes and regard each entry as a binding contract. We can also see whether the existence of a certain class is justified: If we cannot assign any responsibility to a class, we can remove it.

CRC Cards

Wirfs-Brock suggests the use of CRC cards, which can be regarded as extended class dictionary entries because they describe the responsibilities and collaborators of a class. To save some paper or files on our hard disk, we decide to combine the class dictionary and CRC cards so that a CRC card contains not only the name of the class but also its complete description. We also suggest omitting the default functions that exist for almost every class: create, delete, and update. However, some classes depend on those functions. For example, as you can see in Table 2 and Table 3, we cannot delete a buyer who initiated a sale transaction that has not been canceled or confirmed.

Table 2. Extended CRC Cards for Buyer	
Description	Person who wants to buy a property
Attributes	ID name telephone address income preferences
Responsibilities	**Collaborators**
delete	Sale transaction

Table 3.	Extended CRC Cards for Property
Description	Real estate managed by the agency
Attributes	ID address area number of bedrooms number of bathrooms number of stories size (square feet) cooling type heating type textual description video price price per square foot commission commission rate down payment rate down payment value number of days on the market status
Responsibilities	**Collaborators**
search	Buyer (preferences)

Table 4.	Extended CRC Cards for Sale Transaction
Description	Recorded information for the business process sale
Attributes	date agreement form buyer identifier agent identifier property identifier
Responsibilities	**Collaborators**
initiate cancel confirm	Property Buyer

Defining Interactions and Relations

The characters in your novel do not live in isolation; they establish relationships among themselves. Before you start writing, you outline when your characters meet with other characters and determine whether these meetings have any effect on the subsequent action. The relationships may create or resolve conflicts and increase suspense and expectation. Most importantly, you must synchronize the sequence of the encounters. Some encounters have more influence on the behavior of a person than others. Some can even completely change a character.

You must take into consideration that when you deal with two characters who have a relationship, there are two conflicts from each character's point of view. If another character appears—you might think of a love triangle—you must manage six conflicts, as each of the characters has two relationships.

To keep track of the dynamics, you will want to record encounters and current and future relationships in your fact file. If you must handle a more complex constellation, you will want to make some sketches on a piece of paper that visually document the connections. The relationships are not necessarily of the real world; they could be a figment of one's imagination.

During the software analysis phase we build static and dynamic models that illustrate, respectively, the interactions and the relationships or links among objects.

Interactions

VMT applies two different kinds of diagrams to form the dynamic model: the event-trace diagram and the state-transition diagram. The event-trace diagram describes how the participating objects interact during the execution of a use case. We must create such a diagram for each use case to gain an overall view of the system's functions. We can then summarize all functions or responsibilities with their parameters that are related to a particular object. Because several people might be involved in creating the diagrams, the names of the functions and the number and sequence of their parameters must be homogenized. The diagram (Figure 29) represents objects as vertical bars and the events as a horizontal link between the objects.

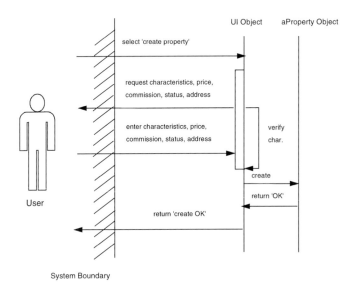

Figure 29. Event-Trace Diagram for the Record Property Use Case

The state-transition diagram focuses on one object only, regarding it as a finite state machine. It shows every state that the object takes on as the result of an executed function. Each object has an initial state, one or more intermediate states, and, optionally, a final state. Each state is implemented as a distinct value of an attribute of the object. The diagram represents the states as nodes and the event that causes the change of the state as an arc between the original state and the resulting state (Figure 30).

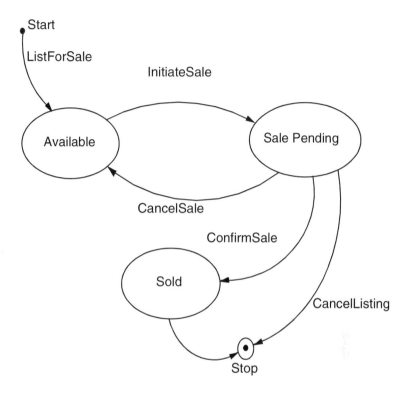

Figure 30. State Transition Diagram of Property Status

To avoid having to develop an overwhelming number of diagrams, we are interested only in objects with state changes that are significant for the process flow. A negligible state change would be when the age of a buyer switches from 39 to 40 (although it is of some importance for the person concerned); an important state change would be when the age of a sale agreement form switches from 9 days to 10. We check the state-transition diagram against every event-trace diagram in which our object is involved to ensure completeness and consistency.

Relationships

The static object model, often simply called the "object model," shows the hierarchy and the coherence of the objects. The coherence is the static relationship, also called the *association*, among the objects. VMT adopts Rumbaugh's notation to draw the object model and the associations (Figure 31 and Appendix B, "OMT Notation," on page 343). We assign meaningful names to the relationships so that we can formulate a complete sentence when we take the name of the first object as the sentence's subject, the name of the relationship as the predicate, and the name of the second object as the sentence's object. For example: The link between Buyer and Property is established by the buyer's preference, so we name the link "prefers" and read the link as "Buyer prefers Property." There are different forms of associations: one-to-one, one-to-many, and many-to-many.

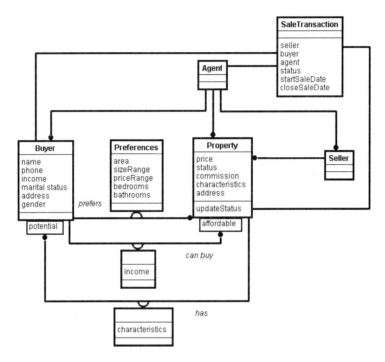

Figure 31. Analysis Object Model of the Visual Realty Application

A special relationship between two classes is inheritance (see "Inheritance" on page 8). We could have constructed subclasses of Property, namely, Building and Plot, but we found that the agency does not differentiate between these two kinds of real estate.

In Figure 31, you see six classes and ten associations. The relevant classes are Buyer, Property, and Sale Transaction. The relevant associations are Buyer can buy Property; Buyer prefers Property; Property attracts Buyer; Sale Transaction involves a Buyer, a Property, and an Agent; Seller sells a Property; and Agent manages a portfolio of Properties, Buyers, and Sellers.

> **Attention**
>
> For the purpose of completeness, Figure 31 shows the Agent and Seller objects and their links. As mentioned in the introduction, the application does not manage the seller. In addition, the application depicts a fictitious real estate agency where only one agent works. Therefore, the application does not manage the agent information.

Defining Contexts

The time during which your story unfolds and where it takes place are of great importance, as they influence the behavior of your characters. For example, if your novel is set in some past era, your characters will necessarily have to speak in a vocabulary that is noncontemporary. The time and location of your novel will undoubtedly require that you do some research and look in libraries for relevant documents. The benefit of this bigger effort might be that you attract those readers who are especially interested in learning something about life in other cultures or epochs; you might think of Noah Gordon's novel, The Medicus, *a medieval epoch that aroused his readers' enthusiasm and their thirst for a sequel.*

Here it might be difficult to draw an analogy with OOA. However, when we must analyze an existing application that we want to adopt in our new system, is it not appropriate to research the past? The existing software was developed in the past, so we must consult the documentation (which sometimes exists) and look in the software libraries for the underlying functions of the system. We can also ask former developers how they planned the implementation and maintenance of the system. As for the location of our application, we must consider the hardware and software platforms and many other parameters that relate to the implementation.

OOA excludes reflections on the implementation environment, as we want to achieve an analysis model that is independent of any constraints. Certainly, we must consider the feasibility of our project in terms of the time frame and available financial resources. In addition, we should know something about the user interfaces of the system. Because we and our customers must clearly understand the analysis model, it cannot contain descriptions that are too formal or drawings that are too complex.

The primary goal of the analysis model is to use it to communicate with our users, who are not necessarily acquainted with our software terminology. Thus, we must name the objects and their attributes and functions with terms that our users understand. Therefore, we use the same terms that appear in the problem statements, so that sometimes the analysis model is also called the semantic model. Actually, it is a symbolic representation of the formulated requirements specifications. We should be able to translate the analysis model into the specifications without difficulty. On the one hand, the model represents the requirements that have been completed and normalized; on the other hand, it serves as a generalized description of the implementation.

As mentioned before, we develop the analysis model without regard to the constraints that the implementation environment would impose on the system. Thus, we can use the same model when we want to implement our application on different platforms. That is why you have not read much about VisualAge for C++ in this chapter. Before we start implementing the application, we must further refine all of the deliverables of the analysis phase to adapt them to the target platform, which in our case is OS/2 Warp. We call this phase of refinement *object-oriented design* (OOD).

4

Designers at Work

If you design something that even a fool can use, then only a fool will use it.

- Murphy's Law

The design phase of software development begins when we start thinking about the implementation specifications. We cannot say exactly when the analysis phase ends and the design phase begins, but there is a difference between analysis and design (Figure 32 and Table 5). The analysis model is a conceptual picture of *what* the system provides, whereas the design model is an abstraction of *how* the system is really built. During design, we take a closer look at the details so that we can implement the final solution.

Object-oriented design (OOD) encompasses both system design and object design activities. System design in a client/server environment is a vast and complex topic. Fortunately, the Visual Realty application is a stand-alone software system, although it can generate export files for uploading and downloading data to or from a server.

In this chapter we present the approach we used to design our application with VisualAge for C++. The approach is adapted from VMT.

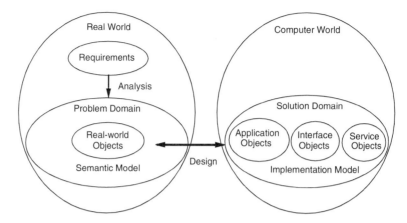

Figure 32. From Analysis to Design

During system design, we decompose the analysis object model into subsystems. The decomposition process is comparable to the process of partitioning the whole application into subapplications. System design also includes the task of choosing a platform and enabling technology as the basis for deriving a high-level architecture. In this chapter, we limit the system design to describing the subsystems of our application. Our main focus is on object design with VisualAge for C++.

Table 5. Deliverables of Analysis and Design

Analysis Deliverable	Design Deliverable
Use cases, external (user's) view	Use cases, internal (designer's) view
User interface specifications and prototype	Design prototype
Object model	Extension to the object model to include interface and service classes
Class dictionary	Extension to the class dictionary to include interface and service classes
CRC cards	More detailed CRC cards are more detailed, and new CRC cards describe the classes required for the implementation
Event-trace diagrams (external view)	Event-trace diagrams (internal view)
State-transition diagrams (global level)	State-transition diagrams (detailed level; only for objects with relevant state changes)

Legacy code is an issue when moving to the design phase, because we must integrate it into our application. We must postpone all fine tuning of overall system performance, because we tend to draw incorrect conclusions if the implementation has not completed. Here the parallel development of a design prototype can help measure run-time behavior, so that we can change our database design as early as possible. The programming language might or might not support object-oriented facilities such as inheritance and polymorphism. It is possible to extend each programming language to an object-oriented language. However, if this is a first project, the task is formidable, as coding rules must be defined and functions that "simulate" object-orientation must be implemented. In our case, however, we need not worry because VisualAge for C++ provides those functions.

System Design

You have already sketched the thread of the plot, and now you define further subplots that support the main flow of action. You structure the overall action by partitioning it. Some authors partition their novels into parts, they further divide the parts into chapters, and sometimes they even subdivide the chapters into subchapters. Optionally, you can assign a title to each chapter and part, so that readers can learn the structure of the action by reading the chapter and part titles. You can also regard a chapter as entirely self-contained, because the actions taking place in it are so closely related that it can exist independently of the book. Indeed, you can assign the writing of such chapters to another author.

System design is the design of a high-level architecture for the proposed solution. It includes a definition of the major system building blocks and their high-level connectivity. It also includes an application architecture that organizes the solution in subsystems.

Our main tasks during the system design stage are to:

❑ Partition the object model into subsystems
❑ Map subsystems to VisualAge for C++ subapplications
❑ Select the implementing platform
❑ Define data placement and data processing

Partition Object Model into Subsystems

We partition the system into two or more subsystems, mainly to reduce complexity. You can compare a subsystem to a self-contained chapter of your novel; we also want our subsystem to be self-contained. We choose objects for a subsystem that are closely coupled by relationships or that form a functional unit (for example, if one object is a collaborator for a function of another object). We can read the functional units from the CRC cards, and we can see the relationships when we look at the object model. As a rule of thumb, we can assign the use cases belonging to one actor to one subsystem. If one actor can invoke several use cases, we then focus on the objects. If some of the use cases use a certain group of objects, we build a subsystem including that group of objects. The objects inside a subsystem are only loosely related to objects outside the subsystem. If some single objects cannot be grouped into any subsystem—objects that are responsible for exception handling, for example—we treat each of them as a special subsystem.

There is one difference when we compare a subsystem to a self-contained chapter in your novel: Some subsystems are regarded as an extension of the base system and are sold separately as service packs. *Your readers would be very unhappy if they had to pay extra for the last chapter of your novel....*

We can split the effort of system design by developing and implementing subsystems simultaneously with more than one team. As the objects in different subsystems are only loosely coupled, the message flow between subsystems is much simpler than the message flow within subsystems, and the teams can thus work rather independently. We can further partition the subsystems into more low-level subsystems.

We partition the Visual Realty application into three major subsystems:

Property:	This subsystem provides agents with all of the functions they need to manage their property portfolios.
Buyer:	This subsystem provides agents with all of the functions they need to manage their buyer portfolios.
Sale transaction:	This subsystem provides agents with all of the functions they need to manage the sale process.

Map Subsystems to VisualAge for C++ Subapplications

With VisualAge for C++ we can make a relatively smooth transition from subsystems to subapplications, as the application design tool of VisualAge for C++, the Visual Builder, isolates subapplications in so-called Visual Builder Binary (VBB) files.

We can consider the following VBB files:

❏ VRPROP.VBB contains the parts required for the property sub-system.

❏ VRBUY.VBB contains the parts required for the buyer subsystem.

❏ VRSALE.VBB contains the parts required for the sale transaction subsystem.

❏ VRSERV.VBB contains the parts required to perform basic services (upload and download data)

❏ VRCOMM.VBB contains common parts (for example, logon view and address view) that can be reused several times in the application.

Select the Implementing Platform

The analysis model is the ideal model, but our computer world is not ideal. The components of the actual implementation environment, namely, the programming language, operating system, database management system (DBMS), networking system, and other software packages, impose some constraints. The design model must include these components, but the goal is to make our problem domain objects as independent of the platform particulars as possible, particularly if we intend to implement our product on different platforms. Rather, we create new service objects that serve as an intermediate layer between the functions of the actual platform and our business objects.

An example is database access: If a function of a business object directly invokes an SQL query, we will have to change and recompile the object when we (or the customer) bring in another DBMS. You could justly retort that a new DBMS always involves a change, whether it concerns the business object or the service object, so we would have to expend the same amount of effort no matter which object we change. We agree, for the current implementation. If we think of reusability and maintenance, however, we prefer the solution with the intermediate object, because then our core objects, which deal with the business logic, are independent of the underlying DBMS. If we are lucky and land a new customer who needs the same application, we can stay cool and ask: "What would you like, DB2 or Poet?" Even if the customer wants a brand-new, fuzzy-logic-oriented, PCM-CIA-based, 128-bit DBMS, we will still deliver the same core objects. (All we have to do is buy a bigger coffeemaker and create an incentive for our programmers, who will have the dubious pleasure of implementing the new service object.)

To make the application workable and manageable, we must select the system platform or infrastructure. In our case, the implementing platform is assumed to be a DB2/2 local area network (LAN) environment.

The enabling technology and component selections for our system building blocks were predetermined by both the available supporting platform for VisualAge for C++ when we wrote this book and the needs of our application (Figure 33).

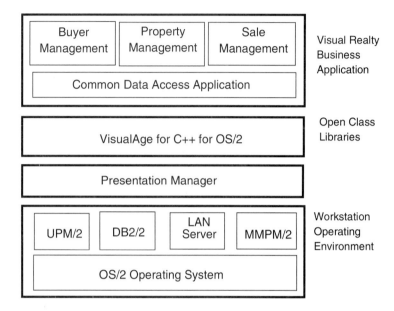

Figure 33. Visual Realty System Platform

The Visual Realty application is simple. It uses a stand-alone database so that the agent can carry his or her laptop when visiting customers. The agent can update the local database and generate export files. Back at the agency, the agent can import the files to the central database.

Define Data Placement and Data Processing

The initial decisions for data placement and data processing are made during system design and can be reassessed during the object design stage. These decisions would include whether the data should be stored in a local or remote database.

Refine Contexts

You have already decided when and where your story takes place. Now you must describe the context more distinctly, like a camera that zooms in on a scene. You place your characters in a period setting or describe the particulars of the landscape. Now is the time to consider how you

want to embellish your novel. Do you want to describe a sunset, or per-
haps a rebellion of gnomes? Remember that the environment you
describe influences the personality, behavior, and speech of your char-
acters. All elements must fit together well so that your readers can
immerse themselves in your fictional world.

Object Design

The object design phase includes a refinement and a fleshing out of
the object details. Of course, the level of detail for the object descriptions can vary.

Our main tasks during the object design phase are to:

❑ Design the solution domain classes
❑ Design the nonvisual parts
❑ Design the GUI with the visual parts
❑ Design the persistent data

Design the Solution Domain Classes

The set of classes that make up an application is usually much larger
than the set of classes identified during the analysis phase. As we consider the circumstances of the implementation environment, we find
objects that we must include in our model. New objects emerge that
help implement the services or serve as an interface between the
application and the world outside the system, namely, the users or
connected devices. The initial set of semantic application classes identified in the analysis object model represents only the "core" business
behavior of the application. Other solution domain classes must be
designed to provide the concrete functions of the application. Interface
classes that represent the user interface and service classes that provide service functions such as data input validation or database access
are some examples of additional classes required for the implementation of the application.

We can compare the visibility of the analysis model with the top of an
iceberg, the main part of which is hidden under water. Our design
model reveals the hidden objects (Figure 34). To maintain traceability,
we translate every object into a part that we later implement, using
VisualAge for C++, in a separate source module. The solution domain
classes and services class are mapped to nonvisual parts, whereas
Interface classes are mapped to visual parts. The core is and should
remain the analysis model. The supporting objects are settled around
this core, providing the services that are necessary to embed the system in the implementation environment.

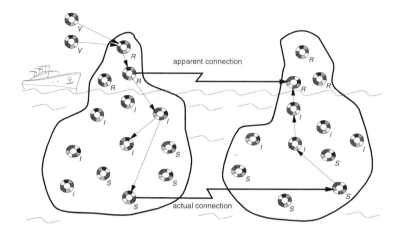

Figure 34. Design Model: Reveal Hidden Objects

The design of solution domain classes is iterative, as is everything else in object-oriented development. For example, in the Visual Realty application, we must have a service class to access the database and control database access with a login procedure. This need does not come out at the very first time of the design phase but after several iterations. As you will see in Chapter 6, "Mapping Relational Tables Using Data Access Builder," on page 127, this service is provided by the IDatastore part.

In the detailed design object model, objects are represented as non-visual or visual parts to facilitate a straightforward implementation that uses the Composition Editor of VisualAge for C++. To avoid complexity, we do not draw all of the parts. However, we show them in the different event-trace diagrams for the subsystem we describe.

Design the Nonvisual Parts

Once we have determined the required solution domain classes, we are ready to flesh out their details and map them to nonvisual parts. To help us in this task, we use the object model, the prototype interface, and the event-trace diagrams for the use case scenarios for each subsystem. The user interfaces enable us to flesh out some base attributes or derived attributes. The event-trace diagrams detail the message flow between the objects and reveal missing objects or missing methods.

Let us take our CRC cards containing the class attributes and responsibilities. We complete the cards by adding the data types of the attributes, naming the functions that carry out the responsibilities, and defining the number, sequence, and data types of the parameters of those functions.

As you will see in Chapter 6, "Mapping Relational Tables Using Data Access Builder," on page 127, the Visual Realty application is data-centric. Thus, most of the nonvisual parts we use are mapped from database tables. Nevertheless, when designing a nonvisual part, you must pay attention to the following issues:

❑ Choosing the right data structures to support object relationships. VisualAge for C++ provides you with a set of predefined data structures (see Chapter 2). The choice is dictated by semantic considerations. For example, an association with multiplicity 0 or 1 between class A and class B is represented by an attribute in each part interface referencing class A or class B. An association with multiplicity 1-m between class A and class B is represented by an attribute of type *collection of class B* in class A and by an attribute of type *class A* in class B.

❑ Designing derived attribute policies. Indeed, it is often useful to make a distinction between primitive attributes that cannot be derived from other attributes and derived attributes that can be derived from other attributes (for example, price per square foot is an attribute that can be derived from price and size).

❑ Designing the data integrity policy. The programmer devotes a great deal of time to building controls on user data. Two main alternatives can be devised:

➢ Target objects expect that data is valid when passed to them and the sender object is in charge of checking the data.
➢ Target objects verify data when they are asked to modify their state.

As you will see in "Event Handler" on page 220, we adopt the first alternative, hooking event handlers to some entry fields at the view level.

Design the GUI with the Visual Parts

During the analysis stage, we have defined the analysis object model with only nonvisual parts. In the design and detailed design phases, we must define the visual parts.

We recommend a bottom-up approach to achieve part reusability. You start at the bottom of the class hierarchy and build one or more elementary visual parts for each nonvisual part that we have created. (Visual parts are also referred to as *views* in this book.) You build the elementary visual parts by using primitive GUI controls (such as entry fields, list boxes, and push buttons). Then you can aggregate these views to build more complex views, which represent the final assembly of the final end-user interface.

Design the Persistent Data

We use Data Access Builder to map our database tables to nonvisual parts. Because our application is data-centric, our Data Access Builder parts play the role of the business nonvisual parts. However, some nonvisual parts, such as MarketingInfo, are built to hold some logic that is relevant to the agency's business rules. The relationships between the parts are simulated by means of joins with primary and foreign keys. For example, the address information of a property is not located in the property table; it is located in a separate table. When the property information is accessed, the address information is retrieved at the same time and displayed in the property view.

In the next section, we select the Property subsystem and explain how to refine its design model to come up with a detailed model that is ready to be implemented by use of VisualAge for C++.

Refining the Design Model

You know exactly when and where your story takes place and you know your characters. Now the time has come to make things happen. Relationships and encounters imbue your story with decisive impulses. You have already defined the relationships in your outline and fact files, but they are static. Now you must make them dynamic. Encounters, meetings, appointments, dates, and coincidences, fictional or real, enliven relationships and further develop the action. They increase the tension, but you can also use them to slow down the main action and let your readers take a few deep breaths.

One of the tasks that will challenge you the most is creating vivid and clear dialog. As in real life, not all is said that is thought. Sometimes you have to let your reader read between the lines.

Now the hard work starts for us: We must draw a detailed dynamic model for all of our use cases, but now we must also consider all participating objects and all objects that we may discover later. During the analysis phase we described only those use cases that an actor directly initiates, and we reflected only the business objects. Now we must also consider those use cases that are created "under the covers" and reflect the objects that are invisible to the user. We can see on the event-trace diagrams how the objects interact with one another. Initially, actors create events (according to Jacobson, *Object-Oriented*

Software Engineering. A Use Case Driven Approach by I. Jacobson et al. p. 147, they "send stimuli") when they give any input. These events are partially handled by the interface objects, as the actor should receive an immediate feedback, but the interface object passes the event to another object that is responsible for carrying out the actor's request. Events, in fact, are function calls to other objects, which in turn should provide information or carry out a service. We must define the names and parameters of every event with meaningful names to facilitate maintenance and reuse.

Each use case has a normal course and several alternative courses that handle exceptions. Sometimes we find abstract use cases that are comparable to subprocedures. (An abstract use case is a sequence of operations that can be reused in one or more "real" use cases.) When we build a big application, several designers develop the dynamic model simultaneously. Thus, we must homogenize the model (that is, we must find the smallest number of methods, detect methods with common behavior, and give them a unique name.)

After we have developed all event-trace diagrams for one object, we can start implementing the object. The diagrams give a complete picture of the object's interfaces. We also can draw each object's state-transition diagram to show which method has an impact on the object's state. As a rule of thumb, we can say that each object maps to one class. If the object plays several roles, however, we should map it to several classes. Object-oriented languages help us to seamlessly translate the dynamic model into source code. As the translation can be done in a straightforward manner, a code generator can be applied here. Humans must still make the final refinements.

From the different views we have sketched in the user interface prototyping phase (see Figure 28 on page 71, for example), we can envision the visual parts we need to implement all of the use cases. Furthermore, from the event-trace diagrams we can chain these different views and discover some nonvisual parts that we need to complete the process. For example, to search a property by its characteristics, users access a primary window where they can choose the search option. This option brings them to a secondary window where they select several characteristics of "their" property. Then they launch the search. The result is displayed by means of a table.

For our purposes, we consider the three main functions of the property subsystem: property retrieving, property creation, and property update.

As previously mentioned, refining the design object model is an iterative process that involves the existing use cases, their corresponding event-trace diagrams, and the design object model itself. On the basis of the part available in the implementation tool and the detailed description of each use case, we evaluate the parts required to complete our process. We apply this refinement process for each event-trace diagram and then modify the design object model.

In the sections that follow, we illustrate the refinement process for the property retrieving, property creation, and property update use cases. We start from a first cut of the property subsystem object model (Figure 35), which is based on the following assumptions:

❏ The property information is divided into separate objects that are stored in separate relational tables.

❏ A Property object is represented on the screen as a notebook.

❏ A distinctive object, PropertyManager, is required to manage a set of properties. In effect, requirement specifications 5 and 6 (see "Requirement Specifications" on page 64) imply the need for a property set structure that must be managed somehow.

❏ A set of properties is shown to the user as a container control that holds one or several container objects. A container object is a particular view of a Property object (the other view is the notebook view).

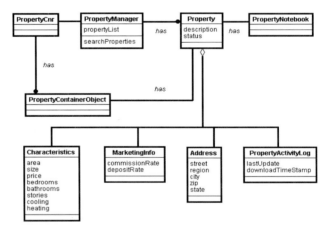

Figure 35. Design Object Model of the Property Subsystem: First Cut

The links between the different objects represent association relationships. The *has* link expresses an association between two objects. For example, the Property and Address objects are associated to express that a Property *has* an Address. The link between PropertyManager and Property indicates that a PropertyManager manages one-to-many properties.

Refining the Property Retrieving Scenario

The use case corresponding to a property search is expressed as follows:

When the user selects the search option, he or she is prompted to enter his or her criteria search, such as price range, size range, area, number of bedrooms, number of bathrooms, number of stories, type of cooling, and type of heating. Once the user provides the information, the user activates the search. The properties that match the criteria are displayed in tabular form.

In this use case scenario, we feel the need for some extra views to complete the process. We can then refine the first event-trace diagram, adding three views that help the user navigate through the application:

❑ PropertyManagementView is a primary window that enables users to choose the search option.

❑ PropertySearchParameterView is a secondary window that enables users to enter their search criteria.

❑ PropertySearchResultView is a window that displays a table of properties that match the users' criteria.

At the detailed design stage, we must take into account the presentation characteristics of the target platform. In our case, the application runs on a stand-alone system under OS/2. Taking advantage of the PM controls, we use the detailed view representation of a container to display the properties as a table.

When the user selects the *search* option from PropertyManagementView, a secondary window is created: PropertySearchParameterView (Figure 36). This secondary window prompts the user to enter his or her criteria. The criteria are sent as a clause to PropertySearchResultView. This clause is used by PropertyManager to extract the matching properties. Then, PropertyManager refreshes the property container, which is displayed by PropertySearchResultView. (Although not shown on Figure 36, PropertyManager is embedded in PropertySearchResultView to refresh the property container.) Thus, PropertySearchParameterView and PropertySearchResultView are associated by the clause. We can then refine the design object model by adding these two classes, which are associated by a link attribute clause.

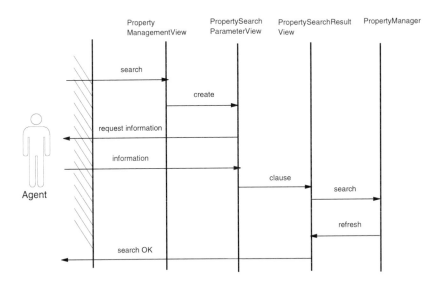

Figure 36. Event-Trace Diagram for the Property Search Use Case

Furthermore, PropertyManagementView is the first panel that is displayed to the user when he or she accesses the Property subsystem. It is linked to PropertySearchParameterView by a *use* relationship called *create*. The create relationship states that the user can access the *Search* option from the PropertyManagementView. During the user interface prototyping phase, it is decided that the user must close the secondary window to access the primary window. (In PM it is said that the secondary is shown modally.) For this reason, the relationship clause is a one-to-one association.

Remember that in the first design stage we had to introduce the PropertyManager class to manage a set of properties. The visual representation of the class was a container control, and the representation of each property was a container object control.

In the second cut (Figure 37) we can aggregate the PropertyManager and the PropertyCnr classes to the PropertySearchResultView. PropertyManager and PropertyCnr are associated by the *show* relationship, which states that "PropertyCnr shows the contents of the Property list managed by PropertyManager." In addition, PropertyCnr holds one-to-many PropertyContainerObjects, each of which is associated with a Property instance by the *has* link attribute.

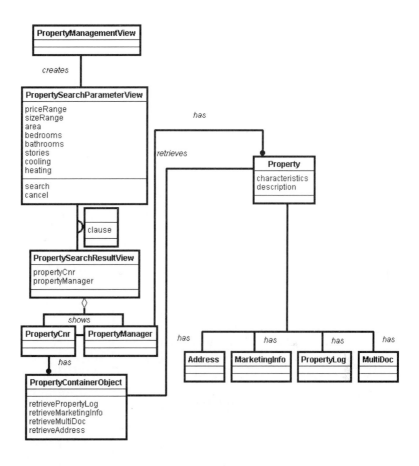

Figure 37. Design Object Model of the Property Subsystem: Second Cut

Refining the Property Creation Scenario

From PropertyManagementView, the agent can select the *create* option to record a new property in the portfolio. To provide the agent with a way of entering the property information, we must again define one extra view, PropertyCreateView. According to the first design object model of the property subsystem, this view presents the property information as a notebook. To reuse this notebook in other scenarios (see "Refining the Property Update Scenario" on page 101), we decide to make this notebook a separate view: PropertyView. Thus, PropertyCreateView contains PropertyView.

The user enters the property information in PropertyView and creates the property in the portfolio by selecting the *create* option of Property-CreateView (Figure 38). The create order is sent to the Property part in charge of creating a new instance. It is also dispatched to the other nonvisual parts to create an instance of each respective part:

❑ Address holds the location information.

❑ MarketingInfo holds the marketing information, such as the price per square foot or agent commission.

❑ PropertyLog holds two time stamps: one for the creation and one for the last update. The time stamps are used during database upload and download.

❑ MultiDoc holds the path name and file name of the video file.

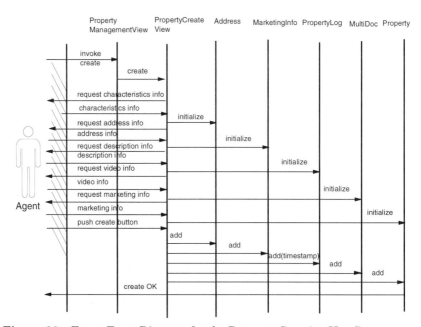

Figure 38. Event-Trace Diagram for the Property Creation Use Case

For the third cut, we refine the design object model as follows (Figure 39):

❑ PropertyCreateView is added and linked to PropertyManagement-View by a *creates* relationship.

❑ PropertyView is added and linked to the PropertyCreateView by a *containment* relationship.

❑ Each notebook page is added as a separate view and aggregated with PropertyView to make up the notebook.

The PropertyView notebook consists of five pages:

❑ Characteristics page displays the property characteristics (area, size, price, bedrooms, bathrooms, stories, cooling and heating).

❑ Address page contains all of the location information about the property.

❑ Description page describes the environment of the property.

❑ Video page allows the user to watch a video of the property.

❑ Marketing page displays some marketing information (for example, price per square foot, sale commission) correlated with one another.

Figure 39 shows the four components of Property: Address, MarketingInfo, PropertyLog, and MultiDoc. Each component is associated with its corresponding page. The Characteristics page contains the descriptive information contained by the Property object itself. The user may ask for some adjustment in the user interface. For example, one page is added for the description of the property, although this attribute is part of the Property object. This is an implementation choice; it does not involve any changes to the model itself.

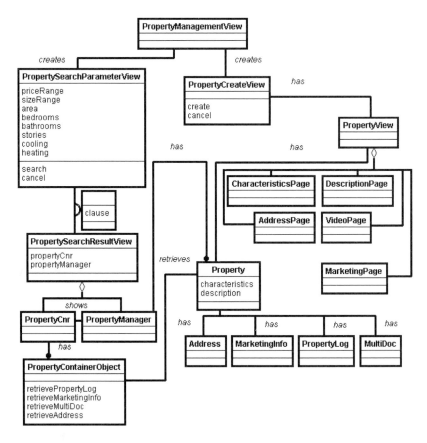

Figure 39. Design Object Model of the Property Subsystem: Third Cut

Refining the Property Update Scenario

A property search results in a set of matching properties that are displayed in a container. The users can update a property of their choice by selecting the *update* option from the PropertyCnr pop-up menu. Thus, from PropertySearchResultView, users must access an extra view, PropertyUpdateView, which displays the property information and enables them to update it if necessary. This view is based on the PropertyView notebook, which we reuse (Figure 40).

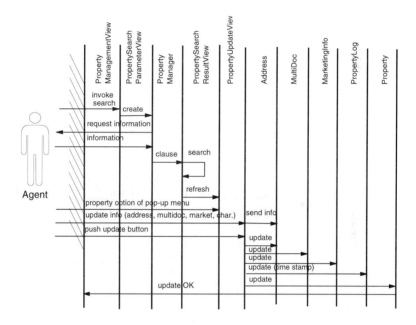

Figure 40. Event-Trace Diagram for the Property Update Use Case

PropertyContainerObject is linked to PropertyUpdateView by the *creates* association. PropertyUpdateView holds PropertyView with the *has* containment relationship (Figure 41).

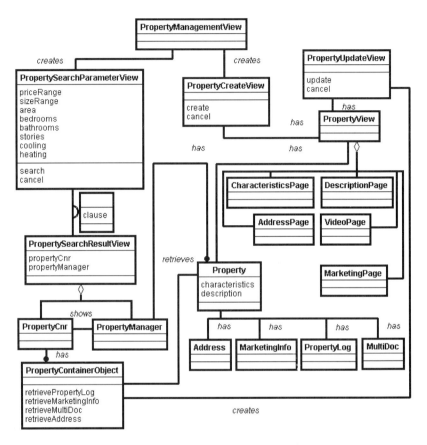

Figure 41. Design Object Model of the Property Subsystem: Fourth Cut

Refining Roles

The fact file that you keep for each character who plays a major or minor role in your novel describes his or her main traits rather superficially. Now, you must elaborate on those and add others to make the character come alive. Your reader should almost hear your characters breathing. You reveal what the characters think, describe their inner monologs, and depict in detail how they react to certain situations. Your readers eventually come to know a certain character as well as another character in your novel knows him or her.

At this stage, you may introduce new characters to illustrate something about the background of your protagonist. Because some of these new characters play a supporting role only, you might describe them shallowly. Perhaps they appear on a few pages and are never mentioned again. Other new characters may have a greater impact on the course of the story, and therefore you describe them more thoroughly. For example, if your novel is about a baseball trainer, you will describe how he handles his team members, thus revealing his ability or inability to do his job. Suppose that one of the team members has some personal problems, which the trainer helps him resolve. The team member with problems has a more important role in your novel than his comrades have, so you describe his traits and experiences, but not those of the rest of the team. In other words, you focus on characters who carry on the plot.

Part 3

Building the Visual Realty Application

By now you must be eager to see how to build the Visual Realty application, so we give you the opportunity to do so in Part 3. Of course, we do not fully detail the implementation of the entire application; rather, we provide you with the keys to build it yourself.

To help you avoid some traps and pitfalls, we focus the development on one subsystem, the Property subsystem, whose main functions are creating, updating, deleting, and retrieving properties. All of those functions take full advantage of the user interface and data access parts that come with the IBM Open Class Library, shipped with VisualAge for C++.

From the detailed design object model, each class is mapped to its corresponding part in Visual Builder: The views are mapped to visual parts, and the business classes are mapped to nonvisual parts.

In the chapters that follow we show you how to build the subsystem in five steps:

1. You set up your development environment and configure the Visual Realty application project, using WorkFrame/2.

2. You map relational tables to nonvisual parts, using Data Access Builder. Later, you use these parts with Visual Builder to enable persistency in the application. We provide you with hints and tips that help you design a good mapping and use the classes necessary to interact with the database.

3. You build the different visual parts that are required in the Property subsystem, using Visual Builder. We show you how to build simple visual parts by assembling primitive parts. (See "Using Visual Builder" on page 27. The primitive parts are also called *controls*.) Then we teach you how to reuse the simple parts to build more complex composite parts. We provide you with some design tips to improve the look and feel of your application and explain how to use such complex controls as containers, notebooks, viewports, and multicell canvases.

4. Although most of the nonvisual parts are generated by Data Access Builder and can be used as is, we show you how to design your own nonvisual parts and take advantage of the notification framework.

5. Using specific connections, you assemble all of your parts. We justify the need for variables, explain the consequences of using the promoting part feature, and demonstrate how to take advantage of dynamic memory allocation by means of the factory part.

5

Setting Up the Development Environment

In this chapter we present step-by-step instructions for creating and configuring your development environment with WorkFrame/2 and Project Smarts. You will use the WorkFrame/2 Build facility to create the appropriate make files and build the application's executable files and libraries. WorkFrame/2 concepts are introduced in Chapter 2, "Getting Started in a VisualAge for C++ Environment," on page 19. If you are not familiar with VisualAge for C++, you should read Chapter 2 first.

We assume that the VisualAge for C++ product as well as the Visual Realty application are installed on your D: drive. For portability, all file names have been built according to the file allocation table (FAT) format. If you are running high-performance file system (HPFS) partitions, you might want to change the file names to be more self-explanatory.

Explanations given throughout this chapter assume that you have some experience with the OS/2 environment. If you do not, use the tutorial that accompanies the operating system.

Read this! ─────────────────────────────────

Throughout this chapter, we use the terms *classes* and *actions*. We do not use them in the "traditional" sense of classes from the object-oriented world or Visual Builder actions. Rather, we use them in the special sense of Work-Frame/2 class and action definitions.

To configure your development environment in the way that is described in this chapter you must install the following Corrective Service Diskettes (CSDs, see VisualAge for C++ Support on page xxviii):

❏ **CTV303** or higher for the Visual builder
❏ **CTW301** or higher for the WorkFrame/2

In the design phase, we identified the different subsystems that make up the Visual Realty application. If you apply the subsystem organization of the application to the WorkFrame/2 environment, you can map one subsystem to a project. In this chapter, we show you how to customize the Property subsystem projects and subprojects.

The Property subsystem manages the creating, deleting, updating, and retrieving properties in the Visual Realty application. Persistent data of the Property subsystem is managed by DB2/2 and accessed from Visual Builder through the parts generated by Data Access Builder

WorkFrame/2 Project Organization

To organize the development environment for the Property subsystem, you first have to identify the project elements, that is, the data files that are required to build the subsystem. The Property subsystem data files can be classified as follows:

❏ Nonvisual and visual parts that are used to build the Property subsystem; Visual Builder can generate those parts, or you can create them

❏ Nonvisual parts created by Data Access Builder that are reused by Visual Builder to manage the Property subsystem persistent data

❏ Visual Realty application common data, that is, the data that all subsystems require, such as some dialog windows

❏ Service subsystem data

Once you have identified the project elements, you then have to identify the dependencies among those elements to determine the project hierarchy. Clearly, the Visual Builder data depends on the Data Access Builder data; you cannot compile the Visual Builder files if the Data Access Builder files have not been generated. In such cases, you must define the project Dacslib that manages the Data Access Builder parts as a subproject of the project that manages the Visual Builder parts. The Property subsystem also uses the Common and Service project data, which implies that the Common and Service projects are to be built first for the Property project to be completed.

Therefore, you must configure the Property project such that it accesses the header files and libraries generated in the Dacslib, Common and Service projects.

You also have to create a main project that manages the application main() entry point, the Property subproject and a Help subproject for the application. The main project is called *Visual Realty*. Figure 42 depicts its project organization.

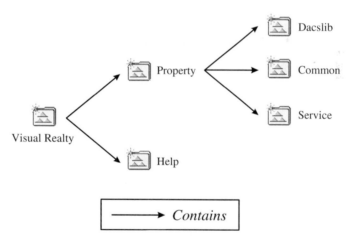

Figure 42. Project Organization for the Visual Realty Application

File Organization

The project organization of the various subsystems does not necessarily reflect the organization of the physical files managed by the Visual Realty projects (see Figure 43). Do not forget that a single project can manage several file locations. However, a project has a single working directory, which is where it creates files.

We chose to develop our application on a single machine, but Work-Frame/2 also handles files located on a LAN.

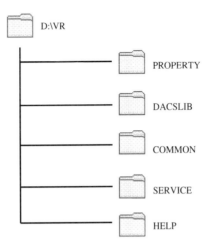

Figure 43. Files Organization for the VisualRealty Application

In the sections that follow, we describe the steps to:

1. Create and customize a specific project—DACSPRJ—to create libraries from the data generated by Data Access Builder

2. Create and customize the Help project

3. Create and customize the Common, Property, and Service projects, as well as the Visual Realty main project with Project Smarts

4. Create and customize the DACS library (Dacslib) project for the Property subsystem

Creating and Customizing the DACSPRJ Project

The DACSPRJ project is used to manage data created from Data Access Builder. The strategy is to map the different DB2 tables used in a subsystem such as Property to C++ classes and group all of those classes in a single library. Thus, you create a specific project, DACSPRJ, which defines the basic actions and types to generate the library. Then, you use the DACSPRJ project as a base for the Dacslib project, which handles the Data Access Builder Property subsystem data.

The purpose of this step is not to reinvent the wheel but to reuse the VisualAge for C++ default project. You simply make slight modifications to the default project to correctly build a Data Access Builder DLL. In fact, when you use Data Access Builder, you are using both C files (generated by the SQL precompiler) and C++ files (generated by Data Access Builder itself). The default VisualAge for C++ project defines a single action (Compile::C++ Compiler) for C and C++ files. Because you have to specify different compilation flags for C and C++ files, you must create your own actions for compilation in the DACSPRJ project.

The VisualAge for C++ default project is located on the D:\IBM-CPP\MAINPRJ drive and is called VACPP. Modifications to VACPP will affect any project you create from Project Smarts. Therefore, we recommend that you copy the VACPP project under a different name, such as DACSPRJ, and modify the copy.

To copy the project, you can either:

❑ Open an OS/2 window, go to the D:\IBMCPP\MAINPRJ directory, type **copy VACPP DACSPRJ**, and press Enter.

or

❑ Double-click on the Drives folder, open the D:\IBMCPP\MAINPRJ folder, select the VisualAge for C++ project, click on it with the right mouse button, and select **Copy**. In the notebook that is now opened, enter DACSPRJ in the *New name* entry field and click on **Copy**.

Technical Information!

The VACPP project is used by default as the base project for any project created from Project Smarts or the VisualAge for C++ project template. Other tools, such as the class browser, use the VACPP project settings. For example, if you want to edit a class definition from the Browser, you start the default editor defined in the VACPP project. If you want to change the default project in your system, you modify the value of the IWF.DEFAULT_PROJECT environment variable (which was defined at installation time in your CONFIG.SYS file).

Modify the DACSPRJ project as follows:

❑ Add a CPPSource file type to handle C++ files only, that is, files with the *.cpp extension.

❑ Modify the existing CSource file type to handle C files, that is, files with the *.c extension.

❑ Add a C Compiler action that takes CSource file types as input.

❑ Modify the C++ Compiler action to take CPPSource file types as input.

❑ Change the default SQLPREP flags.

❑ Change the default flags for the C Compiler and C++ Compiler actions.

❑ Change the default linking flags.

❑ Set the correct Build options.

Adding the CPPSource File Type

You have to create a new source type specific to the C++ Compiler action. This type is called CPPSource and corresponds to files with the .cpp extension. Here are the steps to add the CPPSource type to the DACSPRJ project tools setup:

1. Open the Drives folder, open the D:\IBMCPP\MAINPRJ folder, and double-click on the DACSPRJ project to open it.

2. Open the DACSPRJ project tools setup, switch to the Types view, and select *Types→Add*.

3. Enter the following data:

Class	FileMask
Name	CPPSource
Filter	*.cpp

Tip!

 If you want to reuse types, you can use the OS/2 drag-and-drop facility to copy a type from another project's tools setup to your tools setup. Make sure that you have registered the classes that correspond the types you are reusing.

Modifying the CSource File Type

In the VACPP project, the C++ Compiler action applies to the CSource file type that groups files with the *.c and *.cpp file masks. You must change the CSource file type to include *.c files only:

1. Open the DACSPRJ project tools setup and switch to the Types view.

2. Select the **CSource** type and click with the right mouse button to bring up a contextual menu. Choose the **Change** item. Modify the CSource type description as follows:

   Class   FileMask

   Name   CSource

   Filter   *.c

3. Click on **Change** to commit the changes.

Adding the C Compiler Action

To create the C Compiler action, open the DACSPRJ project tools setup and switch to the Action view. Because the C Compiler action is very similar to the C++ Compiler action, you create it from the C++ Compiler action definition. Select the C++ Compiler action in the compile action class, click on it with the right mouse button, and select **Copy**. Then, complete the fields as shown in Figure 44 and click on **Copy**.

Figure 44. Change Action Dialog Window: C Compiler

Modifying the C++ Compiler Action

You have to modify the settings of the C++ Compiler action to replace the CSource source type with the CPPSource file type. Here are the steps to modify the C++ Compiler action in the DACSPRJ project:

1. Open the DACSPRJ project tools setup and switch to the Actions view.

2. Select the C++ Compiler action in the Compile class and select *Actions→Change....*

3. Switch to the Types notebook page and replace the original CSource source type with the CPPSource type.

Changing SQL Precompile Action Flags

Because Data Access Builder uses static SQL, the SQLPREP action must be configured to automatically generate bind files (.bnd files) as well as the database packages. In other words, the /B and /P flags must be turned on:

1. Open the DACSPRJ project tools setup and switch to the Action view.

2. Select the SQL Precompile action from the Compile class and click on it with the right mouse button to bring up a contextual menu. Select *File Options→Change* from this menu.

3. In the SQLPREP option window, change the output option to **Both (/B /P)**.

4. Click on **OK** to commit the changes.

Changing Compilation and Linking Flags

The next step is to configure the DACSPRJ project so that the compilation and linkage are correctly set to generate a DLL from the Data Access Builder data.

Flags for C Compiler Action

Open the DACSPRJ project and choose *Options→Compile→C Compiler* from the Options menu bar item. In the C Compiler options dialog, you can graphically change most of the compiler options.

Set up the following options:

❏ Target type: **DLL** (on the Processing notebook page)
❏ Library selection: **multithread** (on the Object page)
❏ Library linkage: **dynamic** (on the Object page)

Flags for C++ Compiler Action

Open the DACSPRJ project and choose *Options→Compile→C++ Compiler* from the Options menu bar item. In the C++ Compiler options dialog you can specify the following options:

❏ Target type: **DLL** (on the Processing notebook page)
❏ Library selection: **multithread** (on the Object page)
❏ Library linkage: **dynamic** (on the Object page)

Select the **Do not generate library info** toggle button (on the Object/Details notebook subpage).

Flags for Link Action

As you have specified not to generate the default libraries information for the C++ Compiler action, you must specify the list of libraries that are required at link time. To specify the list of libraries:

1. Open the linking options by selecting *Options→Link*.

2. Switch to the File Names page and enter the following list of libs in the *Libraries to use* entry field:

   cppooc3i.lib cppoov3i.lib sql_dyn.lib cppods3i.lib

You also have to specify that the generated library is using templates:

Switch to the Templates page, choose the **Templates used** toggle button, and then choose **Compile::C++ Compiler** action as the associated action.

Setting the Build Facility Options

The Build facility creates a make file for the project and tries to build the project from it. To correctly generate the make file, you have to set up the list of actions that the MakeMake facility uses. To configure the Build action, open the DACSPRJ project, select *Options→Build→ Build Normal*, and select the following actions:

❑ Compile::C Compiler
❑ Compile::C++ Compiler
❑ Compile::SQL Precompile
❑ Link::Linker
❑ Lib::Import Lib

Creating and Customizing the Visual Realty Projects

The DACSPRJ project is now ready for use. The next step is to create the main project, Visual Realty, and the various subsystem projects.

Creating the Visual Realty Main and Subsystem Projects

The various projects for each subsystem are created from Project Smarts and inherit from the default VisualAge for C++ project, VACPP. To create the Property project:

1. Open the VisualAge for C++ folder.

2. Double-click on the **Project Smarts** icon.

3. Select **Visual Builder** application from the available project list.

4. Click on **Create**.

5. In the dialog window, enter the following data:

Project	Property
Directory	D:\VR\PROPERTY
Folder	Desktop (or your local desktop name)

Repeat steps 3 and 4 to create the Common, Service, and Visual Realty projects with the following data:

Project	Directory	Folder
Common	D:\VR\COMMON	Desktop
Service	D:\VR\SERVICE	Desktop
Visual Realty	D:\VR	Desktop

─── **Attention** ───

When you create a project with Project Smarts, such as a Visual Builder or a IPF context-sensitive project, some sample files are created for you. You can use those files as a startup point, or just delete them if they are not of any use for your projects.

Project Smarts does not support the creation of composite project. You therefore have to manually move the Service, Common, and Property projects into their respective "parent" project. The Property project has to be moved inside the Visual Realty project, while the Service and Common projects must be moved inside the Property project. Do not forget that projects are files and that defining project B as a subproject of project A is equivalent to copying project B inside the project A working directory.

To move the Service and Common projects inside the Property project:

1. Open the Property project

2. Select the Service and Common projects on your desktop (**Ctrl +** left mouse button), drag and drop them in the client area of the Property project.

You can also:

1. Select the Service and Common projects on your desktop (**Ctrl +** left mouse button), click with the right mouse button on one of the selected projects, and select **Move**. A notebook is now opened.

2. Switch to the Drives page and select **D:\VR\PROPERTY.**

3. Click on **Move**.

If you now open the Visual Realty project, it should look similar to Figure 45.

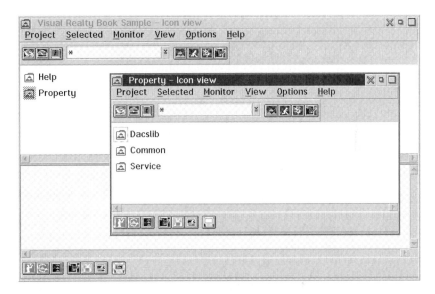

Figure 45. The Visual Realty Project View

Creating the Help Project

The Help project is aimed at managing the context-sensitive help files of the application. It is defined as a subproject of the Visual Realty project. This project is also created from Project Smarts and inherits from the default VisualAge for C++ project, VACPP. To create the Help project:

1. Open the VisualAge for C++ folder.

2. Double-click on the **Project Smarts** icon.

3. Select **IPF Context-Sensitive Help** from the available project list.

4. Click on **Create**.

5. In the dialog window, enter the following data:

Project	Help
Directory	D:\VR\HELP
Folder	Desktop (or your local desktop name)

Click on **OK.** A window pops up prompting you for some variables names. You do not need to fill those variables in if you do not use the default files generated for you by Project Smarts.

Once the Help project is on the desktop, you drag and drop it inside the Visual Realty project. You can also:

1. Select the Help project on your desktop (left mouse button), click with the right mouse button and select **Move**. A notebook is now opened.
2. Switch to the Drives page and select **D:\VR.**
3. Click on **Move**.

Now you must change the settings of each project to change its target name and make file name. For each project, open the project settings, switch to the Target notebook page, and change the target name and make file name as follows:

Project	Target Name	Make File
Property	vrprop.dll	vrprop.mak
Service	vrserv.dll	vrserv.mak
Common	vrcomm.dll	vrcomm.mak
Visual Realty	vrmain.exe	vrmain.mak

You are now ready to customize the Visual Realty projects.

Customizing the Visual Realty Main and Subsystem Projects

To correctly compile the Service, Property, and Visual Realty projects, you must set the values of the LIB and INCLUDE environment variables for the compiler to find the correct header files and libraries. You also can set various variables and flags to activate the trace facility in the User Interface Class Library.

Modifying the LIB and INCLUDE Environment Variables

In the Visual Realty application, common parts are grouped in the Common project. Both the Service and Property subsystems use those common parts. You therefore must update the LIB and INCLUDE variables to include the path where common includes and libraries are located for the Property and Service projects. The Property subsystem also uses the Service and Property Dacslib subsystems. The LIB and INCLUDE variables must be completed accordingly.

> ┌─ **Attention!** ───
>
>
>
> The new value of an environment variable is known only *within the scope* of the project. If your make file requires the newly defined INCLUDE variable to correctly build the application, you must start the make action from the Work-Frame/2 project. If you start the make action from an OS/2 session window, the INCLUDE value is as defined in the OS/2 CONFIG.SYS file.

To define the LIB and INCLUDE variables for the Property project:

1. Open the Property project tools setup, switch to the Variables view, and select *Variables→Add*.

2. Enter the following information to add the LIB variable and click on **Add**.

Name   LIB

String   D:\VR\COMMON;D:\VR\SERVICE;D:\VR\DACS-LIB;%LIB%

The %LIB% statement is equivalent to the current value of the LIB variable, as defined in your CONFIG.SYS file.

Enter the following information to define the INCLUDE variable and click on **Add**.

Name   INCLUDE

String   D:\VR\COMMON;D:\VR\SERVICE;D:\VR\DACS-LIB;%INCLUDE%

Repeat steps 1 and 2 to define the LIB and INCLUDE variables for the Visual Realty projects and define the HELP variable for the Help project as follows:

Project Name	Variable Name	Variable String
Visual Realty	LIB	D:\VR\COMMON;D:\VR\SERVICE;D:\VR\PROP-ERTY;D:\VR\DACSLIB;%LIB%
Visual Realty	INCLUDE	D:\VR\COMMON;D:\VR\SERVICE;D:\VR\PROP-ERTY;D:\VR\DACSLIB;%INCLUDE%
Visual Realty	HELP	D:\VR\HELP;%HELP%

Setting Up the Subsystem Projects to Generate a DLL

Each Visual Realty subsystem is compiled and linked to generate a DLL. Therefore, you must change the compile and linking flags and then create a module definition file (.DEF) for each subsystem.

For each subsystem project (Common, Service, and Property), open the project and choose *Options→Compile*. Switch to the Processing notebook page and do the following:

1. In the Processing Step group box, select the **Perform compile only** radio button.
2. In the Target group box, select the **DLL** radio button.
3. Click on **OK** to commit the changes.

Then, for each subsystem, use your favorite editor to create a .DEF file according to the following template, where vrxxxx is respectively, vrprop, vrserv, and vrcomm for each subproject:

```
LIBRARY vrxxxxx INITINSTANCE
DESCRIPTION 'vrxxxxx dll'
PROTMODE
DATA MULTIPLE NONSHARED LOADONCALL
EXPORTS
```

Setting Up the Linking Action Options

Select *Options→Link*, switch to the File Names notebook page, and modify the data for each project as follows:

Project Name	Libraries to Use	Definition File Name
Common	os2386.lib	vrcomm.def
Service	os2386.lib	vrserv.def
Property	os2386.lib vrcomm.lib vrdacs.lib vrserv.lib	vrprop.def
Visual Realty	os2386.lib vrcomm.lib vrdacs.lib vrserv.lib vrprop.lib	(none)

Then, switch to the Templates page. Ensure that the **Templates used** toggle button is checked and associated with the Compile::C++ Compiler action.

Setting Up the Build Facility Options

To correctly generate the make file, you have to set up the list of actions that the MakeMake facility uses. To configure the Build action, open each of the Service, Common, and Property projects, select *Options→Build→Build Normal*, and select the following actions:

- ❑ Compile::C++ Compiler
- ❑ Link::Linker
- ❑ Lib::Import Lib (except for the Visual Realty project, whose target is an executable file, not a library).

For the Visual Realty project, select the following actions:

- ❑ Bind::Resource Bind
- ❑ Compile::C++ Compiler
- ❑ Compile::Resource Precompile
- ❑ Compile::Resource Compiler
- ❑ Link::Linker

Repeat these two steps for the *Build→Rebuild All* option.

Setting Up a Project for Trace Support

If you want to take advantage of the trace facility in the user interface class library, follow these steps:

1. Compile your code with the IC_TRACE_DEVELOP preprocessor macro. You can set this macro from the Build Smarts facility:

   a. Open Build Smarts and select the **Development** toggle button

   b. In the *Define* entry field, enter IC_TRACE_DEVELOP.

2. Set the ICLUI TRACE and ICLUI TRACETO environment variables to enable the trace functions. The ICLUI TRACE variable enables or disables the trace according to its value (ON/OFF), and the ICLUI TRACETO variable enables you to redirect the trace output to a file or a standard output. Redirect the output to STDOUT so that you can see it from the project monitor window.

   To set the ICLUI TRACE and ICLUI TRACETO variables you can either:

   - Add the following statements to your CONFIG.SYS file:

     ```
     SET ICLUI TRACE=ON
     SET ICLUI TRACETO=STDOUT
     ```

   or

- Add the variables in the project tools setup:

  Open the project tools setup and switch to the Variables view. Enter the following information to define the ICLUI TRACE variable and click on **Add**:

  Name   ICLUI TRACE

  String   ON

  Proceed in the same way to define the ICLUI TRACETO variable:

  Name   ICLUI TRACETO

  String   STDOUT

Setting Up a Project for Visual Builder

After you have used Visual Builder for a while, you might find it annoying to have to manually load the necessary VBB files for your application. Do not despair, however. Visual Builder provides a facility for automatically loading the correct VBBs when you start the tool. All you have to do is create a VBLOAD.DAT file, using your favorite editor. A VBLOAD.DAT file is a flat file in which you list the VBB files you want to load at startup. The VBLOAD.DAT file for the property subsystem looks like this:

```
D:\IBMCPP\DDE4VB\VBDAX.VBB
D:\IBMCPP\DDE4VB\VBMM.VBB
D:\IBMCPP\DDE4VB\VBSAMPLE.VBB
D:\VR\PROPERTY\VRPROP.VBB
D:\VR\COMMON\VRCOMM.VBB
D:\VR\SERVICE\VRSERV.VBB
```

You must specify the full path name for each VBB. Note that you do not have to specify the VBBASE.VBB file because Visual Builder always loads it at startup.

For each Visual Realty project, create a VBLOAD.DAT file as follows:

Project Name	VBLOAD.DAT File Contents
Service	D:\IBMCPP\DDE4VB\VBDAX.VBB D:\IBMCPP\DDE4VB\VBSAMPLE.VBB D:\VR\COMMON\VRCOMM.VBB D:\VR\COMMON\KBDHDR.VBB D:\VR\SERVICE\VRSERV.VBB
Common	D:\IBMCPP\DDE4VB\VBSAMPLE.VBB D:\VR\COMMON\VRCOMM.VBB

Project Name	VBLOAD.DAT File Contents

Visual Realty	`D:\IBMCPP\DDE4VB\VBDAX.VBB`
	`D:\IBMCPP\DDE4VB\VBSAMPLE.VBB`
	`D:\VR\COMMON\VRCOMM.VBB`
	`D:\VR\SERVICE\VRSERV.VBB`
	`D:\VR\SERVICE\VRPROP.VBB`
	`D:\VR\VRMAIN.VBB`

Creating and Customizing the Dacslib Project

To create the DACS library (Dacslib) project for the Property project, open the Templates folder and drop the WorkFrame 3.0 Project template on your OS/2 desktop. Open the settings notebook for this new project and provide the following:

❑ **Target page**

➢ *Target:* **vrdacs.dll**. Each project must have a single target, such as an EXE or a DLL file.

➢ *Make file:* **vrdacs.mak**. The name of the file used by the nmake tool to build the target.

❑ **Location page**

➢ *Source Directories for project files* **D:\VR\DACSLIB**. If you specify several source directories, you must indicate which directory is the working directory. The working directory is used to store any files created in the project.

❑ **Inheritance page**

➢ *Inherit from* **DACSPRJ**. To specify from which project you inherit, click on the **Add** push button and use the file dialog window. If you have moved the DACSPRJ project to your desktop directory, the path which locates your project is `C:\DESKTOP` (assuming OS/2 is installed on your C disk).

❑ **General page**

Change the name of the project to **Dacslib**.

After you have provided the above information, move the Dacslib project inside the Property subsystem:

1. Select the Dacslib project and click on it with the right mouse button to get a contextual menu.

2. Select **Move**.

3. Switch to the Drives notebook page and select **D:\VR\PROPERTY**.

4. Click on **Move**.

Technical Information!

If you inherit from multiple projects, you must use the Promote and Demote functions to manage project precedence. The rule is that the latest project in the inheritance list prevails over all other projects if there is a conflict, for example, if several projects define the same action but with different options.

Setting Up the Linking Flags

You have to specify the name of the .DEF file used by the linker. Open the link options dialog, and in the *Definition File Name* field, enter **vrdacs.def**.

Click on **OK** to commit the changes.

Creating a Library Definition File

Once the code is generated from Data Access Builder, you have to erase the various .DEF files and create a unique DEF file. Use your favorite editor to create the VRDACS.DEF file in the D:\VR\DACSLIB directory, with the following contents:

```
LIBRARY vrdacs INITINSTANCE
DESCRIPTION 'vrdacs dll'
PROTMODE
DATA MULTIPLE NONSHARED LOADONCALL
EXPORTS
```

For details on DEF files, refer to the *C/C++ Programming Guide*.

Naming Conventions

We used the following name conventions throughout the development of the Visual Realty application (see Appendix D, "Class Dictionary," on page 353):

1. All file names are built according to the FAT format (eight letters for the file name, three letters for the file extension).

2. All file names are built according to the VRSXXXXX format, where:

- VR is an invariant for Visual Realty
- S is the subsystem name
    - B, for the Buyer subsystem
    - P, for the Property subsystem
    - T, for the Sales Transaction subsystem
    - C, for the Common subsystem
    - S, for the Service subsystem
- XXXXX identifies the file contents.

Run-time Considerations

For the application to run, the necessary DLLs must be located in one of the directories listed in the LIBPATH variable. We can therefore create a D:\VR\DLL directory where all of the Visual Realty application DLLs will be moved. This directory must be added to the LIBPATH variable in the CONFIG.SYS file.

6

Mapping Relational Tables Using Data Access Builder

Data Access Builder lets you create object-oriented applications quickly and reliably by generating the parts that you need to access your relational tables. For each part, Data Access Builder generates all of the required methods (add, update, delete, and retrieve) as well as the embedded SQL code.

You can use the generated parts directly in your programs or import them into Visual Builder. If you use Visual Builder to connect the parts to other parts, you can quickly create applications that efficiently access your databases.

Some of the key features of Data Access Builder are:

❏ Table to parts mapping: You can create new parts, using your existing database tables. You can create one part, or many parts, from any table. Both C++ and SOM IDL code are supported.

❏ Quick and custom mapping: The quick map feature lets you do a column-to-attribute mapping. By using inheritance, you can customize their classes to suit your needs.

❏ Visual display of mappings: Data Access Builder displays the mapping of your database tables to the object classes. This display supports visual editing.

❏ Connection and transaction services: These services are provided for connection and disconnection from your databases. In addition, commit and rollback operations are provided to handle transaction services.

❏ DATABASE 2 OS/2 support: You can use DB2/2 in a stand-alone environment or through the DB2 Client Application Enabler.

In the design object model (Figure 41 on page 102), *property* is described by the following classes and their relationships:

Property   Holds the general information of property:

  Property registration identifier
  Size
  Number of stories
  Number of bathrooms
  Number of bedrooms
  Cooling type
  Heating type
  Description

Address   Holds the location information for the property:

  Street
  City
  Area
  State
  Zip code

MarketingInfo   Holds the marketing information for the property:

  Price
  Days on the market (elapsed time between the last update and the creation date)
  Commission rate (agent commission rate)
  Down payment rate (buyer payment rate)

PropertyLog   Holds the logging information:

> Creation time stamp
> Last update
> Status (available, pending, or sold)

MultiDoc   Holds the multimedia information for the property:

> Type (bitmap or video; only the video features are implemented in the sample application)
> File name

To store this property information, we define the following five tables (see Appendix C, "Database Definition," on page 347 for details):

❏ PROPERTY
❏ PROPERTY_ADDRESS
❏ MARKETING_INFO
❏ PROPERTY_LOG
❏ MULTI_DOC

The relationships between Property and the other classes are represented by a foreign key in each table. In addition, we create two views:

❏ PROP_AD_LOG is built by joining the PROPERTY, PROPERTY_ADDRESS, MARKETING_INFO and PROPERTY_LOG tables on PROPERTY_ID and ADDRESS_ID. It is used to simultaneously display, in a container, the information from the four tables (see "Using a Container" on page 182).
❏ LIST_AREA is built by joining the PROPERTY_ADDRESS and PROPERTY_LOG tables and contains, in alphabetic order, the distinct areas of properties that have the "available" status.

Mapping Tables to Parts

You can start Data Access Builder in three ways:

❏ Click on the appropriate icon in the tools folder.
❏ Start the product from an OS/2 session.
❏ Start the product from WorkFrame/2.

With the first method, the source files are generated in the directory that is specified in the notebook settings of the program. By default, the files are produced in the `D:\IBMCPP\WORKING` directory (assuming you have installed VisualAge for C++ on your D drive). If you want to generate your code in the `D:\REAL` directory (assuming you have created a `\REAL` directory to hold all files related to your application), open the settings of Data Access Builder and set the working directory to `D:\REAL`.

With the second method, the code is generated in the directory from which you start Data Access Builder. Therefore, if you want to generate your code in D:\REAL, simply change to the D:\REAL directory and type the icsdata command to start Data Access Builder.

You use the third method to start Data Access Builder. In Chapter 5, "Setting Up the Development Environment," on page 107, you defined a Dacslib project for the Property subsystem. From Dacslib you can start Data Access Builder in four ways:

❏ Select the *Database* option from the Project pull-down menu.
❏ Select the *Database* option from the project's pop-up menu.
❏ Use the accelerator keys: **Ctrl+Shift+A**.
❏ Double-click on a Data Access Builder session file (extension .DAX).

Data Access Builder generates the files in the directory that you specified on the Location page of the Dacslib project settings notebook, that is, D:\VR\DACSLIB.

Open the DACS library project and start Data Access Builder. The startup window presents you with the following selections:

Create Classes   To create new classes from relational tables

Open   To open a Data Access Builder file and resume the work of a saved session

Cancel   To quit Data Access Builder

Help   To access the online help

To create a mapping from scratch, click on the **Create Classes...** push button. When you select *Create Classes...*, Data Access Builder accesses your database directory and presents a list of all database names cataloged on your machine (see Figure 46). From the list, you can select the database with which you want to work.

Figure 46. Data Access Builder Create Classes Window

Select the REAL database and click on **Connect**.

When you click on *Connect*, Data Access Builder tries to connect to the selected database. If Database Manager is not already running, it is started. If you are not logged on, you are asked to give the userid and password of the database creator (in our case, the userid is USERID, and the password is PASSWORD).

Once the database connection is established, Data Access Builder lists the tables and views, prefixed with USERID (Figure 46). Click on each table or view you want to map to a part. In our case, select only the tables and views related to the Property subsystem:

- ❑ USERID.LIST_AREA
- ❑ USERID.MARKETING_INFO
- ❑ USERID.MULTI_DOC
- ❑ USERID.PROPERTY
- ❑ USERID.PROPERTY_ADDRESS
- ❑ USERID.PROPERTY_LOG
- ❑ USERID.PROP_AD_LOG

Then, click on **Create classes** to get to the main window, which shows the mapping of each table on the free-form surface (Figure 47).

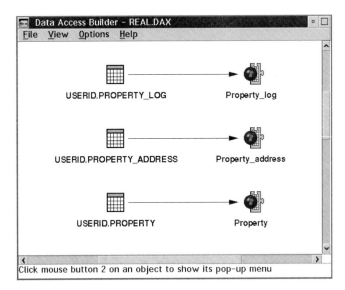

Figure 47. Data Access Builder Main Window

To access the pop-up menu of each table, click on a table with the right mouse button or, as a shortcut, double-click with the left mouse button.

Before you generate the code for each part, you can check the associated file names. For each part, the following files are generated:

- ❏ *.hpp, header for the parts
- ❏ *.cpp, code for the parts
- ❏ *.sqc, embedded SQL to access the table
- ❏ *.vbe, import file for Visual Builder
- ❏ *.def, definition file for creating the DLL
- ❏ *.mak, make file for building the DLL and LIB files

The make file produces a DLL and the import library required to access the database. The DLL provides the code to access the relational tables. The import library is used during link-editing to resolve the external references for the database access.

We strongly recommend that you use a file stem length of no more than seven characters so that you can manipulate your source code with either HPFS or the FAT file system. You can modify the file stem with the following names:

- ❏ ListAreV for LIST_AREA
- ❏ MarkInfV for MARKETING_INFO
- ❏ MultidoV for MULTI_DOC
- ❏ PropertV for PROPERTY

❏ PropAddV for PROPERTY_ADDRESS
❏ PropLogV for PROPERTY_LOG
❏ PropALoV for PROP_AD_LOG

If you use Data Access Builder to generate one target for each table mapping, make sure that the file names are unique for each target generated. In our example, if you generate one DLL for each class, you will avoid confusing Property, Property_address, and Property_log. Each of them would generate a makefile that would produce the same targets: PropertV.dll and PropertV.lib. In addition, the maximum length for a database package is eight characters in DB2/2 1.2. Thus, you should avoid file names with more than eight characters.

Notice that the *C++ Target Library* check box is not checked. Because Data Access Builder is started from the WorkFrame/2 environment, the target library should be set at the project level on the Target page of the project settings notebook.

The *Data identifier* (Figure 48) is used to identify a row. Before the update, delete, and retrieve operations, the unique values of the data identifiers must be set to locate the row in the relational table. When the *Data identifier* check box of an attribute is selected, that attribute is used to identify a row in the table. By default, each primary key is an identifier. If the table does not have a primary key, the first attribute is selected as the default data identifier. You must ensure that the attribute contains unique values. If the values in a data identifier identify more than one row, errors occur during the retrieve operation, and multiple rows are affected during the update and delete operations. Table 6 lists the identifiers for each relational table.

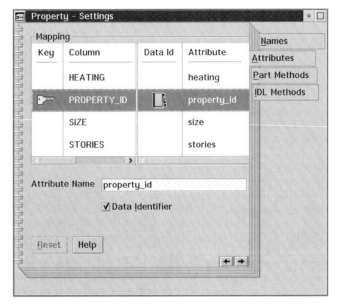

Figure 48. Data Access Builder Page Attribute of the Settings Notebook

Table 6.	Relational Table Identifiers
Table	**Identifier**
LIST_AREA	AREA
MARKETING_INFO	PROPERTY_ID
MULTI_DOC	MULTIDOC_ID
PROPERTY	PROPERTY_ID
PROPERTY_ADDRESS	ADDRESS_ID
PROPERTY_LOG	PROPERTY_ID
PROP_AD_LOG	PROPERTY_ID

Select *Generate* on the pop-up menu of each part to generate the C++ code in the Dacslib project folder (Figure 49).

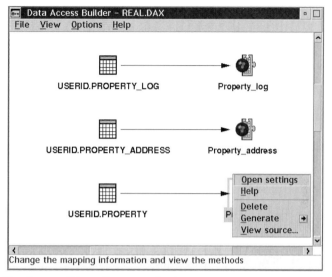

Figure 49. Pop-up Menu Generate Option

Notice that, after the source code has been generated for a part, an orange jigsaw puzzle icon is added underneath the blue ball icon (Figure 49). Later, these icons remind you that the code has already been generated. Close Data Access Builder and save the session under the REAL.DAX file name.

You can now build the library and the corresponding DLL, using the Build option from your project folder (Make sure DB2 is started before building the application to prevent the SQL precompile action from failing.) Notice that you can also generate the library from the *Build* option of the Property project because the Dacslib Project is embedded in the Property project.

Parts Produced

When you map a table, T, to a part, two parts are generated: the T part and the TManager part, also called the manager part.

The T part is derived from the IPersistentObject class and represents a row of the T table. Using the T part, you can access the information of the table, because each column is mapped to a corresponding part attribute (Data Access Builder handles type conversion between DB2/2 and C++). Data Access Builder generates a method to get and set the value of each attribute as well as check or set the attributes to NULL (if allowed for that column). Those attributes are enabled for notification (see Chapter 10, "If You Want to Know More about Visual Builder...," on page 323) and return IString() representations. In this way, attributes can be connected to other visual parts, with each attribute reflecting the change to the other parts. In addition, the T part supports the actions you usually apply on a table row: add, delete, update, and retrieve.

These database access methods use static SQL for efficient access. Before using these methods, you must indicate the attribute you will use to retrieve the entire row (see Figure 48 on page 134 and Table 6 on page 134) and then check the **Data identifier** check box. You can have several data identifiers.

The TManager part is derived from IPOManager and accesses multiple rows of data. Using this part, you can retrieve several rows of the table. Use the Refresh method to retrieve all rows of the table, and use the Select method to retrieve a selected set of rows according to an SQL clause.

The rows are maintained through an attribute of type IVSequence<T*>*, called iItems. As you will see in the section below, the iItems attribute is used through attribute-to-attribute connections with other visual parts, such as a container or a list box, to display the contents of a set of rows.

In the current release of Data Access Builder, you must only use the Select method of the manager part to limit the number of rows that are read from a table and added to the IVSequence of the Manager part.

All SQL access is executed through the exception handler framework. In this way, exceptions are thrown by the parts whenever an error occurs, and your application can catch the exceptions to react accordingly.

Using Data Access Builder Parts with Visual Builder

For each mapping, Data Access Builder produces a Visual Builder export file (VBE extension), which is used to import the parts definition in Visual Builder.

In the Visual Builder main window select ***Import part information...*** from the *File* menu item to import all of your VBE files. For each VBE file, a VBB file that consists of two parts is created. If you want to reorganize your files, you can move parts from one VBB file to another. For example, you may decide to move all Data Access Builder parts related to the property subsystem in the VRPROP.VBB file.

To use the parts, you must establish a database connection. For this purpose, Data Access Builder provides specific parts in the VBDAX.VBB file. This file is located in the D:\IBMCPP\DDE4VB\ directory. You must load it in Visual Builder to access its different parts:

❑ IDSConnectCanvas—used as a general dialog to connect to a database, **A**. This part can be reused to connect to a database in providing the following information (Figure 50):

> Database name
> Access mode (share or exclusive mode)
> Userid
> Password

IDatastore—a general-purpose part that gathers many of the services you need to establish and manage and database connection, **B**.

The attributes of IDatastore are:

> isConnected, connection status (TRUE if connected, FALSE otherwise)
> dataStoreName, database name
> shareModeExclusive, flag enabled for exclusive mode, flag reset for share mode
> userName, userid for the connection
> authentication, password for the connection

The events IDatastore can generate are:

> Connected, sent when the connection is established
> Disconnected, sent when the connection is terminated
> Transacted, sent when the connection is completed (rollback or commit), false otherwise

The actions of IDatastore are:

> Connect, connect to the database
> Disconnect, disconnect from the database
> Commit, commit pending transaction
> Rollback, roll back pending transaction

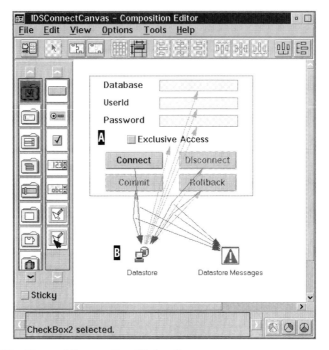

Figure 50. General Connection Dialog Canvas

Now that you are more familiar with Data Access Builder, let us build a simple application (Figure 51). This time, you do not use the Work-Frame/2 environment to organize your code. Instead, you start Data Access Builder from an OS/2 session. To create a database connection, follow these instructions (we assume that VBDAX.VBB is loaded and the Data Access Builder parts created for the Dacslib project have been imported in Visual Builder):

1. Open an OS/2 session.

2. Change to the `D:\VR\DACSLIB` directory, where the Data Access Builder library for the Property subsystem has been generated.

3. Start Visual Builder from this directory by issuing the `icsvb` command. The Visual Builder window is displayed, and the working directory is set to the current directory.

4. Create a new visual part with IFrameWindow as the base class:

   • From the Visual Builder window, select *Part → New...* option.

- Fill in the entry fields as follows:

Field	Value
Class name	TinyApp
Description	Sample application with DACS
File name	TINY
Part type	visual part
Base class	IFrameWindow

- Click on the **Open** push button. An IFrameWindow* part is displayed on the free-form surface.

5. Add an IDatastore* part on the free-form surface, **A** (use *Option → Add parts...* from the Composition Editor menu bar).

6. Open its settings notebook and set its attributes as follows (we assume that a user, USERID, with a password, PASSWORD, can connect to the REAL database):

Field	Value
dataStoreName	REAL
userid	USERID
authentication	PASSWORD

7. Connect the **Ready** event of the application to the **Connect** action of IDatastore, **1**. (The event is accessible from the free-form surface pop-up menu.)

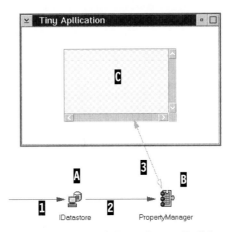

Figure 51. Simple Application with Data Access Builder

You can then use the database connection to interact with the relational tables. If you want to display the contents of the PROPERTY table in a list box:

1. Add a PropertyManager* part on the free-form surface, **B** (use *Option → Add parts...* from the Composition Editor menu bar).

2. From the Visual Builder palette, select an ICollectionViewList-box* part in the *Lists* category and drop it on the IFrameWindow* part. (An ICollectionViewListBox part is a general-purpose list box that displays objects of any type in a collection.)

3. Open the settings notebook of the ICollectionViewListBox* part and on the General page set the *Item type* to **Property***, **C**. The items attribute maintained by the collection list box is set to the IVSequence<Property*>* type and matches the type of the items attribute held by PropertyManager (see the attribute-to-attribute connection **3** in Figure 51 on page 139).

4. Connect the **Connected** event of IDatastore to the **Refresh** action of PropertyManager, **2**.

5. Connect the ***items*** attribute of PropertyManager to the ***items*** attribute of the list box, **3**.

6. Switch to the Class Editor and fill in the *.LIB File Name* entry field with DACSLIB.LIB. A pragma statement is added to the class header file generated by the Visual Builder to inform the linker to link the application with the DACSLIB.LIB library.

7. Save your part and generate its code:

   - To generate the source code of the part, select the *Save and Generate → Part source* option from the *File* pull-down menu of the Visual Builder window.

   - To generate the make file of your tiny application, select the *Save and Generate → main()* for part option from the *File* pull-down menu of the Visual Builder window.

Hackers!

When you drop a part on the free-form surface by using *Options → Add Parts...*, you cannot enter a part's class name without a trailing star (* for the dereferencing operator). If you omit the star, you can only drop a variable of the part. Also, if you drop a part from the palette, you may notice that its type is a pointer to the part itself. In fact, you cannot drop on the free-form surface a part that is not a pointer.

The relationship between a part and its subparts is an association of *containment by reference*; that is, the class of the subpart is not embedded in the class of its composite part. Rather, a pointer on the subpart is defined as an attribute of the composite part. This subtle difference facilitates development of the parts because you do not have to provide a copy constructor (although we strongly recommend that you provide one for all of your parts (see item 11 of *Effective C++* from Scott Meyers).

In fact, when you make connections between parts, you define a class that contains methods requiring parts as parameters (*Initialize* is one of them; see Chapter 9, "Connecting the Parts," on page 227). By default, a parameter is passed to a C or C++ function by value. Thus, the parameter is copied into the stack before the call and restored when the function terminates.

If you want to pass a part as a parameter, you must provide the part with a copy constructor. If you do not provide a copy constructor, you end up with compilation errors. To avoid this problem, each part you drop on the free-form surface must be a pointer whose base class holds a copy constructor!

You can now compile the code and run the application to see the contents of the table displayed in the collection list box:

❑ Switch to the OS/2 session window and make sure that D:\VR\DAC-SLIB is your current directory. (The compiler must have the Property.hpp file to compile and the linker must have the DACSLIB to link-edit the tiny application.)

❑ On the command line, enter: **nmake tinyapp.mak**.

❑ Once the code has been compiled and linked, run the application by typing **tinyapp** on the command line.

All of the columns are displayed, separated by a period, in the list box. In "Overriding the String Generator of the Collection List Box" on page 191, we explain how to choose the contents of the list box.

Read this!

 Each time your application uses the IDatastore part, you must bind the DAXSCL.BND file to any databases that your application accesses. This bind file allows IDatastore to connect, disconnect, and complete transactions against the database. To bind the file, enter the following command:

```
SQLBIND D:\IBMCPP\BND\DAXSCL.BND
database /G=PUBLIC
```

where database is the name of your database.

Now that we have mapped the tables to nonvisual parts, let us tackle Visual Builder and begin to build the visual parts of the property subsystem.

7

Creating Visual Parts

A visual part is a visual representation of the application objects you defined during the design phase (see "Object Design" on page 89). The set of visual parts you define makes up the user interface of the application.

To get acquainted with the different views you are going to build, you can run the Visual Realty application that is provided as a CD-ROM with this book (see Figure 52).

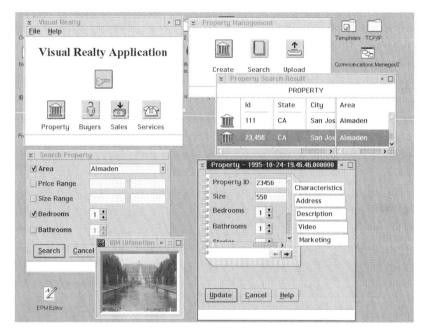

Figure 52. Visual Realty Application in Action

You will find all of the information you need to install and run this application in Appendix A, "Installing the Application," on page 341. You can also consult the READ.ME file on the CD-ROM for the latest information.

> ─ **Attention!** ───────────────────────────
>
> All of the visual parts that you build are prefixed with the letter *A* (for example, PropertyView is built as the APropertyView part). With this naming convention, the visual parts will be listed first in the Visual Builder window visual part list box.
>
> Also, in this chapter, *view* and *composite visual part* are synonyms.

To create visual parts, we strongly suggest that you begin from the simplest parts and work up to the more complex parts. For example, to build the visual parts of the Property subsystem, start from the simplest view, AAddressView, and work up to the main view of the application: ARealMainView. You can easily apply this building process by following the *view hierarchy structure*, which depicts the use relationship between the parts (see Figure 53). For example, according to the hierarchy, AAddressView is built before APropertyView because AAddressView is used by APropertyView, which in turn is used by APropertyUpdateView, and so forth.

Figure 53. View Hierarchy

As is evident in the view hierarchy, use of the Property subsystem requires that you build the following visual parts:

AAddressView displays an address. It is used in the Buyer and Property subsystems.

APropertyView displays the property information.

APropertyCreateView displays the property information when a new property is created.

APropertyUpdateView displays the property information when a property is updated.

ADeleteDialogView displays a warning message before deleting records from the database. It is reused by the Buyer, the Property, and the Sale transaction subsystems.

APropertySearchResultView displays a list of properties that match the buyer's criteria.

APropertySearchParameterView displays and collects the buyer's criteria to select properties in the database.

AUpLoadView triggers the generation of the database export files.

APropertyManagementView is the primary window of the Property subsystem and provides access to the property management options.

ALogonView collects the user's authentication to establish a database connection.

ARealSettingsView enables the user to update the application settings.

ARealMainView is the main window application and enables the user to log on to the database and to access the different subsystems.

In the sections that follow, we describe how to use Visual Builder to build the visual parts. We assume that you have some basic knowledge of the tool (for a Visual Builder "crash course", refer to "Using Visual Builder" on page 27) and are familiar with the OS/2 environment. We also assume that the following files are loaded in Visual Builder:

❑ VBDAX.VBB, database access parts
❑ VBMM.VBB, multimedia parts
❑ VBSAMPLE.VBB, general-purpose parts
❑ KBDHDR.VBB, general-purpose event handler for the keyboard

If you have installed VisualAge C++ on your D drive and you also have installed the samples component, you will find the first three files in the D:\IBMCPP\DDE4VB directory. The last file is provided on the CD-ROM that accompanies this book. Refer to "Setting Up a Project for Visual Builder" on page 122, where you will find instructions for building the VBLOAD.DAT file to load automatically these files in Visual Builder when starting Visual Builder within each subproject.

Make sure that you read Chapter 5, "Setting Up the Development Environment," on page 107 to get acquainted with the WorkFrame/2 development environment, which serves as a base for organizing our sample application. From each subproject (property, service, common, and main) that you define, you can access the Visual Builder window by selecting the **Visual** action from the Project pull-down menu or the project pop-up menu. You can also use the accelerator keys **Ctrl+Shift+V**.

When you construct your visual parts, you will have to configure some parts, such as set canvas or multicell canvas, to enable them to evenly display, when they resize, the controls they contain. These controls are also called *child windows*. The settings for these canvases assume that you use the default font for your controls: System Proportional - 10. Because our application has been developed on an SVGA resolution machine (1024 x 768 pixels in 256 colors), your panels may not look exactly the same if you run the application on a machine that has a different resolution.

Also, when you add an entry control, such as an entry field or a list box, to another part or the free-form surface, the number of characters you can type for the control has a default value. When you change the default, the control is not resized accordingly, except when it is dropped on a multicell canvas. You can change the width of the entry control to reflect its actual limit by selecting the *Reset to default size* option in its pop-up menu. For example, suppose the entry field control you drop on the free-form surface has a default limit of 32 characters—this limit is kept in the *limit* attribute. When you change the default to 10 characters, the width of the entry field control is not updated accordingly. To resize the controls, select the control and click on it with the right mouse button to display its pop-up menu. Then select the ***Reset to default*** *size* option to adjust its width to 10 characters.

In the sections that follow, you build the visual parts of the Visual Realty application by using entry controls that hold data. The data width—the specific number of characters—is given by the corresponding attribute of its relational table (see Appendix C, "Database Definition," on page 347). Make sure that you reset the control's size to the default size after changing the limit of characters it can accept. As mentioned above, this constraint does not apply when you drop a control in a multicell canvas. In this case, setting the limit of the control automatically sets its width.

Finally, "adding a part" to the Composition Editor means selecting the part from its palette category and dropping it on the free-form surface or another part. The first time you have to add a part that you have not used, we will give you its category name. This rule always applies except when we tell you to use *Option → Add part...* from the menu bar of the Visual Builder window.

It is now time to build your first visual part.

AAddressView

AAddressView represents the primary view for the Address class. It consists of a multicell canvas—IMultiCellCanvas part is the name of the part that you use in Visual Builder—on which you lay out several entry fields—IEntryField part—to display the *Street*, *Area*, *City*, and *ZipCode* attributes of the Address class and a combo box—IComboBox part—to display its *State* attribute (see Figure 54).

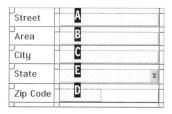

Figure 54. AAddressView Part

Instead of using a standard ICanvas part, you build AAddressView as a subclass of the IMultiCellCanvas part. This canvas enables the controls that you drop onto it to expand or shrink when it is resized.

An IMultiCellCanvas part is a set of cells organized in rows and columns. A multicell canvas is like a spreadsheet; each cell can contain a part, and a part can span multiple rows and columns. The cells are adjusted to vary the text length of the control. Multicell canvases enhance NLS and facilitate the use of the application in different graphical resolutions.

Each time you create a visual part that inherits from the IFrame-Window part, the canvas of its client area is a standard canvas, ICanvas part. The controls you place in such a canvas cannot be resized when the canvas expands or shrinks. However, multicell canvases enable your controls to resize when changing fonts or screen resolution. Thus, we recommend that you replace the ICanvas part with an IMultiCellCanvas part in all frame windows of the Visual Realty application.

You can work with a multicell canvas in two ways:

❑ You can choose to use a multicell canvas to enable the controls that you drop into it to resize when the user resizes the multicell canvas. For this purpose, you can select the columns and the rows that you want to be expandable in your multicell canvas. Each control that you drop in one of these rows or columns can then grow or shrink according to the dimension of the multicell canvas. For example, suppose you have an entry field that contains the fully qualified name of a file. Let us say that this entry field can accept a name that is 45 characters long. You can add this entry field in a multicell canvas column that you can set to be expandable, and you can set the limit attribute of the entry field to 45. Then, you can resize the length of the entry field to your liking—this size is known as the *minimum size* of your control. The multicell canvas memorizes this size as the limit below which the control is clipped if the user continues to shrink the multicell canvas.

(That is why a multicell canvas is also known as a *minimum size canvas*.) When users want to type a long file name, they can stretch the canvas so that the entry field stretches accordingly. You will use this facility in "Building the Video Page" on page 166.

❑ You can choose to use a multicell canvas to enable your application to be portable across different screen resolutions or font settings. In this case, the multicell canvas does all the work for you. All you do is drop your controls on the multicell canvas. Each time you change the font type or the label of those controls, they are resized according to the minimum size the control returns to the multicell canvas.

To adjust the size of a parent window to the size of its canvas in any type of resolution, the parent window must execute a moveSizeTo-Client action before displaying. This action requires, as a parameter, an IRectangle object that describes the position and the minimum size of the client. The action can be executed by triggering a custom logic connection (see "Using Custom Logic" on page 249) from the ready event of the free-form surface to the parent window:

```
target → moveSizeToClient(IRectangle(target → position(),
                                      target → client()
                                            → minimumSize()));
```

If you use a multicell canvas as the client canvas, you can adjust the size of the multicell canvas to the size of the parent window by setting its outermost columns and rows to be expandable. This is the method you will use in this book (see, for example, "ADeleteDialogView" on page 178).

> ── **Attention!** ──────────────────────
>
>
> When you resize a control by using its handles—the handles are the four small black boxes that appear on the corners of the control when you select it—make sure that you do not set the minimum size to a fixed value. If a fixed minimum size is set for the control and the control is used in combination with a minimum size canvas, it will not resize properly when the screen resolution is changed because its minimum size is not calculated at execution time. To ensure that the minimum size is calculated at execution time, open the control's settings notebook and, on the Size/Position page, select the **Calculate at execution time** radio button. This precaution is not necessary if you do not use the control in a minimum size canvas.

In a multicell canvas, the width of a given column is the width of the largest control in that column. Likewise, the height of a row is the height of the highest control in that row. Thus, you may encounter some trouble if, for example, you are seeking to drop two controls with a different width in the same column. The smaller control will adjust to the width of the larger. You can prevent the smaller control from resizing in two ways:

❑ Add another column in your multicell canvas and make the longest control span two columns. Use the **ALT** key to drag your control over multiple columns or rows. Then set the second column to be expandable. In this way, the control expands across the second column, and the shortest control is not resized. The problem with this approach is that you make the first control expandable even though expansion might not be needed. The second approach resolves this issue.

❑ Use another canvas in the multicell canvas and drop the shortest control on it. The constraint here is that you must use a minimum size canvas that manages the minimum size attribute of its controls. You can use the set canvas, the toolbar canvas, and the multicell canvas as the minimum size canvas. Whichever canvas you use, ensure that the visual part that you build will support different screen resolutions and font settings. Use an ISetCanvas part to add the zip code entry field in AAddressView. The ISetCanvas part is a set of cells organized in rows and columns called *decks*. It can be used to provide adjustable cells in rows or columns within canvases.

A final word of advice: When you use a multicell canvas, do not place controls in the first and last rows and in the first and last columns. Reserve them for the left and right and top and bottom margins. You can set the columns and rows to be expandable so that the controls in the multicell canvas remain centered when it is resized.

To build AAddressView, follow the step-by-step instructions in Table 7.

Table 7. (Part 1 of 3) Constructing AAddressView Part	
Step	**Action**
1	Start Visual Builder from the Common project (select *Project* → *Visual* in the menu bar).
2	From the Visual Builder window, select *Part* → *New...* option.
3	Fill in the entry fields as follows:

Step 3 detail:

Field	Value
Class name	AAddressView
Description	General-purpose address view
File name	VRCOMM
Part type	visual part
Base class	IMultiCellCanvas

Click on the **Open** push button. An IMultiCellCanvas* part is displayed on the free-form surface.

Table 7. (Part 2 of 3) Constructing AAddressView Part

Step	Action
4	Open the settings notebook of the IMultiCellCanvas* part and configure it as follows: ❑ Number of rows: 11 ❑ Number of columns: 5 ❑ Expandable rows: 1, 11 ❑ Expandable columns: 1, 5 Close the settings notebook.
5	Select the **Sticky** check box, ▣, below the palette. When the *Sticky* check box is selected, the mouse pointer remains loaded with the last part that has been dropped on the free-form surface. This is a convenient way of dropping several parts of the same type without moving the mouse pointer back and forth from the palette to the free-form surface.
6	Add five IStaticText* parts to the IMultiCellCanvas* part, as shown in Figure 54 on page 148, and name then appropriately. Change their text attributes as follows: Street, Area, City, State, and Zip Code. (The IStaticText* part is located in the *Data entry* category.) Notice that, with the *Sticky* check box selected, the IStaticText* part remains loaded in the mouse pointer after it has been dropped. Because you are going to add four entry fields, keep the *Sticky* check box selected.
7	Add four IEntryField* parts (▣, ▣, ▣, ▣) to cells (2, 4), (4, 4), (6, 4), and (10, 4) of the IMultiCellCanvas* part. (The IEntryField* part is located in the *Data entry* category.)
8	Open the settings notebook of each IEntryField* part and set the names and limits as follows: **Part** **Name** **Limit** A EntryFieldStreet 20 B EntryFieldArea 20 C EntryFieldCity 20 D EntryFieldZipCode 10 Close the settings notebooks. Refer to Appendix C, "Database Definition," on page 347 for the structure of the PROPERTY_ADDRESS table. When you add a part to another part or to the free-form surface, Visual Builder automatically assigns a name to the part. It is good practice to rename the parts to more meaningful names if you want to refer to them from other parts. You change the part's name from its settings or its pop-up menu.
9	In step 10, you are going to add only one IComboBox* part in the IMultiCellCanvas* part. Thus, you can deselect the *Sticky* check box now.

Table 7. (Part 3 of 3) Constructing AAddressView Part

Step	Action
10	Add an IComboBox* part to cell (8, 4) of the IMultiCellCanvas* part. (The IComboBox* part is located in the *Lists* category.)
11	Open the settings notebook of the IComboBox* part, **E**, set its type to **Read-only drop-down** and its name and limit as follows: **Part** **Name** **Limit** E ComboStateBox 20 Close the settings notebook. Refer to Appendix C, "Database Definition," on page 347 for the structure of the PROPERTY_ADDRESS table.
12	Add an ISetCanvas* part to cell (10, 4) of the IMultiCellCanvas* part. This canvas will hold the entry field for the zip code. (The ISetCanvas* part is located in the *Composers* category.)
13	Open the settings notebook of the ISetCanvas* part and, on the General page, set the width and height of the margin to **0**. Then close the settings notebook.
14	Select the IMultiCellCanvas* part and from its pop-up menu select the **Reset to default size** option to adjust its size to the controls it holds.

Note: Reverse highlighted letters are keyed to Figure 54 on page 148.

You can improve your visual part so that the user can use the keyboard to move the input focus from one subpart to another.

Tabbing from One Part to Another

From a part's pop-up menu you can select the *Tabbing and Depth Order* option to control the order in which the user tabs between its subparts.

When you select the *Tabbing and Depth Order* option of a part, the tabbing order list of the part is displayed. From this list you can:

❑ Change the position of parts to reflect their order in the Composition Editor. In effect, the order in which parts are placed on a canvas part determines their tabbing order. You probably need to change the order of the list as you add or rearrange parts. You move one line of the list by dragging and dropping it to the location of your choice.

❑ Set groups and tab stops. To enable the user to move the input focus to a part by using the **Tab** and **Backspace** keys, select the **Tab stop** check box to the left of the part you want to be tabbed. If you want the user to be able to move the input focus to a part with the keyboard arrow keys, you must define a group of parts by selecting the **Group** check box to the left of the first part in the group—this part is called the group part. In the Tabbing and Depth Order dialog box, each part under the group part is in the group; the user can select each part by using the arrow key. To start another group, select the **Group** check box for the part you want to be the first part in that group. If you select both the **Group** and **Tab stop** check boxes for a part, the user can tab to the first part in the group and then use arrow keys to move to other parts in the group. The user moves from one group to another, using **Tab** and **Shift Tab** keys. In a group, the user moves from one part to another, using the keyboard arrow keys.

❑ Perform operations on parts as you do in the Composition Editor. You can access the pop-up menu of a part from the order list. You will find this operation useful when you want to access a part that you cannot see in the Composition Editor.

To enable the user to move from one input control to another by using the keyboard keys, modify the AAddressView part as follows:

1. Select the IMultiCellCanvas* part.

2. Select the *Tabbing and Depth Order* option from its pop-up menu.

3. If necessary, reorder the entry fields and the combo box to match their order in the view (you can drag and drop a line in the list).

4. Select the **Group** check box of EntryFieldStreet to define a group.

5. Select the **Tab stop** check boxes for all entry fields and the combo box as shown in Figure 55.

6. Close the window.

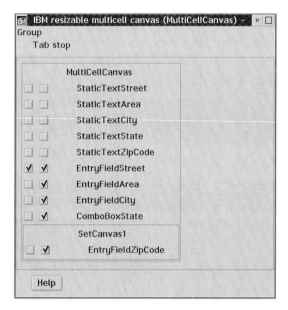

Figure 55. Tabbing Order for AAddressView

AAddressView is reused by APropertyView to display the address of a property. Therefore, APropertyView must have access to the contents of each entry field of AAddressView and to the contents of its combo box.

Promoting a Part Feature

Promoting a part feature is a way of exposing the feature to another part. When a feature is promoted in part A, it can be accessed from another part, B, when part A is embedded as a subpart within part B. Thus, to use AAddressView as a subpart and access the contents of its entry fields and its combo box in another part, you must promote the *text* attribute of these controls.

When you define a part in Visual Builder, the new features you add to the part are not available from other parts unless you promote them. You can promote the feature of a part in two ways:

❏ Select the part and use the *Promote part feature...* option from the part's pop-up menu.

❏ Use the Promote page in the Class Editor.

Let us promote the *text* attribute of EntryFieldStreet:

1. Select EntryFieldStreet (◻ in Figure 54 on page 148) and click on it with the right mouse button.
2. Select the *Promote part feature ...* option.
3. Promote the *text* attribute (Figure 56).

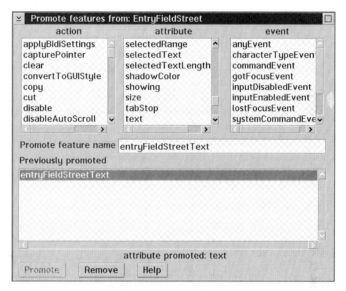

Figure 56. Promote EntryFieldStreetText Attribute of AAddressView

Now that you have promoted your first feature, you must promote the *text* attribute of the other controls: ComboBoxState, EntryFieldArea, EntryFieldCity, and EntryFieldZipCode.

When you have promoted all features, switch to the Class Editor and fill in the *Code generation file* group box as follows:

❑ C++ header file (.hpp): **vrcadrv.hpp**
❑ C++ code file (.cpp): **vrcadrv.cpp**

Save your part. At this time it is not necessary to generate the code because the connections have not been drawn.

APropertyView

APropertyView is the view of the Property class. In the design object model of the Property subsystem (Figure 41 on page 102), the Property class is represented as an association of four different classes:

❏ Address
❏ MarketingInfo
❏ PropertyLog
❏ MultiDoc

To reflect this association, you design the view of Property as a notebook whose pages represent the respective view of each class component (see Figure 57).

Note that the PropertyLog class is not represented as a notebook page because it does not have any visual representation. It is used to hold the time stamp of each creation or update in the database. In addition, a Description page is added to display information that is related to the Property class but does not fit on the Property page.

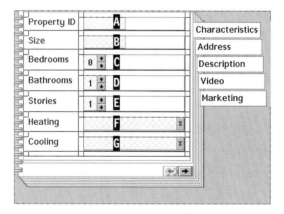

Figure 57. APropertyView Part

In the sections that follow, you build APropertyView by using a notebook part and then enhance it with the multicell canvas and the viewport parts.

> ── **Reminder** ────────────────────────────
> You must promote all field attributes of the APropertyView part because the part is reused in APropertyCreateView and APropertyUpdateView, and these attributes must be accessible.

Using a Notebook Control

The INotebook* part is a software representation of a physical note-book. It presents information on tabbed pages that the user can display sequentially or randomly. For an example of a notebook control, open any Visual Builder settings editor.

When building a notebook, you can use its various settings to tailor its appearance. You can:

❑ Select the type of binding (spiral or solid).
❑ Define the tab appearance, tab size, and tab text alignment.
❑ Define the page button size.

Once you have tailored the appearance of the notebook, you can add pages by selecting an add page choice from its pop-up menu. If the notebook does not have any pages, your only choice is to add a first page with the *Add Initial Page* option. If the notebook has one or more pages, select a page and choose **Add Page After** or **Add Page Before**. When a notebook is added to the Composition Editor, it already has one page (Figure 58).

Figure 58. Notebook for APropertyView

To build APropertyView as a notebook, follow the step-by-step instructions in Table 8.

Table 8. (Part 1 of 2) Building APropertyView As a Notebook

Step	Action
1	Start Visual Builder from the Property project (select *Project → Visual* in the menu bar).
2	From the Visual Builder window, select *Part → New...* option.

Table 8. (Part 2 of 2) Building APropertyView As a Notebook	
Step	**Action**
3	Fill in the entry fields as follows: **Field** — **Value** Class name — APropertyView Description — Property primary view File name — VRPROP Part type — visual part Base class — INotebook Click on the **Open** push button. An INoteBook* part is displayed on the free-form surface with one initial page.
4	Open the settings notebook of the INotebook* part and set its appearance as follows: **Setting** — **Value** Binding — Spiral Tab shape — Square Status area — Left Tab — Center Close the settings notebook.
5	Add four more pages, using the *Add Page After* option.

Building the Pages of a Noteboook

You can construct a notebook page by using one of two methods:

❏ Assemble controls on a separate canvas and drop the canvas on the page client area. Use this method if the visual part for the notebook page is reusable. For example, you built the AAddress-View part (Figure 54 on page 148) as a reusable part and can drop it on the Address page (Figure 61 on page 164). It is good practice to build your notebook page on a separate canvas, especially when the pages are complex. Furthermore, you can encapsulate non-visual parts at the page level.

❏ Assemble controls directly on the notebook page. Use this method if the visual part for the notebook page is not reusable or the page is simple enough to be built directly in the notebook. Because the Marketing, Characteristics, Video, and Description pages of our Visual Realty application are fairly simple, you build them directly in the notebook (Figure 64 on page 169).

Although you build the Marketing, Characteristics, Video, and Description pages as nonreusable canvases, you should always design your parts as reusable. In actuality, you might not reuse a specific part in your application, but you never know when you will need the part in another application. Building for reuse implies building for other applications.

Enhancing the Notebook Page

When you add a page to a notebook, the page is created with an ICanvas* part as a client area. On this canvas, you can add several parts to enhance your page. As you know, the standard canvas is suitable for most situations, but it does not allow the controls to be evenly distributed when it resizes. Thus, to enhance the notebook, you use a multicell canvas for all pages.

The multicell canvas is not a panacea for all resizing problems, however. In effect, every canvas, whatever its type, has a fixed minimum size that corresponds to the size of the canvas in the Composition Editor. Thus, the use of a multicell canvas for a notebook page does not prevent the user from getting clipping effects when the notebook is downsized.

In order for the user to scroll the page to access information when the page is clipped, you must use a viewport in the notebook page. The IViewPort part belongs to the *Composers* category. It is a scrollable framework for any type of canvas (Figure 59). The user interacts with the controls placed inside the viewport and can scroll both horizontally and vertically if the control does not fit in the frame window.

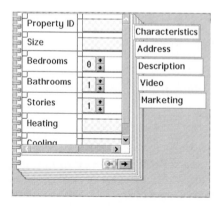

Figure 59. Characteristics Page Using a Viewport

In the Visual Realty application, you use an IViewPort part for each notebook page. In addition, you must attach a specific handler, IVB-MinSizeViewPortHandler, to each viewport. This handler ensures that when a viewport grows in size, its child part will grow with it. In our case, the child part is a multicell canvas that "knows" how to enlarge proportionally. Without the handler, the multicell canvas would not enlarge to fit the dimensions of the viewport.

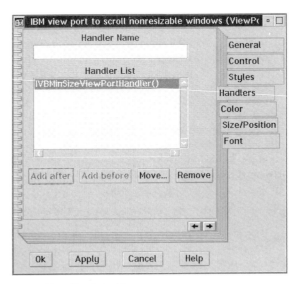

Figure 60. Event Handler List Box

Tip!

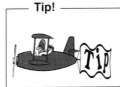

To select a page in a notebook, click in between the two horizontal lines at the bottom of a page. The two lines provide you with visual help to locate the page within the notebook. They are not shown at run time.

Building the Characteristics Page

The characteristics page is built from basic controls such as entry fields, combo boxes, and numeric spin buttons. It serves as a good example of the use of different controls for different needs. You build this part in the same way you built AAddressView. This time, you use the ISetCanvas part for each control that you drop on the multicell canvas because the width of the control differs.

To build the characteristics page, follow the step-by-step instructions in Table 9.

Table 9. (Part 1 of 3) Building the Characteristics Page

Step	Action
1	Select the first notebook page and change its tab label to **Characteristics**.
2	Open the settings notebook of the INotebook* part and set the tab parameters as follows: **Setting** **Value** Major tab width 130 Major tab height 30 Close the settings notebook. The tab length is adjusted to fit the largest label of the notebook. Usually you choose the tab length after you have entered its labels. Use the **Apply** push button of the settings notebook to adjust the length of the tabs.
3	Click inside the page to select the canvas and remove it.
4	Add an IViewPort* part to the page. (The IViewPort* part is located in the *Composers* category.)
5	Open the settings notebook of the IViewPort* part and, on the Handlers page, add the IVBMinSizeViewPortHandler handler to the handler list (Figure 60 on page 160). Close the settings notebook.
6	Add an IMultiCellCanvas* part in the IViewPort* part. (IMultiCellCanvas* part is located in the *Composers* category.) Configure the IMultiCellCanvas part as follows: ❑ Number of rows: 15 ❑ Number of columns: 5 ❑ Expandable rows: 1, 15 ❑ Expandable columns: 1, 5
7	Add seven IStaticText* parts to the IMultiCellCanvas* part as shown in Figure 57 on page 156 and change their text attributes as follows: Property ID, Size, Bedrooms, Bathrooms, Stories, Heating, and Cooling.
8	Add seven ISetCanvas* parts in cells (2, 4), (4, 4), (6, 4), (8, 4), (10, 4), (12, 4), and (14, 4) of the IMultiCellCanvas* part.

Table 9. (Part 2 of 3) Building the Characteristics Page

Step	Action
9	Add two IEntryField* parts (**A**, **B**) to the ISetCanvas* parts in cells (2, 4) and (4, 4) of the IMultiCellCanvas* and set their names and limits as follows:

Part	Name	Limit
A	EntryFieldPropertyID	5
B	EntryFieldSize	5

Step	Action
10	Add three INumericSpinButtons* parts (**C**, **D**, **E**) to the ISetCanvas* parts located in cells (6, 4), (8, 4), and (10, 4) (the INumericSpin-Button* part is located in the *Data entry* category) and set them up follows:

Part	Name	Limit	Lower	Upper	Value
C	NumericSpinButtonBedrooms	1	0	6	0
D	NumericSpinButtonBathrooms	1	1	4	1
E	NumericSpinButtonStories	1	1	3	1

A property with no bedrooms is a studio.

Step	Action
11	Add two IComboBox* parts (**F** and **G**) to the ISetCanvas* parts in cells (12, 4) and (14, 4) and set their names and limits as follows:

Part	Name	Limit
F	ComboBoxHeating	20
G	ComboBoxCooling	20

Step	Action
12	Open the settings notebook of ComboBoxHeating and set its contents as follows:

- ❑ No Heating
- ❑ Gas Electric
- ❑ Propane Gas
- ❑ Bottled Gas
- ❑ Solar
- ❑ Oil Central
- ❑ Forced Air Wall
- ❑ Furnace Floor
- ❑ Furnace Radiant
- ❑ Baseboard
- ❑ Steam or Hot Water
- ❑ Heat Pump
- ❑ Other

Select ***Read-only drop-down*** in the *Combo box type* group box. Close the settings notebook.

Step	Action
	Table 9. (Part 3 of 3) Building the Characteristics Page
13	Open the settings notebook of ComboBoxCooling and set its contents as follows: ❏ No Cooling ❏ Central Conditioner ❏ Room Conditioner ❏ Evaporative Cooler ❏ Other Select **Read-only drop-down** in the *Combo box type* group box. Close the settings notebook.
14	Select the IMultiCellCanvas* part and open the Tabbing and Depth Order dialog box. Set the tabbing groups as follows (see "Tabbing from One Part to Another" on page 152): **Group Tab Feature** X X EntryFieldPropertyID X EntryFieldSize X NumericSpinButtonBedrooms X NumericSpinButtonBathrooms X NumericSpinButtonStories X ComboBoxHeating X ComboBoxCooling Close the dialog box.

Note: Reverse highlighted letters are keyed to Figure 57 on page 156.

Building the Address Page

To build the address page, reuse AAddressView as shown in Figure 61.

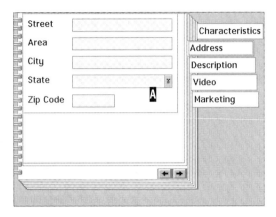

Figure 61. Address Page

Follow the step-by-step instructions in Table 10.

Step	Action
Table 10. Building the Address Page	
1	Select the second notebook page and change its tab label to **Address**.
2	Click inside the page to select the canvas and remove it.
3	Add an IViewPort* part to the page.
4	Open the settings notebook of the IViewPort* part and, on the Handlers page, add the IVBMinSizeViewPortHandler handler to the handler list (Figure 60 on page 160). Close the settings notebook.
5	Add an AAddressView* part in the IViewPort* part (*Option → Add parts...* from the Composition Editor menu), A. The AAddressView* part is added to the page. Notice that you cannot access its sub-parts.

Note: The reverse highlighted letter is keyed to Figure 61.

Building the Description Page

The description page (Figure 62) consists of three controls: a viewport, a multicell canvas, and a multiple-line edit (MLE) control. The MLE control provides users with a basic word processor that enables them to briefly describe the property.

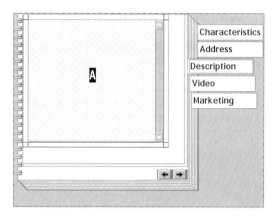

Figure 62. Description Page

To build the description page, follow the step-by-step instructions in Table 11.

Step	Action
Table 11. Building the Description Page	
1	Select the third notebook page and change its tab label to **Description**.
2	Click on the page to select the canvas and remove it.
3	Add an IViewPort* part to the page.
4	Open the settings notebook of the IViewPort* part and, on the Handlers page, add the IVBMinSizeViewPortHandler handler to the handler list (Figure 60 on page 160). Close the settings notebook.
5	Add an IMultiCellCanvas* part to the IViewPort* part. Stretch the part to fill in the page and configure it as follows: ❑ Number of rows: 3 ❑ Number of columns: 3 ❑ Expandable rows: 2. ❑ Expandable columns: 2 The MLE control will grow when the page is resized.
6	Add an IMultiLineEdit* part to the IMultiCellCanvas* part (IMultiLineEdit* part is located in the *Data entry* category) and change its name to MultiLineEditDescription, Ⓐ. Stretch the part to fill in the page.

Note: The reverse highlighted letter is keyed to Figure 62.

Building the Video Page

The video page (Figure 63) enables the buyer to watch a video of the property. The page is built from a visual representation of a VCR command control: the IMMPlayerPanel part. For this part to be added to the Composition Editor, the VBMM.VBB file must be loaded in Visual Builder (*File → Load* from the Visual Builder window).

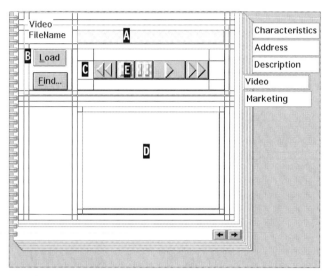

Figure 63. Video Page

This time, you build the part by using several multicell canvases, each of which is in charge of handling the resizing of a specific portion of the page. On the Video page, the *file name entry* field and the canvas where the video is displayed are expandable. A group box is used to logically group the video controls and the entry field.

To build the video page, follow the step-by-step instructions in Table 12.

Table 12. (Part 1 of 3) Building the Video Page	
Step	**Action**
1	Select the fourth notebook page and change its tab label to **Video**.
2	Click inside the page to select the canvas and remove it.
3	Add an IViewPort* part to the page.

Table 12. (Part 2 of 3) Building the Video Page

Step	Action
4	Open the settings notebook of the IViewPort* part and, on the Handlers page, add the IVBMinSizeViewPortHandler handler to the handler list (Figure 60 on page 160). Close the settings notebook.
5	Add an IMultiCellCanvas* part to the IViewPort* part. Stretch the part to fill in the page and configure it as follows: ❑ Number of rows: 11 ❑ Number of columns: 9 ❑ Expandable rows: 1, 10, 11 ❑ Expandable columns: 1, 5, 9 Use Figure 64 on page 169 to position the controls in the IMultiCell-Canvas* part. Notice that row 10 and column 5 are set to expandable so that the entry field and the multicell canvas used for the video canvas can expand.
6	Add one IStaticText* part to cell (4, 3) of the IMultiCellCanvas* part and change its text attribute to Filename.
7	Add one IEntryField* part to cell (4, 5) of the IMultiCellCanvas* part and set its name to EntryFieldVideo and its limit to 40, **A**.
8	Open the settings of EntryFieldVideo and, on the Styles page, set the *readOnly* radio button to **On** to prevent the user from entering a file name in the entry field. To set the contents of the entry field, the user must use the *Find...* push button.
9	Add an ISetCanvas* part, **B**, to cell (6, 3) of the IMultiCellCanvas* part. This canvas will contain two push buttons.
10	Open the settings notebook of the ISetCanvas* part and, on the General page, set the deck orientation to **Vertical** and the margin width to **0**. The push buttons dropped onto the canvas will line up vertically.
11	Add an IMultiCellCanvas* part, **C**, to cell (6, 5) of the first IMulti-CellCanvas* part and configure it as follows: ❑ Number of rows: 3 ❑ Number of columns: 3 ❑ Expandable rows: 1, 3 ❑ Expandable columns: 1, 3 This canvas will contain the IMMPlayerPanel part and will ensure that the panel remains centered underneath the entry field when the page is resized.

Table 12. (Part 3 of 3) Building the Video Page

Step	Action
12	Add an IMultiCellCanvas* part, **D**, to cell (10, 5) of the first IMulti-CellCanvas* part and configure it as follows: ❑ Number of rows: 3 ❑ Number of columns: 3 ❑ Expandable rows: 2 ❑ Expandable columns: 2 This canvas will contain the canvas for the video and will grow when the page is resized.
13	Add an ICanvas* part to cell (2, 2) of the IMultiCellCanvas* part, **D**. (ICanvas* part is located in the *Composers* category.) The video is displayed inside.
14	Add two IPushButton* parts to the ISetCanvas* part, **B**, and change their labels as shown in Figure 63. (The IPushButton* part is located in the *Buttons* category.)
15	Open the settings notebook of the *Load* push button and set its name to *PushButtonLoad*. Close the settings notebook.
16	Open the settings notebook of the *Find...* push button and set its name to **PushButtonFind**. Then switch to the Styles page and set the *defaultButton* radio button to **On**. Close the settings notebook.
17	Add one IMMPlayerPanel* part, **E**, to the cell (2, 2) of the IMulti-CellCanvas* part (*Option → Add part...* from the Composition Editor menu).
18	Add an IGroupBox* part on the first IMultiCellCanvas* part and change its name to **Video**. (The IGroupBox* part is located in the *Data entry* category.) Extend the group box from cell (2, 2) to cell (7, 6) to span the IEntryField* and IMMPlayPanel* parts. (Use the **ALT** key to extend the group box beyond the multicell canvas cell boundaries.)
19	Select the first IMultiCellCanvas* part and open the Tabbing and Depth Order dialog box. Define two tabbing groups as follows (see "Tabbing from One Part to Another" on page 152): **Group** **Tab** **Feature** X X EntryFieldVideo X X PushButtonLoad X PushButtonFind Close the dialog box.

Note: Reverse highlighted letters are keyed to Figure 63 on page 166.

Building the Marketing Page

The marketing page (Figure 64) displays the marketing information about the property. It is built from basic controls such as entry fields and static text controls. The static text controls **A**, **B**, **C**, and **D** are updated by the nonvisual part, AMarketingInfo, which computes their value according to the contents of entry fields **E**, **F** and **G**.

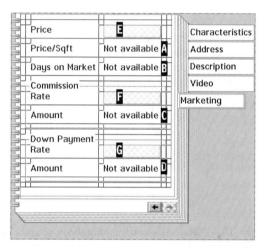

Figure 64. Marketing Page

To build the marketing page, follow the step-by-step instructions in Table 13.

Step	Action
	Table 13. (Part 1 of 3) Building the Marketing Page
1	Select the last notebook page and change its tab label to **Marketing**.
2	Click on the page to select the canvas and remove it.
3	Add an IViewPort* part to the page.
4	Open the settings notebook of the IViewPort* part and, on the Handlers page, add the IVBMinSizeViewPortHandler handler to the handler list (Figure 60 on page 160). Close the notebook settings.

Table 13. (Part 2 of 3) Building the Marketing Page	
Step	**Action**
5	Add an IMultiCellCanvas* part to the IViewPort* part. Stretch the part to fill in the page and configure it as follows: ❑ Number of rows: 22 ❑ Number of columns: 7 ❑ Expandable rows: 1, 22 ❑ Expandable columns: 1, 7 Use Figure 64 on page 169 to position the controls in the IMultiCell-Canvas* part.
6	Add seven IStaticText* parts to the second column of the IMultiCell-Canvas* as shown in Figure 64 on page 169 and set their text attributes as follows: ❑ Price ❑ Price/Sqft ❑ Days on Market ❑ Rate ❑ Amount ❑ Rate ❑ Amount
7	Add four more IStaticText* parts (**A**, **B**, **C**, **D**) to cells (5, 5), (7, 5), (13, 5), and (20, 5) of the IMultiCellCanvas* part and set their part names as follows: **Part**　　**Name** A　　StaticTextPriceSqft B　　StaticTextDaysOnMarket C　　StaticTextCommssionValue D　　StaticTextDownPaymentValue
8	Change the text attribute of IStaticText* parts **A**, **B**, **C**, and **D** to **Not Available** and their respective limit to **7**, **3**, **7**, and **7**. Their contents will be calculated later by the nonvisual part, AMarketingInfo (see "AMarketingInfo" on page 214).
9	Add three IEntryField* parts (**E**, **F** **G**) to cells (3, 5), (11, 5), and (18, 5) of the IMultiCellCanvas* part and set their part names and limits as follows: **Part**　　**Name**　　**Limit** E　　EntryFieldPrice　　7 F　　EntryFieldCommissionRateSize　　5 G　　EntryFieldDownPaymentRate　　5
10	Add two IGroupBox* parts to group the commission rate and amount and the down payment rate and amount. The commission group box extends from cell (9, 2) to cell (14, 6), and the down payment group box extends from cell (16, 2) to cell (21, 6).

Table 13. (Part 3 of 3) Building the Marketing Page

Step	Action
11	Select the first IMultiCellCanvas* part and open the Tabbing and Depth Order dialog box. Define two tabbing groups as follows (see "Tabbing from One Part to Another" on page 152): **Group** **Tab** **Feature** X X EntryFieldPrice X X EntryFieldCommissionRate X EntryFieldDownPaymentRate Close the dialog box.

Note: Reverse highlighted letters are keyed to Figure 64 on page 169.

To reuse APropertyView in other parts, you must promote some of its features. Switch to the Part Interface Editor and select the Promote page. Promote the features listed in Table 14.

Table 14. (Part 1 of 2) Promoted Features of APropertyView

Promote Feature Name	Subpart Name	Feature Type	Promoted Feature
addressViewComboBoxState-Text	AddressView	attribute	ComboBoxState-Text
addressViewEntryFieldAreaText	AddressView	attribute	EntryFieldArea-Text
addressViewEntryFieldCityText	AddressView	attribute	EntryFieldCity-Text
addressViewEntryFieldStreet-Text	AddressView	attribute	EntryFieldStreet-Text
addressViewEntryFieldZipCode-Text	AddressView	attribute	EntryFieldZip-CodeText
commissionRate	EntryFieldCommission-Rate	attribute	valueAsDouble
daysOnMarket	StaticTextDaysOnMarket	attribute	text
downPaymentRate	EntryFieldDownPayment-Rate	attribute	valueAsDouble
price	EntryFieldPrice	attribute	valueAsDouble
bathrooms	NumericSpinButton-Bathrooms	attribute	value

Table 14. (Part 2 of 2) Promoted Features of APropertyView			
Promote Feature Name	**Subpart Name**	**Feature Type**	**Promoted Feature**
bedrooms	NumericSpinButtonBed-rooms	attribute	value
size	EntryFieldSize	attribute	valueAsDouble
propertyID	EntryFieldPropertyID	attribute	text
cooling	ComboBoxCooling	attribute	text
heating	ComboBoxHeating	attribute	text
videoFileName	EntryFieldVideo	attribute	text
Note: Notice that the numeric attributes are promoted as *valueAsDouble*.			

Now you can save APropertyView. First, switch to the Class Interface Editor and fill in the *Code generation file* group box as follows:

❑ C++ header file (.hpp): **vrpprpv.hpp**
❑ C++ code file (.cpp): **vrpprpv.cpp**

Then save the part.

APropertyCreateView

APropertyCreateView (Figure 65) is a composite part that consists of APropertyView and three push buttons:

❑ **Create**, for creating a new property in the database
❑ **Cancel**, for canceling the operation and closing the window
❑ **Help**, for accessing on-line help

The base class of this part is an IFrameWindow part. You tailor this main window, adding an info area, IInfoArea part, to its frame and changing the standard canvas to a multicell canvas. The info area is used to display help information related to some parts of the view. We explain the use of the info area with the fly-over help facility in "Adding Fly-over Help to a Control" on page 247.

The three push buttons are added to a set canvas.

Figure 65. APropertyCreateView

To build APropertyCreateView, follow the step-by-step instructions in Table 15.

Table 15. (Part 1 of 3) Constructing APropertyCreateView Part	
Step	**Action**
1	Start Visual Builder from the Property project (select *Project → Visual* in the menu bar).
2	From the Visual Builder window, select *Part → New...* option.
3	Fill in the entry fields as follows: **Field** **Value** Class name APropertyCreateView Description View to create a property in the database File name VRPROP Part type visual part Base class IFrameWindow Click on the **Open** push button. An IFrameWindow* part is displayed on the free-form surface.
4	Change the IFrameWindow* part title to **New Property**.
5	Delete the ICanvas* part in the IFrameWindow*.
6	Add an IMultiCellCanvas* part to the IFrameWindow*.

Table 15. (Part 2 of 3) Constructing APropertyCreateView Part

Step	Action
7	Open the settings notebook of the IMultiCellCanvas* part and configure it as follows: ❑ Number of rows: 4 ❑ Number of columns: 3 ❑ Expandable rows: 2, 3 ❑ Expandable columns: 2 When you set the row 3 to expandable, the ISetCanvas* part that holds the three push buttons is kept in the bottom of the window when the view is resized.
8	Switch to the Color page and select the **Colors** radio button of the *Color selection* group box. Then select **paleGray** in the *Color values* drop-down list box. In this way, all controls dropped in the multicell canvas have a pale gray background. Close the settings notebook.
9	Add an IInfoArea* part, **A** to the IFrameWindow* part. (The IInfoArea* part is located in the *Frame extensions* category).
10	Add an APropertyView* **B**, to cell (2, 2) of the IMultiCellCanvas* part as shown in Figure 65 on page 173 (*Option → Add parts* from the Composition Editor menu).
11	Add an ISetCanvas* part, **C**, to cell (4, 2) of the IMultiCellCanvas* part as shown on Figure 65 on page 173.
12	Add three IPushButton* parts to the ISetCanvas* part and set their names as follows: ❑ PushButtonCreate ❑ PushButtonCancel ❑ PushButtonHelp
13	Change the *text* attribute of the three push buttons as follows: ❑ ~Create for PushButtonCreate ❑ ~Cancel for PushButtonCancel ❑ ~Help for PushButtonHelp Notice the use of ~ for the key accelerator.
14	Open the settings notebook of PushButtonHelp and switch to the Styles page. Set the *help* radio button to **On** to turn this regular push button into a help push button. Set the *noPointerFocus* radio button to **On** to prevent the help push button from getting the input focus when the user clicks on it. In this way, the application can display help for the part that has the input focus when the user clicks the *help* push button. Close the notebook settings.

Table 15. (Part 3 of 3) Constructing APropertyCreateView Part

Step	Action
15	Select the ISetCanvas* part and open the Tabbing and Depth Order dialog box. Define a tabbing group for the three push buttons as follows (see "Tabbing from One Part to Another" on page 152):

Group	Tab	Feature
X	X	PushButtonCreate
	X	PushButtonCancel
	X	PushButtonCreate

Close the dialog box.

Note: Reverse highlighted letters are keyed to Figure 65 on page 173.

Now you can save APropertyCreateView. First, switch to the Class Editor and fill in the *Code generation file* group box as follows:

❑ C++ header file (.hpp): **vrpcrtv.hpp**
❑ C++ code file (.cpp): **vrpcrtv.cpp**

Then, save the part.

APropertyUpdateView

APropertyUpdateView (Figure 66) is a composite part that consists of APropertyView and three push buttons:

❑ **Update,** for updating property information in the database
❑ **Cancel**, for canceling the operation and closing the window
❑ **Help,** for accessing online help (Figure 66)

You build the APropertyUpdateView in the same way you built APropertyCreateView.

Figure 66. APropertyUpdateView

To build APropertyUpdateView, follow the step-by-step instructions in Table 16.

Step	Action
Table 16. (Part 1 of 3) Constructing APropertyUpdateView Part	
1	Start Visual Builder from the Property project (select *Project* → *Visual* in the menu bar).
2	From the Visual Builder window, select *Part* → *New...* option.
3	Fill in the entry fields as follows:

Fill in the entry fields as follows:

Field	Value
Class name	APropertyUpdateView
Description	View to update property information in the database
File name	VRPROP
Part type	visual part
Base class	IFrameWindow

Click on the **Open** push button. An IFrameWindow* part is displayed on the free-form surface.

Step	Action
4	Change the IFrameWindow* part title to **Property**.
5	Delete the ICanvas* part in the IFrameWindow* part.
6	Add an IMultiCellCanvas* part to the IFrameWindow*.

Table 16. (Part 2 of 3) Constructing APropertyUpdateView Part

Step	Action
7	Open the settings notebook of the IMultiCellCanvas* part and configure it as follows: ❑ Number of rows: 4 ❑ Number of columns: 3 ❑ Expandable rows: 2, 3 ❑ Expandable columns: 2
8	Switch to the Color page and select the **Colors** radio button of the *Color selection* group box. Then select **paleGray** in the *Color values* drop-down list box. In this way, all controls dropped in the multicell canvas have a pale gray background. Close the settings notebook.
9	Add an IInfoArea* part, **A**, to the IFrameWindow* part.
10	Add an APropertyView* part, **B**, to cell (2, 2) of the IMultiCell-Canvas* part as shown in Figure 66 on page 176 (*Option → Add parts* from the Composition Editor menu).
11	Add an ISetCanvas* part, **C**, to cell (4, 2) of the IMultiCellCanvas* part as shown on Figure 66 on page 176.
12	Add three IPushButton* parts to the ISetCanvas* part and set their names as follows: ❑ PushButtonUpdate ❑ PushButtonCancel ❑ PushButtonHelp
13	Change the *text* attribute of the three push buttons as follows: ❑ ~Update for PushButtonUpdate ❑ ~Cancel for PushButtonCancel ❑ ~Help for PushButtonHelp Notice the use of ~ for the key accelerator.
14	Open the settings notebook of PushButtonHelp and switch to the Styles page. Set the *help* radio button to **On**. Set the *noPointerFocus* radio button to **On**. Close the settings notebook.

Table 16. (Part 3 of 3) Constructing APropertyUpdateView Part	
Step	**Action**

15	Select the ISetCanvas* part and open the Tabbing and Depth Order dialog box. Set the Tab check boxes as follows (see "Tabbing from One Part to Another" on page 152):
	
	Group **Tab** **Feature**
	X X PushButtonUpdate
	   X PushButtonCancel
	   X PushButtonCreate
	
	Close the dialog box.

Note: Reverse highlighted letters are keyed to Figure 66 on page 176.

Now you can save APropertyUpdateView. First, switch to the Class Editor and fill in the *Code generation file* group box as follows:

❏ C++ header file (.hpp): **vrpupdv.hpp**
❏ C++ code file (.cpp): **vrpupdv.cpp**

Then, save the part.

APropertyView and APropertyUpdateView look quite similar; they differ in their push button labels. Reusing APropertyView saves a lot of time and brings consistency to the whole application.

ADeleteDialogView

ADeleteDialogView is a simple visual part (Figure 67) that is used throughout the application. It provides a way of warning users when they go to delete a record in the database.

Figure 67. ADeleteDialogView

Because you will reuse this part across different subsystems, do not embed any Data Access Builder parts. Instead, promote two features:

❑ The buttonClickEvent of the *OK* push button. The part that reuses ADeleteDialogView needs this promoted feature to know when the button has been clicked and to perform the appropriate action.

❑ The *text* attribute of the textOfRecord static text control. This promoted feature is used to display, in the dialog box, the identifier of the record to be deleted (see Table 17 on page 180 and Figure 67 on page 178).

ADeleteDialogView is used as a dialog window. It is not resizable, but you still have to use the IMultiCellCanvas* part to make this view portable across different screen resolutions and different font settings.

Even though this view is not resizable, you must set some rows and columns of the IMultiCellCanvas* part to be expandable. In effect, when running the application under different screen resolutions, this view is resized to fit the new resolution and the canvas might be a bit distorted. In setting the outermost columns and rows to be expandable, you minimize the distortion.

Tip!

When using a multicell canvas for your view, you can directly observe the effect of resizing the view in the Composition Editor and anticipate the appearance of your view in different resolutions.

Notice that you use an IIconControl part to display an icon in the dialog window. The icon displayed is set by updating the *DLL name* and *resource ID* fields in the IIconControl General settings page. Be aware that an icon is not resized on either a set canvas or a multicell canvas when the canvas is resized.

In our sample application, you use the ABTICONS.DLL provided with VisualAge C++. It contains predefined icons that you can use for your own needs.

If you want to use your own specific icons, you can use Project Smarts to create a Resource Dynamic Link Library project to build your own DLL. In the complete application that accompanies this book, we use our own specific DLL, REALICON.DLL, which you can reuse for your future applications. To ensure that your application can access either one of these DLLs, put them in a directory that your LIBPATH accesses (check the LIBPATH environment variable in your CONFIG.SYS file).

To build ADeleteDialogView, follow the step-by-step instructions in Table 17.

Table 17. (Part 1 of 3) Building ADeleteDialogView

Step	Action
1	Start Visual Builder from the Common project (select *Project → Visual* in the menu bar).
2	From the Visual Builder window, select *Part → New...* option.
3	Fill in the entry fields as follows: **Field** **Value** Class name ADeleteDialogView Description General purpose delete dialog view File name VRCOMM Part type visual part Base class IFrameWindow and click on the **Open** push button. An IFrameWindow* part is displayed on the free-form surface.
4	Change the IFrameWindow* part title to **Delete Record**.
5	Open the settings notebook of the IFrameWindow* part and change the style setting as follows: **Setting** **Value** dialogBorder On maximizeButton Off minimizeButton Off sizingBorder Off systemMenu Off Close the settings notebook. The window turns into a nonresizable dialog box.
6	Delete the ICanvas* part in the IFrameWindow* part.
7	Add an IMultiCellCanvas* part to the IFrameWindow* part.
8	Open the settings notebook of the IMultiCellCanvas* part and configure it as follows: ❑ Number of rows: 7 ❑ Number of columns: 3 ❑ Expandable rows: 3, 5 ❑ Expandable columns: 1, 3
9	Switch to the Color page and select the **Colors** radio button of the *Color selection* group box. Then select **paleGray** in the *Color values* drop-down list box. Close the settings notebook.

Step	Action
	Table 17. (Part 2 of 3) Building ADeleteDialogView
Step	**Action**
10	Add an ISetCanvas* part, **A**, to cell (2, 2) of the IMultiCellCanvas* part. This set canvas will contain an icon and a static text control lined up horizontally.
11	Add an IIconControl* to the ISetCanvas* part. (The IIconControl* part is located in the *Data entry* category.)
12	Open the settings notebook of the IIconControl* part. Set the DLL name to **abticons** and the resource ID to **531**. Close the settings notebook.
13	Add an IStaticText* part to the ISetCanvas* part and change its label to **Delete**.
14	Open the settings notebook of the ISetCanvas* part, set its alignment to center (select the middle radio button in the *Alignment* group box), and adjust its margin and pad dimensions as follows: **Field** **Value** Margin Width 0 Margin Height 0 Pad Width 10 Pad Height 0 Close the settings notebook.
15	Add an IStaticText* part to cells (5, 2) of the IMultiCellCanvas* part and change its label to **RecordIdentifier**.
16	Open the settings notebook of the RecordIdentifier IStaticText* part and change the part's name to **RecordID**. On the same page, set the static text alignment to center (select the middle radio button of the *Alignment* group box). Close the settings notebook.
17	Promote the ***text*** attribute of the RecordID part.
18	Add an IMultiCellCanvas* part, **B**, to cell (7, 2) of the IMultiCellCanvas* part and configure it as follows: ❏ Number of rows: 3 ❏ Number of columns: 5 ❏ Expandable rows: none ❏ Expandable columns: 1, 3, 5
19	Add two IPushButton* parts to cells (2, 2) and (2, 4) of the IMultiCellCanvas* part, **B**, and change their labels as shown in Figure 67 on page 178.

Table 17. (Part 3 of 3) Building ADeleteDialogView	
Step	**Action**
20	Change the push button names to **PushButtonOK** and **Push-ButtonCancel**.
21	Promote the **buttonClickEvent** event of *PushbuttonOK*.
22	Set **PushbuttonOK** as the default push button (set defaultButton to **On** in the Styles page of the settings notebook).
23	Select the IMultiCellCanvas* part, **B**, and open the Tabbing and Depth Order dialog box. Set the Tab check boxes as follows (see "Tabbing from One Part to Another" on page 152): **Group**　　**Tab**　　　　**Feature** 　　　　X　　　　PushButtonOK 　　　　X　　　　PushButtonCancel

Note: Reverse highlighted letters are keyed to Figure 67 on page 178.

Now you can save ADeleteDialogView. First, switch to the Class Editor and fill in the *Code generation file* group box as follows:

- ❑ C++ header file (.hpp): **vrcdelv.hpp**
- ❑ C++ code file (.cpp): **vrcdelv.cpp**

Then, save the part.

APropertySearchResultView

APropertySearchResultView (Figure 68) displays a list of properties that match the buyer's criteria. To display these properties in tabular form, use an IVBContainerControl part, which represents a container control.

Using a Container

An IVBContainerControl part is a control used to display nonvisual interface objects. As a container, it shows different views of the objects it holds:

Text and flowed text view The objects are represented as text in single (text view) or multiple (flowed text view) columns.

Name and flowed name view The objects are represented as small icons followed by text in single (name view) or multiple (flowed name view) columns.

Icon view The objects are represented as icons.

Tree view The objects are represented hierarchically.

Details view The objects are represented as a table, with one row for each object and a column for each object attribute. This is the view you use to display the property list (Figure 68).

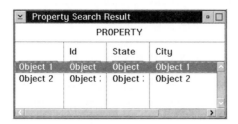

Figure 68. APropertySearchResultView

For our sample application, you will use the details view of the Prop_-ad_log Data Access Builder part. The Prop_ad_log's attributes are displayed in column controls, which are added to the container. The following attributes are displayed: identifier, state, city, and area. In addition, you tailor the container by adding an icon of a property.

APropertyResultView is built from an IFrameWindow part. An IMultiCellCanvas part is used as the client area in place of the standard ICanvas part.

You build the view in two steps: First you tailor a container to suit your needs, then you add five columns to the container and tailor each of them to display the necessary information (an icon of the property, the property status, the city, the state, and the area).

To build the container, follow the step-by-step instructions in Table 18.

Table 18. (Part 1 of 2) Building APropertySearchResultView: Building a Container	
Step	**Action**
1	Start Visual Builder from the Property project (select *Project →Visual* in the menu bar).

Table 18. (Part 2 of 2) Building APropertySearchResultView: Building a Container

Step	Action
2	From the Visual Builder window, select *Part → New...* option.
3	Fill in the entry fields as follows: **Field** **Value** Class name APropertySearchResultView Description View of a property list File name VRPROP Part type visual part Base class IFrameWindow
4	Change the IFrameWindow* part title to **Property Search Result**.
5	Delete the ICanvas* part in the IFrameWindow* part.
6	Add an IMultiCellCanvas* part to the IFrameWindow* part.
7	Open the settings notebook of the IMultiCellCanvas* part and configure it as follows: ❑ Number of columns: 1 ❑ Number of rows: 1 ❑ Expandable columns: 1 ❑ Expandable rows: 1 You do not have to add extra rows and columns in the IMultiCell-Canvas* part, because the container can fill in the entire window client area.
8	Add an IVBContainerControl* part to the IMultiCellCanvas* part. (The IVBContainerControl* part is located in the *Lists* category.)
9	Open the settings notebook of the IVBContainerControl* part and set the following values (Figure 69 on page 185): Field Value Subpart name PropertyContainer Title PROPERTY Show title selected Show title separator selected Title alignment centered View type showDetailsView Item type Prop_ad_log* Text area Icon #IDynamicLinkLibrary("abticons").loadIcon(106) Notice that the item type field is filled in with the type of the Data Access Builder part that maps the PROP_AD_LOG table. The container is tailored by displaying a "house" icon. This icon will be displayed in the icon column that you add later on.

When you enter the type of the object container, you must be aware of the object type that the object provider provides. In the sample application, the container is filled with the objects in the Data Access Builder Prop_ad_logManager part. In this sense, Prop_ad_log-Manager constitutes the object provider. As mentioned in Chapter 6, "Mapping Relational Tables Using Data Access Builder," on page 127, we know that Prop_ad_logManager contains an attribute, *items*, of type IVSequence<Prop_ad_log*>*. This attribute will be connected by an attribute-to-attribute connection to the same attribute of the container. Thus, the container will hold a sequence of objects of Prop_ad_-log* type (Figure 69).

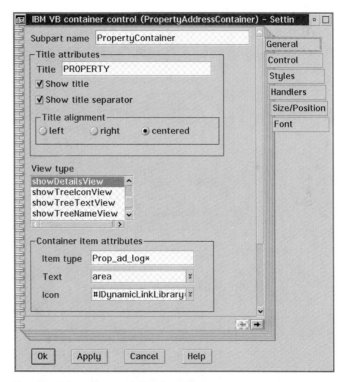

Figure 69. Container General Settings Page

Once the container is set up, you must add container columns to display the information.

Adding Columns to a Container

The detail view requires that you add a container column to the container for each object attribute to be displayed. A container column is represented by the IContainerColumn* part.

You add an IContainerColumn* part to your container by dragging it from the parts palette and dropping it on the container. Then, you edit its settings to reflect the information you want to display (Figure 70).

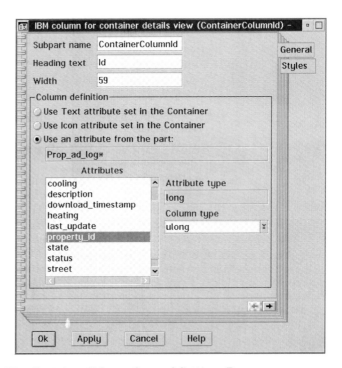

Figure 70. Container Column General Settings Page

To add the columns to your container, follow the step-by-step instructions in Table 19.

Table 19. (Part 1 of 3) Building APropertySearchResultView: Adding Container Columns	
Step	**Action**
1	Add five IContainerColumn* parts in the IContainerControl* part. (The IContainerColumn* part is located in the *Lists* category.)

Table 19. (Part 2 of 3) Building APropertySearchResultView: Adding Container Columns

Step	Action
2	Open the settings notebook of the first IContainerColumn* part and change the fields as follows:

Field	Value
Subpart name	ContainerColumnIcon
Heading text	Icon
Width	59
Use Icon attribute set in the container	selected

The resource identifier set in the IContainerControl* part is used to display an icon in this IContainerColumn* part. Switch to the Styles page and set the verticalSeparator to **On**. Close the settings notebook.

Step	Action
3	Open the settings notebook of the second IContainerColumn* part and change the fields as follows:

Field	Value
Subpart name	ContainerColumnId
Heading text	Id
Width	59
Use an attribute from the part	selected
Attributes	property_id

The property identifier is displayed in this column. Switch to the Styles page and set the horizontalSeparator and verticalSeparator to **On**. Close the settings notebook.

Step	Action
4	Open the settings notebook of the third IContainerColumn* part and change the fields as follows:

Field	Value
Subpart name	ContainerColumnState
Heading text	State
Width	59
Use an attribute from the part	selected
Attributes	state

The property state is displayed in this column. Then, switch to the Styles page and set the horizontalSeparator and verticalSeparator to **On**. Close the settings notebook.

Step	Action

Table 19. (Part 3 of 3) Building APropertySearchResultView: Adding Container Columns

Step	Action
5	Open the settings notebook of the fourth IContainerColumn* part and change the fields as follows:

Field	Value
Subpart name	ContainerColumnCity
Heading text	City
Width	59
Use an attribute from the part	selected
Attributes	city

The property city is displayed in this column. Then, switch to the Styles page and set the horizontalSeparator and verticalSeparator to **On**. Close the settings notebook.

6	Open the settings notebook of the last IContainerColumn* part and change the fields as follows:

Field	Value
Subpart name	ContainerColumnArea
Heading text	Area
Width	59
Use an attribute from the part	selected
Attributes	area

The property area is displayed in this column. Switch to the Styles page and set the horizontalSeparator and verticalSeparator to **On**. Close the settings notebook.

Now you can save APropertySearchResultView. First, switch to the Class Editor and fill in the *Code generation file* group box as follows:

- ❏ C++ header file (.hpp): **vrpsrrsv.hpp**
- ❏ C++ code file (.cpp): **vrpsrrsv.cpp**

Then, save the part.

APropertySearchParameterView

In the Visual Realty application, the user can search properties according to the buyer's preferences. As stated in "Requirement Specifications" on page 64, different criteria are taken into account: area, price range, size range, number of bedrooms, and number of bathrooms. The user may choose to search properties using some or all of these criteria.

One way of designing a visual part that enables the user to construct a search properties clause is to build a part that holds as many input controls as search criteria and use an ICheckBox part to select or deselect each criterion.

Using Check Box Control

An ICheckBox part is a square box with text that represents the settings choice (Figure 71). A mark in the check box indicates that the choice is selected. In our case, you use the ICheckBox part instead of the IRadioButton part because the choices are not mutually exclusive. For example, if the user wants to search all properties that range in size from 500 to 2500 square feet, the user first selects the **Size** checkbox and then enters the size range.

Figure 71. APropertySearchParameterView

The part is built from an IFrameWindow part. An IMultiCellCanvas* part is used in the client area to display the parts when the window is resized. Several ICheckBox* and IEntryField* parts are dropped on the IMultiCellCanvas. An ISetCanvas* holds three IPushButton* parts.

The list of areas is displayed in a collection combo-box control: ICollectionViewComboBox*.

Using Collection Combination-Box Control

An ICollectionViewComboBox part is a control that combines a selection list and an entry field for collection object choices. This selection list displays the records of the LIST_AREA table. You will use the List_areaManager Data Access Builder part to fill in the list. As with an IVBContainerControl part, the ICollectionViewComboBox part must be set up to display objects of a specific type. The type is entered

in the *Item type* entry field of the General page in the ICollectionView-
ComboBox part's settings notebook. The type must be a pointer type of
the part that is displayed in the ICollectionViewComboBox part. In
our case, you must set the type to **List_area***.

The ICollectionViewComboBox part combines the behavior of an
IEntryField part with an ICollectionViewListBox part. It behaves similarly to the ICollectionViewListBox part (ICollectionViewComboBox
and ICollectionViewListBox parts are also called *collection* list box).
When an object is added to an ICollectionViewListBox part or an
ICollectionViewComboBox part, the display of its contents is ruled by
its method: IString asString(). This method returns an IString, which
can be the concatenation of several object attributes.

For example, the parts that Data Access Builder generates have an
asString method that returns the concatenation of all of their
attributes, after conversion if necessary, separated by a dot. This is
why, in the first example that you built in Section "Using Data Access
Builder Parts with Visual Builder" on page 136, the ICollectionView-
ListBox part displays each property part as the concatenation of the
property identifier, property size, number of stories, number of bathrooms, number of bedrooms, type of cooling, type of heating, and
description text. In our example, the only information displayed by the
asString method of the List_area part is the property area, because it
is the only attribute of the corresponding relational view. When the
part does not have an asString method, an evasive IVBase Object is
displayed instead.

You can tailor the information displayed in a collection list box in two
ways:

❑ Override the asString method of the part that must be displayed
  in the collection list box.

❑ Override the string generator of the collection list box.

Overriding the asString Method

Each object that you want to display in a collection list box must be
provided with an asString method to get its equivalent IString form. If
an object is already provided with an asString method, you can override it with your own method by subclassing its corresponding class.
The asString() method need only return an IString object.

The only way to override the asString method of a Data Access Builder
part is to edit the code directly. In effect, you cannot derive a class
from the generated part because you would also change the type of the
items attribute managed by the manager class.

Do not edit the Data Access Builder part directly because you will lose all of your changes if you generate the code from the same part later.

Back to the small application you developed in Section "Using Data Access Builder Parts with Visual Builder" on page 136. You can modify the property code—the code is located in the property.cpp file—as shown in Figure 72 to have only the property identifiers displayed in the collection list box.

```
//....
public: IString Property::asString()
{
    return IString(Property_id());
}
//....
```

Figure 72. Overriding the asString Method

Overriding the String Generator of the Collection List Box

You can override the ICollectionViewListBox or the ICollectionView-ComboBox string generator that customizes the part information to be displayed. A string generator, IStringGenerator<Element>, is a template class that manages the translation of Element objects to their IString form. It can provide strings for collection elements that are used in the ICollectionViewListBox part or ICollectionViewComboBox part.

To use the IStringGenerator, you must define a subclass of the IString-GeneratorFn<Element> template class and override the pure virtual function: virtual IString stringFor(Element const& pElement). The IStringGeneratorFn template class is an abstract base class that defines the protocol for storing and calling functions that generate IString objects. Objects of this class represent functions that are called when the stringFor function is called. The stringFor function accepts an object reference of the template class type.

It is a good idea to override the string generator of a collection list box when using the collection list box in tandem with Data Access Builder parts. In effect, you do not have to edit the source code generated by Data Access Builder to customize the contents of the collection list box.

To have the property identifiers display in the ICollectionViewListBox of the sample detailed in Section "Using Data Access Builder Parts with Visual Builder" on page 136, follow these instructions:

1. Build a new class, IStringGeneratorForPropertyFn, to set a new IStringGenerator for the ICollectionViewListBox (see Figure 73).

2. Open the settings notebook of the ICollectionViewListBox* part.

3. Switch to the General page and fill in the String generator entry field with: **IStringGenerator<Property*>(new IStringGeneratorForPropertyFn())**.

4. Switch to the Class Editor and, in the *Required include files* list box, add the file name where IStringGeneratorForPropertyFn is defined.

Now you can regenerate the code and compile it.

```
// Class used to set a new IStringGenerator for a DAX part when
// used with an ICollectionViewListBox

#include <PropertyV.hpp>      // DAX generated file.
                             // Property is the data object

#include <istrgen.hpp>        // header file for IStringGenerator class

class IStringGeneratorForPropertyFn :
            public IStringGeneratorFn<Property*>
{
  public:
    IStringGeneratorForPropertyFn() {};
    virtual ~IStringGeneratorForPropertyFn() {};

    virtual IString stringFor(Property* const& pProperty)
    {
        // Return the identifier of the property
        return pProperty->Property_id();
    }
}; // IStringGeneratorForPropertyFn
```

Figure 73. IStringGeneratorForPropertyFn Declaration

To build APropertySearchParameterView, follow the step-by-step instructions in Table 20.

Table 20. (Part 1 of 5) Building APropertySearchParameterView	
Step	**Action**
1	Start Visual Builder from the Property project (select *Project →Visual* in the menu bar).
2	From the Visual Builder window, select *Part → New...* option.
3	Fill in the entry fields as follows: **Field** — **Value** Class name — APropertySearchParameterView Description — View to collect the buyer preferences File name — VRPROP Part type — Visual part Base class — IFrameWindow Click on the **Open** push button. An IFrameWindow* part is displayed on the free-form surface.

Table 20. (Part 2 of 5) Building APropertySearchParameterView

Step	Action
4	Change the IFrameWindow* part title to **Search Property**.
5	Delete the ICanvas* part in the IFrameWindow* part.
6	Add an IMultiCellCanvas* part in the IFrameWindow* part.
7	Open the settings notebook of the IMultiCellCanvas* part and configure it as follows: ❑ Number of rows: 12 ❑ Number of columns: 5 ❑ Expandable rows: 11 ❑ Expandable columns: 1, 5 Close the settings notebook.
8	Add five ICheckBox* parts, **A**, to cells (2, 2), (4, 2), (6, 2), (8, 2), and (10, 2) of the IMultiCellCanvas* part (ICheckBox* part is located in the *Buttons* category) and set their settings as follows: **Name** — **Text** CheckBoxArea — Area CheckBoxPrice — Price Range CheckBoxSize — Size Range CheckBoxBedrooms — Bedrooms CheckBoxBathrooms — Bathrooms
9	Add an ICollectionViewListBox* part, **B**, to the IMultiCellCanvas* part and make it span three columns from cell (2, 4) to cell (2, 6).
10	Open the settings notebook of the ICollectionViewListBox* part and set the fields as follows: **Field** — **Value** Name — CollectionViewArea* Item type — List_area* Limit — 20 Combo box type — Read-only drop-down The area is 20 characters wide (see the PROPERTY table structure in Appendix C, "Database Definition," on page 347). The list box is set to read-only to prevent users from typing in a property area that does not exist in the database.
11	Switch to the Control page of the ICollectionViewListBox* part settings notebook and deselect the **Enabled** check box. In "APropertySearchParameterView" on page 283, you will draw connections to enable this control only when the CheckBoxArea is selected. Close the settings notebook.

Table 20. (Part 3 of 5) Building APropertySearchParameterView

Step	Action
12	Add four IEntryField* parts to cells (4, 4), (4, 6), (6, 4), and (6, 6) of the IMultiCellCanvas* part to hold the price and size ranges, **C**, **D**, **E**, **F**
13	Open the settings notebooks of each entry field and configure them as follows:

Name	Limit	Enabled check box
EntryFieldMinPrice	7	unselect
EntryFieldMaxPrice	7	unselect
EntryFieldMinSize	5	unselect
EntryFieldMaxSize	5	unselect

Close the settings notebooks. Deselect the **Enabled** check box of each entry field from the Control page of its settings notebook. In "APropertySearchParameterView" on page 283, you will draw connections to enable this control only when their corresponding check box (CheckBoxPrice or CheckBoxSize) is selected.

Step	Action
14	Add an ISetCanvas* part in cell (8, 4) of the IMultiCellCanvas* part and set its margin width and height to **0**. This setting enables the numeric spin button boundaries for the number of bedrooms to line up with the set canvas boundaries.
15	Add an INumericSpinButton* part to the ISetCanvas* part to hold the number of bedrooms, **G**, and configure it as follows:

Field	Value
Name	NumericSpinButtonBedrooms
Alignment	Center
Limit	1
Lower	0
Upper	6
Value	0
Enabled	unselect

Unselect the **Enabled** check box of the numeric spin button from its settings notebook Control page. In "APropertySearchParameter-View" on page 283, you will draw connections to enable this control only when the corresponding CheckBoxBedrooms check box is selected.

Step	Action
16	Add an ISetCanvas* part in cell (10, 4) of the IMultiCellCanvas* part and set its margin width and height to 0. This setting enable the numeric spin button for the number of bathrooms to line up with the set canvas boundaries.

Table 20. (Part 4 of 5) Building APropertySearchParameterView

Step	Action
17	Add an INumericSpinButton* part to the ISetCanvas* part to hold the number of bathrooms, ⬛, and configure them as follows: **Field** — **Value** Name — NumericSpinButtonBathrooms Alignment — Center Limit — 1 Lower — 1 Upper — 4 Value — 1 Enabled — unselect Unselect the **Enabled** check box of the numeric spin button from its Settings notebook Control page. In "APropertySearchParameterView" on page 283, you will draw connections to enable this control only when the corresponding CheckBoxBathrooms check box is selected.
18	Add an ISetCanvas* part to the IMultiCellCanvas* part and make it span from cell (12, 2) to cell (12, 5) as shown in Figure 71 on page 189, ⬛.
19	Add three IPushButton* parts to the ISetCanvas* part and set their names as follows: ❏ PushButtonSearch ❏ PushButtonCancel ❏ PushButtonHelp
20	Change the *text* attribute of the three push buttons as follows: ❏ ~Search for PushButtonSearch ❏ ~Cancel for PushButtonCancel ❏ ~Help for PushButtonHelp Notice the use of ~ for the key accelerator.
21	Open the settings notebook of PushButtonHelp and switch to the Styles page. Set the *help* radio button to **On** to turn this regular push button into a help push button. Set the *noPointerFocus* radio button to **On** to prevent the help push button from getting the input focus when the user clicks on it. Close the settings notebook.
22	Add an IInfoArea* part to the IFrameWindow*, ⬛.

Table 20. (Part 5 of 5) Building APropertySearchParameterView

Step	Action
23	Select the IMultiCellCanvas* part and open the Tabbing and Depth Order dialog box. Define six tabbing groups as follows (see "Tabbing from One Part to Another" on page 152):

Group	Tab	Feature
X	X	CheckBoxArea
	X	CollectionViewArea
X	X	CheckBoxSize
	X	EntryFieldMinSize
	X	EntryFieldMaxSize
X	X	CheckBoxPrice
	X	EntryFieldMinPrice
	X	EntryFieldMaxPrice
X	X	CheckBoxBedrooms
	X	NumericSpinButtonBedrooms
X	X	CheckBoxBathrooms
	X	NumericSpinButtonBathrooms
X	X	PushButtonSearch
	X	PushButtonCancel
	X	PushButtonHelp

Note: Reverse highlighted letters are keyed to Figure 71 on page 189.

Now you can save APropertySearchParameterView. First, switch to the Class Editor and fill in the *Code generation file* group box as follows:

❑ C++ header file (.hpp): **vrpsrcv.hpp**
❑ C++ code file (.cpp): **vrpsrcv.cpp**

Then, save the part.

AUpLoadView

AUpLoadView (Figure 74) is a dialog window that enables the user to generate DB2/2 import files. These import files can be sent to the real estate server and then uploaded to update its database.

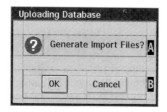

Figure 74. AUpLoadView

To build AUpLoadView, follow the step-by-step instructions in
Table 21.

Step	Action
	Table 21. (Part 1 of 3) Building AUpLoadView
1	Start Visual Builder from the Services project (select *Project* → *Visual* in the menu bar).
2	From the Visual Builder window, select *Part* → *New...* option.
3	Fill in the entry fields as follows: **Field** / **Value** Class name / AUploadView Description / General view to generate DB2/2 import files File name / VRSERV Part type / visual part Base class / IFrameWindow Click on the **Open** push button. An IFrameWindow* part is displayed on the free-form surface.
4	Open the settings notebook of the frame window and change the style attributes as follows: **Attribute** / **Setting** dialogBorder / On maximizeButton / Off minimizeButton / Off sizingBorder / Off systemMenu / Off Close the settings notebook. The window becomes a nonresizable dialog box.
5	Change the IFrameWindow* part title to **Uploading Database**.
6	Delete the ICanvas* part in the IFrameWindow* part.
7	Add an IMultiCellCanvas* part to the IFrameWindow* part.

Step	Action

Table 21. (Part 2 of 3) Building AUpLoadView

Step	Action
8	Open the settings notebook of the IMultiCellCanvas* part and configure it as follows: ❑ Number of rows: 5 ❑ Number of columns: 3 ❑ Expandable rows: 1, 3 ❑ Expandable columns: 1, 3 Close the settings notebook.
9	Switch to the Color page and select the **Colors** radio button of the *Color selection* group box. Then select **paleGray** in the *Color values* drop-down list box. Close the settings notebook.
10	Add an ISetCanvas* part, **A**, to cell (2, 2) of the IMultiCellCanvas* part. This set canvas will hold an icon and a static text control.
11	Add an IIconControl* part to the ISetCanvas* part.
12	Open the settings notebook of the IIconControl* part. Set the DLL name to **abticons** and the resource ID to **531**.
13	Add an IStaticText* part to the ISetCanvas* part and change its labels to **Generate Import Files**.
14	Open the settings notebook of the ISetCanvas* part, set its alignment to center (middle radio button), and adjust the width and eight of the *Margin* and *Pad* group boxes as follows: **Group box** **Width** **Height** Margin 0 0 Pad 10 0 Close the settings notebook.
15	Add an IMultiCellCanvas* part, **B**, to cell (4, 2) of the IMultiCellCanvas* part and configure it as follows: ❑ Number of rows: 3 ❑ Number of columns: 5 ❑ Expandable rows: none ❑ Expandable columns: 1, 3, 5
16	Add two IPushButton* parts to cells (2, 2) and (2, 4) of the IMultiCellCanvas* part **B** and change their labels as shown in Figure 67 on page 178.
17	Change the push button names to **PushButtonOK** and **PushButtonCancel**.
18	Promote the **buttonClickEvent** event of *PushbuttonOK*.

Table 21. (Part 3 of 3) Building AUpLoadView

Step	Action
19	Set **PushbuttonOK** as the default push button (set defaultButton to **On** in the Styles page of the settings notebook).
20	Select the IMultiCellCanvas* part, █, and open the Tabbing and Depth Order dialog box. Set the **Tab** check boxes as follows (see "Tabbing from One Part to Another" on page 152): **Group** **Tab** **Feature** X PushButtonOK X PushButtonCancel Close the dialog box.

Note: Reverse highlighted letters are keyed to Figure 74 on page 197.

Now you can save AUpLoadView. First, switch to the Class Editor and fill in the *Code generation file* group box as follows:

❑ C++ header file (.hpp): **vrsuplv.hpp**
❑ C++ code file (.cpp): **vrsuplv.cpp**

Then, save the part.

APropertyManagementView

APropertyManagementView (Figure 75) is the first window that the user sees when accessing the Property subsystem. It calls the other views you have built previously. By clicking on graphical push buttons, the user can select the following options:

❑ Create a property (APropertyCreateView)
❑ Search properties (APropertySearchParameterView)
❑ Upload property tables (AUpLoadView)

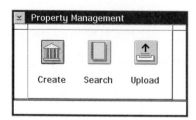

Figure 75. APropertyManagementView

APropertyManagementView derives from an IFrameWindow part. It is set to be nonresizable. Because each control is lined up along two rows and three columns, the set canvas appears to be the canvas to use to hold the different controls. In addition, the set canvas is a minimum size canvas and supports multiple screen resolutions and font settings. To ensure that the set canvas stays centered in the middle of the client area, use a small multicell canvas of three rows and three columns for the client area of the frame window. Set the multicell canvas top row, bottom row, left column, and right column to be expandable and place the set canvas in the middle of the multicell canvas: cell (2, 2).

Using Graphic Push Buttons

An IGraphicPushButton part is a selection button for an action or routing choice. The choice is represented by a graphical image on the push button. The user can click on the push button to perform an action. Usually, you can use an IGraphicPushButton part whenever an action can be represented graphically.

To associate a graphical image with the push button, enter the *DLL name* in the *DLL name* field and the resource ID in the *Resource id* field of the IGraphicPushButton General settings page (Figure 76).

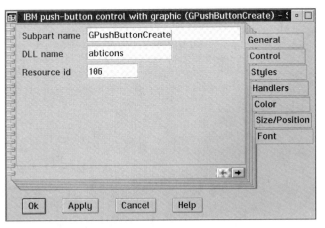

Figure 76. IGraphicPushButton General Settings Page

To build APropertyManagementView, follow the step-by-step instructions in Table 22.

Step	Action
	Table 22. (Part 1 of 2) Building APropertyManagementView
Step	**Action**
1	Start Visual Builder from the Property project (select *Project* → *Visual* in the menu bar).
2	From the Visual Builder window, select *Part* → *New...* option.
3	Fill in the entry fields as follows:

Table 22. (Part 1 of 2) Building APropertyManagementView

Step	Action
1	Start Visual Builder from the Property project (select *Project* → *Visual* in the menu bar).
2	From the Visual Builder window, select *Part* → *New...* option.
3	Fill in the entry fields as follows: **Field** — **Value** Class name — APropertyManagementView Description — Main Window for the property subsystem File name — VRPROP Part type — visual part Base class — IFrameWindow Click on the **Open** push button. An IFrameWindow* part is displayed on the free-form surface.
4	Open the settings notebook of the frame window and change the style attributes as follows: **Attribute** — **Setting** dialogBorder — On maximizeButton — Off minimizeButton — Off sizingBorder — Off Close the settings notebook. The window becomes a nonresizable dialog box. Notice that we keep the system menu to enable the user to close the window.
5	Delete the ICanvas* part in the IFrameWindow* part.
6	Add an IMultiCellCanvas* part to the IFrameWindow* part and configure it as follows: ❑ Number of rows: 3 ❑ Number of columns: 3 ❑ Expandable rows: 1, 3 ❑ Expandable columns: 1, 3
7	Change the IFrameWindow* part title to **Property Management**.

Table 22. (Part 2 of 2) Building APropertyManagementView

Step	Action
8	Add an ISetCanvas* part to cell (2, 2) of the IMultiCellCanvas* part and configure it as follows: **Field** — **Value** Deck Orientation — Horizontal Pack Type — Even Deck Count — 2 Margin Width — 20 Margin Height — 20 Pad Width — 30 Pad Height — 20 Alignment — Centered Use the **Apply** push button of the settings notebook to adjust margins and pads before closing the notebook to undergo the changes.
9	Add three IGraphicPushButton* parts to the client area and change their settings as follows (the IGraphicPushButton* part is located in the *Buttons* category): **Button** — **SubPart** — **DLL** — **Resource Id** Create — GPushButtonCreate — abticons — 106 Search — GPushButtonSearch — abticons — 306 Upload — GPushButtonUpload — abticons — 51
10	Add three IStaticText* parts and change their *text* attributes to **Create**, **Search**, and **Upload**.
	Note: Because the number of decks in the set canvas defines an implicit order, you must add the three graphic push buttons first, then the three static text controls.
11	Add an IInfoArea* part to the IFrameWindow* part.

Now you can save APropertyManagementView. First, switch to the Class Editor and fill in the *Code generation file* group box as follows:

❏ C++ header file (.hpp): **vrpmngv.hpp**
❏ C++ code file (.cpp): **vrpmngv.cpp**

Then, save the part.

ALogonView

ALogonView (Figure 77) is a general logon view that can be used to authenticate a user. When users start the application, they must first connect to the database to access the different subsystems. ALogonView prompts users for their user ID and password. This information is passed to an IDatastore part to establish the connection (see Chapter 6, "Mapping Relational Tables Using Data Access Builder," on page 127).

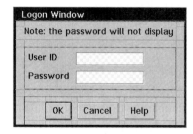

Figure 77. ALogonView

Notice that this view is simple. The only peculiarity is an event handler, which you attach to each entry field to force the user input to be in uppercase. We explain how to construct your own event handler in "Event Handler" on page 220.

To build ALogonView, follow the step-by-step instructions in Table 23.

Table 23. (Part 1 of 3) Building ALogonView	
Step	**Action**
1	Start Visual Builder from the Common project (select *Project* → *Visual* in the menu bar).
2	From the Visual Builder window, select *Part* → *New...* option.
3	Fill in the entry fields as follows: **Field**　　　　**Value** Class name　　ALogonView Description　　General purpose view to log on File name　　　VRCOMM Part type　　　visual part Base class　　　IFrameWindow Click on the **Open** push button. An IFrameWindow* part is displayed on the free-form surface.

Table 23. (Part 2 of 3) Building ALogonView

Step	Action
4	Open the settings notebook of the frame window and change the style attributes as follows: **Attribute** — **Setting** dialogBorder — On maximizeButton — Off minimizeButton — Off sizingBorder — Off systemMenu — Off Close the settings notebook. The window becomes a nonresizable dialog box.
5	Change the IFrameWindow* part title to **Logon Window**.
6	Delete the ICanvas* part in the IFrameWindow* part.
7	Add an IMultiCellCanvas* part to the IFrameWindow* part and configure it as follows: ❑ Number of rows: 6 ❑ Number of columns: 3 ❑ Expandable rows: 3, 5 ❑ Expandable columns: 1, 3
8	Add an IStaticText* part to cell (2, 2) of the IMultiCellCanvas* and change its label to **Note: the password will not display**.
9	Add an ISetCanvas* part in cell (4, 2) of the IMultiCellCanvas* part and change the setting of its attributes as follows: **Attribute** — **Setting** Deck Orientation — Vertical Pack Type — Even Deck Count — 2
10	Add two IStaticText* parts to the ISetCanvas* part and change their labels to **User ID** and **Password**.
11	Add two IEntryField* parts and change their names to **EntryFieldUserID** and **EntryFieldPassword** and their limit to **10**. Reset their size to the default size, using the **Reset to default size** action from their pop-up menu.
12	Promote each *text* attribute of each IEntryField* part. Because ALogonView will be reused in other parts, you must promote these features to have access to the logon information.

Table 23. (Part 3 of 3) Building ALogonView

Step	Action
13	Add an IMultiCellCanvas* part to cell (6, 2) of the first IMultiCell-Canvas* part and configure it as follows: ❑ Number of rows: 3 ❑ Number of columns: 3 ❑ Expandable rows: none ❑ Expandable columns: 1, 3
14	Add three IPushButton* parts and the new IMultiCellCanvas* part in cells (2, 2), (2, 4), and (2, 6) and change their *text* labels, respectively, to **OK**, **Cancel**, and **Help** (Figure 77 on page 203).
15	Change the name of the IPushButton* parts to **PushButtonOK**, **PushButtonCancel**, and **PushButtonHelp**.
16	Open the settings notebook of EntryFieldUserID and, on the Handlers page, add an UpperCaseKbdHandler to the handler list box. Close the settings notebook.
17	Open the settings notebook of EntryFieldPassword and, on the Handlers page, add UpperCaseKbdHandler. Then switch to the Styles page and set the *unreadable* style to **On**. Close the settings notebook.
18	Open the settings notebook of PushButtonHelp and switch to the Styles page. Set the *help* radio button to **On**. Set the *noPointerFocus* radio button to **On**. Close the settings notebook.
19	Set **PushButtonOK** as the default push button (set defaultButton to **On** in the Styles page of the settings notebook).
20	Select the IFrameWindow* part and open the Tabbing and Depth Order dialog box. Set the tabbing groups as follows: | Group	Tab	Feature | |---|---|---| | X | X | EntryFieldUserID | | | X | EntryFieldPassword | | X | X | PushButtonOK | | | X | PushButtonCancel | | | X | PushButtonHelp | Close the dialog box.

Now you can save ALogonView. First, switch to the Class Editor and fill in the *Code generation file* group box as follows:

❑ C++ header file (.hpp): **vrclogv.hpp**
❑ C++ code file (.cpp): **vrclogv.cpp**

Then, save the part.

ARealSettingsView

ARealSettingsView (Figure 78) enables the user to update the Visual Realty application's settings. The settings consist of the directory information where files are uploaded or downloaded from the server:

Movie path   The path where the video files are placed when they are downloaded from the server

Upload path   The path where the export files are produced to be uploaded to the server

Download path The path where the import files are placed when they are downloaded from the server

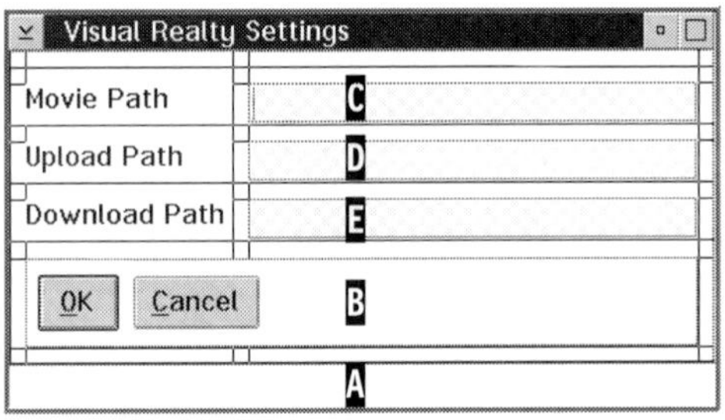

Figure 78. ARealSettingsView

An IProfile part, which stores the directories information, works in tandem with ARealSettingsView. The use of IProfile part is described in "ARealSettingsView" on page 305.

ARealSettingsView is not reused in other parts of the application, so you do not have to promote its features.

To build ARealSettingsView, follow the step-by-step instructions in Table 24.

Step	Action
Table 24. (Part 1 of 3) Building ARealSettingsView	
1	Start Visual Builder from the Common project (select *Project* → *Visual* in the menu bar).
2	From the Visual Builder window, select *Part* → *New...* option.

Table 24. (Part 2 of 3) Building ARealSettingsView

Step	Action
3	Fill in the entry fields as follows: **Field** **Value** Class name ARealSettingsView Description Application settings view File name VRCOMM Part type visual part Base class IFrameWindow Click on the **Open** push button. An IFrameWindow* part is displayed on the free-form surface.
4	Change the IFrameWindow* part title to **Visual Realty Settings**.
5	Delete the ICanvas* part in the IFrameWindow* part.
6	Add an IMultiCellCanvas* part in the IFrameWindow* part.
7	Open the settings notebook of the IMultiCellCanvas* part and configure it as follows: ❏ Number of columns: 5 ❏ Number of rows: 10 ❏ Expandable columns: 4 ❏ Expandable rows: 8 Close the settings notebook.
8	Add an IInfoArea* part to the IFrameWindow* part, **A**.
9	Add an ISetCanvas* part to the IMultiCellCanvas* part as shown on Figure 78 on page 206, **B**.
10	Add two IPushButton* parts to the ISetCanvas* part and set their names as follows: ❏ PushButtonOK ❏ PushButtonCancel
11	Change their labels as follows: ❏ ~OK for PushButtonOK ❏ ~Cancel for PushButtonCancel Notice the use of ~ for the key accelerator.
12	Add three IEntryField* parts and change their names to **EntryFieldMovie**, **EntryFieldUpload**, and **EntryFieldDownload**, **C**, **D**, **E**. Set their limit to 50 characters.

Table 24. (Part 3 of 3) Building ARealSettingsView

Step	Action
13	Set **PushbuttonOK** as the default push button (set defaultButton to **On** in the Styles page of the settings notebook).
14	Select the IFrameWindow* part and open the Tabbing and Depth Order dialog box. Set the tabbing groups as follows:

Group	Tab	Feature
X	X	EntryFieldMovie
	X	EntryFieldUpload
	X	EntryFieldDownload
X	X	PushButtonOK
	X	PushButtonCancel

Close the dialog box.

Note: Reverse highlighted letters are keyed to Figure 78 on page 206.

Now you can save ARealSettingsView. First, switch to the Class Interface Editor and fill in the *Code generation file* group box as follows:

- ❑ C++ header file (.hpp): **vrcsetv.hpp**
- ❑ C++ code file (.cpp): **vrcsetv.cpp**

Then, save the part.

ARealMainView

ARealMainView (Figure 79) is the application main view. From this view, the user can log on to the database and access each subsystem.

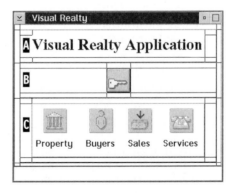

Figure 79. ARealMainView

ARealMainView derives from an IFrameWindow part. It is built from the parts that you already know: IMultiCellCanvas, ISetCanvas, IGraphicPushButton, and IStaticText. The user can resize the window; the IMultiCellCanvas is used intensively to enable the controls to distribute evenly.

To build ARealMainView, follow the step-by-step instructions in Table 25.

Table 25. (Part 1 of 3) Building ARealMainView

Step	Action
1	Start Visual Builder from the Visual Realty project (select *Project* → *Visual* in the menu bar).
2	Create a visual part by using the following settings: **Field** / **Value** Class name — ARealMainView Description — Application main view File name — VRMAIN Part type — visual part Base class — IFrameWindow
3	Change the title of the IFrameWindow* part to Visual Realty.
4	Add an IInfoArea* part to the IFrameWindow* part.
5	Delete the ICanvas* part in the IFrameWindow* part.
6	Add an IMultiCellCanvas* part in the IFrameWindow* part and configure it as follows: ❑ Number of columns: 3 ❑ Number of rows: 5 ❑ Expandable columns: all ❑ Expandable rows: all
7	Add three IMultiCellCanvas* parts in the IMultiCellCanvas* part already in place. The first multicell canvas contains the application title; the second, one graphic push button; and the third, a set canvas with the graphic push buttons and their associated static text controls.

Table 25. (Part 2 of 3) Building ARealMainView

Step	Action
8	Configure each IMultiCellCanvas* part as follows: ❑ IMultiCellCanvas* part **A** — Number of rows: 3 — Number of columns: 3 — Expandable rows: 1, 3 — Expandable columns: 1, 3 ❑ IMultiCellCanvas* part **B** — Number of rows: 3 — Number of columns: 3 — Expandable rows: 1, 3 — Expandable columns: 1, 3 ❑ IMultiCellCanvas* part **C** — Number of rows: 3 — Number of columns: 3 — Expandable rows: 1, 3 — Expandable columns: 1, 3
9	Add an IStaticText* part to cell (2, 2) of the IMultiCellCanvas* part, **A**, and change its *text* attribute to **Visual Realty Application**. This IStaticText* part constitutes the main title.
10	Change the font of the main title to suit your needs. (In Figure 79 on page 208, the font is set to Times New Roman Bold, size 18. The resolution is SVGA.)
11	Add an ISetCanvas* part to cell (2, 2) of the IMultiCellCanvas* part, **C**, and change the setting of its attributes as follows: **Attribute** — **Setting** Pack Type — Even Deck Count — 2 Pad Width — 20 Alignment — Center
12	Add five IGraphicPushButton* parts: one to cell (2, 2) of the IMultiCellCanvas* part, **B**, and four to the ISetCanvas* part.

Table 25. (Part 3 of 3) Building ARealMainView

Step	Action
13	Change the IGraphicPushButton* parts settings as follows: | Button	Subpart	DLL	Res. id	Enabled
--------	---------	-----	---------	---------
Logon	GPushButtonLogon	abticons	153	deselect
Properties	GPushButtonProperty	abticons	106	deselect
Buyers	GPushButtonBuyer	abticons	543	deselect
Sales	GPushButtonSale	abticons	107	deselect
Services	GPushButtonService	abticons	49	deselect	 The last four graphic push buttons must be set to disable by deselecting the **Enabled** check box on the Control page of their settings notebook. This prevents the user from accessing a subsystem as long as there is no database connection established (see "Logging on to the Database" on page 310). When a database connection is established, these graphic push buttons are set enable.
14	Add four IStaticText* parts to the ISetCanvas* part and change their label attributes as shown in Figure 79 on page 208.
15	Set the graphic push button logon as the default push button.
16	Select the IFrameWindow* part and open the Tabbing and Depth Order dialog box. Set the tabbing groups as follows: 	Group	Tab	Feature
-------	-----	---------
X	X	GPushButtonLogon
X	X	GPushButtonProperty
	X	GPushButtonBuyer
	X	GPushButtonSale
	X	GPushButtonService	 Close the dialog box.

Note: Reverse highlighted letters are keyed to Figure 79 on page 208.

Now you can save ARealMainView. Switch to the Class Editor and fill in the *Code generation file* group box as follows:

❑ C++ header file (.hpp): **vrmain.hpp**
❑ C++ code file (.cpp): **vrmain.cpp**

Then, save the part.

 Congratulations! You have finished building your visual parts. In Chapter 8, "Creating Nonvisual Parts," on page 213 you will learn how to build nonvisual parts. Remember that visual programming does not imply no programming at all!

8

Creating
Nonvisual Parts

Nonvisual parts represent application objects that the user cannot see at run time. These objects can be divided into two main categories: business objects and technical objects.

Business objects support the business object model of the application. For example, Property is a business class whose instances are business objects. You can access the views that display some of their features (APropertyView displays the attribute values of Property).

Technical objects support the middleware layer of the application. They can be, for example, transaction management objects, security management objects, or database access objects. For the sample application, all Data Access Builder objects can be considered as technical objects. They provide the application with database access. Sometimes, technical objects can be used for more basic tasks, such as validating user input or handling the appearance of an object according to its contents. Event handlers are an example of such technical objects.

Basically you can handle two kinds of nonvisual parts with Visual Builder: the full, enabled nonvisual part and the class interface part. The full, enabled nonvisual part is always subclassed from the IStandardNotifier class, which provides a concrete implementation of the notifier protocol in the notification framework (see Chapter 10, "If You Want to Know More about Visual Builder...," on page 323). This part can notify other parts, and connections can be drawn from and to it.

The class interface part can inherit from any class but does not support the notification protocol. This nonvisual part cannot notify other parts. Creating a class interface part rather than a nonvisual part is especially useful when you do not want to alter the legacy source code of your own C++ classes that you want to use with Visual Builder. (see Chapter 10, "If You Want to Know More about Visual Builder...," on page 323 for more information about using your legacy code with Visual Builder). However, creating a class interface part has two restrictions: Because you do not integrate any code to enable the notification framework, you cannot use a class interface part as a source for a connection. Also, if a class interface part is the target for an attribute-to-attribute connection, the connection is unidirectional (only the target side is updated). For a complete overview of the notification framework and more information about how to implement a nonvisual part, refer to Chapter 10, "If You Want to Know More about Visual Builder...," on page 323.

In the sections that follow, we describe how to build both full, enabled nonvisual parts and class interface parts. First you will implement the AMarketingInfo nonvisual part, which belongs to the business object category. It holds business rules that apply to the properties in the context of our application. Then you will build a class interface part, the UpperCaseKbdHandler event handler.

AMarketingInfo

The AMarketingInfo part (see the design object model in Figure 41 on page 102) contains some attributes that are not stored in the database; *PricePerSqft* (price per square foot) is one of them. It is calculated from the *Price* and *Size* attributes of the Data Access Builder part, Marketing_info, by using the following formula: PricePerSqft = Price/Size. These attributes are called *derived* attributes because their value can be derived from the values of other attributes.

You can calculate the value of such attributes in two ways:

❑ Extend the AMarketingInfo nonvisual part by subclassing it. In effect, the source code that Data Access Builder generates is not intended to be edited directly. You would lose all of your changes if you regenerated the code from the same class.

❑ Build a separate nonvisual part to hold the derived attributes and calculate their value from the AMarketingInfo part.

With the second way of calculating derived attributes, you do not have to associate the business rules with any implementation choice; that is, you do not have to store the information in a relational database such as DATABASE 2 OS/2. This is the calculation we chose. Building a nonvisual part constitutes an alternative to the custom logic connection that we describe later (see "Using Custom Logic" on page 249).

The AMarketingInfo part consists of seven attributes and their associated get and set methods:

❑ *price*, the property price from the Data Access Builder part

❑ *commissionRate*, the commission rate from the Data Access Builder part (percentage of the total sale)

❑ *downPaymentRate*, the deposit rate the buyer has to pay to hold the property (percentage of the total price)

❑ *size*, the property size from the Data Access Builder part

❑ *commission*, the amount of commission the agent earns in selling the property

❑ *pricePerSqft*, the property price per square foot

❑ *downPayment*, the deposit the buyer has to pay to hold the property

The first three attributes are updated according to the value of the last four attributes. In addition, each time one of these attributes is updated, all of the others are updated accordingly.

To create the AMarketingInfo nonvisual part, assuming Visual Builder has been started from the Property project folder:

1. Select the ***New*** option from the *Part* pull-down menu.

2. Fill in the *Class Name*, *Description*, and *File name* fields, as shown in Figure 80.

3. Select ***Nonvisual part*** in the *Part type* field.

4. Click on the **Open** push button; the Part Interface Editor is loaded for editing the part.

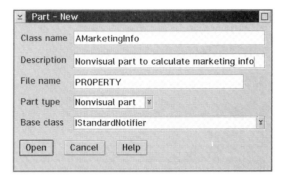

Figure 80. Creating AMarketingInfo Nonvisual Part

To add *pricePerSqft* as a new attribute for the nonvisual part:

1. Enter the attribute name in the corresponding field.

2. Select **double** as the return type of the pricePerSqft get method.

3. Click on the **Defaults** push button. The different fields are filled in with the default member function prototypes for this attribute. Because the value of this attribute is updated by the set member function of the price attribute, you can erase the set member function of pricePerSqft.

4. Fill in the *Description* field with a meaningful comment.

5. Click on the **Add** push button.

You have now added the *pricePerSqft* attribute to the part. You can repeat the process for the *commission* and *downPayment* attributes. Refer to Table 26 for more information.

Because the other attributes have a set member function, you can add them by using the default member function prototypes. Therefore, you can directly click on the **Add with defaults** push button.

Table 26. (Part 1 of 2) Table Attributes				
Name	**Type**	**Get Function**	**Set Function**	**Event ID**
price	double	virtual double price() const	virtual AMarketing-Info& setPrice(double aPrice)	priceId

Table 26. (Part 2 of 2) Table Attributes

Name	Type	Get Function	Set Function	Event ID
commission-Rate	double	virtual double commissionRate() const	virtual AMarketing-Info& setCommission-Rate(double aCommissionRate)	commission-RateId
downPayment-Rate	double	virtual double down-PaymentRate() const	virtual AMarketing-Info& setDown-PaymentRate(double aDownPaymentRate)	downPayment-RateId
size	double	virtual double size() const	virtual AMarketing-Info& setSize(double aSize)	sizeId
pricePerSqft	double	virtual double pricePer-Sqft() const		pricePerSqftId
commission	double	virtual double commis-sion() const		commissionId
downPayment	double	virtual double down-Payment() const		down-PaymentId

Once you have registered all attributes and their associated methods, switch to the Class Editor and fill in the user file fields:

❑ User .hpv file: **vrpmrkt.hpv**
❑ User .cpv file: **vrpmrkt.cpv**

You are ready to generate the code:

1. Select *Save and Generate → Part source* to generate the part source code.

2. Select *Save and Generate → Feature source....* to generate the code for every get and set method registered.

Several files are generated:

- ❏ vrpmrkt.h, constant declaration for the class
- ❏ vrpmrkt.hpp, class declaration (this file includes vrpmrkt.hpv)
- ❏ vrpmrkt.cpp, class definition (this file includes vrpmrkt.cpv)
- ❏ vrpmrkt.hpv, attributes and member functions declaration
- ❏ vrpmrkt.cpv, member functions definition
- ❏ vrpmrkt.rci, resource file

To refine the part and update the pricePerSqft, commission, and downPayment attributes according to the value of the other attributes, you must edit the vrpmrkt.cpv file. Use the LPEX editor, provided with VisualAge for C++, or your favorite editor to update the file, as shown in Figure 81.

```
// Feature source code generation begins here...
//......................
AMarketingInfo& AMarketingInfo::setPrice(double aPrice)
{
  if (!(iPrice == aPrice))
  {
    iPrice = aPrice;
    if( iSize != 0 ) {
      iPricePerSqft = IString(iPrice / iSize);
      iCommission = IString( iCommissionRate *. iPrice / 100);
      iDownPayment = IString( iDownPaymentRate * iPrice / 100);
    }
    else
      iPricePerSqft = "Size is not informed.";
    notifyObservers(INotificationEvent(AMarketingInfo::priceId, *this));
    notifyObservers(INotificationEvent(AMarketingInfo::pricePerSqftId,
*this));
    notifyObservers(INotificationEvent(AMarketingInfo::commissionId,
*this));
    notifyObservers(INotificationEvent(AMarketingInfo::downPaymentId,
*this));
  } // endif
  return *this;
}

//.............
AMarketingInfo& AMarketingInfo::setCommissionRate(double aCommissionRate)
{
  if (!(iCommissionRate == aCommissionRate))
  {
    iCommissionRate = aCommissionRate;
    if( iPrice != 0 )
      iCommission = IString( iCommissionRate * iPrice / 100);
    else
      iCommission = "Price is not informed.";
    notifyObservers(INotificationEvent(AMarketingInfo::commissionRateId,
*this));
    notifyObservers(INotificationEvent(AMarketingInfo::commissionId,
*this));
  } // endif
  return *this;
}

//.................
AMarketingInfo& AMarketingInfo::setDownPaymentRate(double aDownPaymentRate)
{
  if (!(iDownPaymentRate == aDownPaymentRate))
  {
    iDownPaymentRate = aDownPaymentRate;
    if( iPrice != 0 )
      iDownPayment = IString( iDownPaymentRate * iPrice / 100);
```

Figure 81. (Part 1 of 2) MarketingInfo Source Code Detail

```
     else
        iDownPayment = "Price is not informed";
     notifyObservers(INotificationEvent(AMarketingInfo::downPaymentRateId,
*this));
   } // endif
   return *this;
}

//..............
AMarketingInfo& AMarketingInfo::setSize(double aSize)
{
   if (!(iSize == aSize))
   {
      iSize = aSize;
      if( iPrice != 0 )
         iPricePerSqft = IString(iPrice / iSize);
      else
         iPricePerSqft = "Price is not informed.";
      notifyObservers(INotificationEvent(AMarketingInfo::sizeId, *this));
      notifyObservers(INotificationEvent(AMarketingInfo::pricePerSqftId,
*this));
   } // endif
   return *this;
}

// Feature source code generation ends here.
```

Figure 81. (Part 2 of 2) MarketingInfo Source Code Detail

Only the set member function for the *price, size, downPaymentRate,* and *commissionRate* attributes are updated to calculate the other attributes that depend on them. In "Connecting a Nonvisual Part to a Visual Part" on page 233, the MarketingInfo part is connected, by attribute-to-attribute connections, to the Marketing page of APropertyView. The contents of each entry field on this page are updated according to the value of the associated attribute. To keep the contents of the entry fields up to date, a notification must be sent to the attribute-to-attribute connections each time the value of an attribute changes. Considering a connection as an *observer,* the notification is triggered by the notifyObservers() method, which you must call in the get method of each attribute (see Chapter 10, "If You Want to Know More about Visual Builder...," on page 323). The notifications enable a global change on the Marketing page of APropertyView when necessary.

Event Handler

The parts you can create with Visual Builder provide standard behaviors that should meet most of your needs. At times, however, you may want to use an event handler to modify or extend the default behavior.

Below, we describe how to build a simple event handler to convert to uppercase letters the input that the user types in ALogonView to uppercase letters (see "ALogonView" on page 202) and "wrap" it as a class interface part to reuse it with Visual Builder. For more information about building event handlers, refer to the *Open Class Library User's Guide*.

Handlers are registered with parts and set up in the Handlers pages of the settings notebook. You can attach several handlers to the same part. They will be executed in the reverse order in which they are attached to the part.

The management of events and event handlers is based on the IBM Open Class Library architecture. Basically, the architecture uses events and handlers to encapsulate the message architecture of OS/2 PM in an object-oriented way. PM messages are sent as event objects to the window or control that received the event. The window then invokes the handler attached to it, passing the event object as a parameter. The handlers are called sequentially, with the most recently added handler called first. When an event handler completes the event processing, it returns a Boolean value of TRUE. If none of the handlers can process the event, it is passed up to the owner chain.

The distinction between window classes and handler classes lets you separate the event handling logic from the rest of the application. Thus, you can reuse the logic in several applications. For example, you can build an event handler that verifies the social security number format whenever an entry field accepts the social security number. You define this handler only once. Each time you want to use an entry field to enter the social security number information, you can attach the event handler to the entry field.

You can use the IHandler part to control the event handler action on a specific part.

You build an event handler in two steps:

1. Write the code of your event handler class.

   - Derive your event handler class from one of the predefined event handler classes. If none of them is suitable for your needs, you still can derive your handler from the IHandler part.

   - Each handler class has one or more virtual functions that are called to process the events. You provide your own function to override these virtual functions and tailor its logic to your needs.

   - Compile the new event handler class and create a library that you will link later on when building the application.

2. Convert your event handler class to a class interface part that you can use with Visual Builder.

Writing the Code for Your Event Handler Class

To write the code for your UpperCaseKbdHandler class, you first have to choose the handler class from which to derive your own event handler. Because the event handler is to be used when entering information from the keyboard, it seems natural to choose IKeyboardHandler as the class from which to derive your own event handler. Of course, you also could choose an event handler associated with the editing process, such as IEditHandler, but you would not be able to reuse it with other types of controls, such as a list box. In our example, you derive UpperCaseKbdHandler from IKeyboardHandler (Figure 82), and you overload the virtual function, characterKeyPress, to meet your needs (Figure 83).

```
#ifndef _KBDHDR_
#define _KBDHDR_
//*************************************************************
// Reusable Handlers - Keyboard Handler
//
// Copyright (C) 1994, Law, Leong, Love, Olson, Tsuji.
//
// Adapted for use with VisualAge C++ by: Peter Jakab
//
// All Rights Reserved.
//*************************************************************
#include <ikeyhdr.hpp>
#include <istring.hpp>
#include <iwindow.hpp>

#ifndef __NO_DEFAULT_LIBS__
  #pragma library("kbdhdr.lib")
#endif

// Keyboard handler example to convert lowercase characters
// to uppercase as the user types.
class UpperCaseKbdHandler : public IKeyboardHandler
{
protected:
   virtual Boolean characterKeyPress ( IKeyboardEvent& event );
};
#endif                                    /* _KBDHDR_ */
```

Figure 82. UpperCaseKBDHandler Header File

You overload the characterKeyPress function to ensure that every character typed from the keyboard is converted to an uppercase character.

```
#include "kbdhdr.hpp"

Boolean UpperCaseKbdHandler :: characterKeyPress ( IKeyboardEvent& event
{
  Boolean dontPassOn = false;
  IString strChar = event.mixedCharacter();

  if (strChar.isSBCS()  &&  strChar.isLowerCase())
  {                                            /* Single-byte 'a'-'z'.*/
    // Generate the uppercased character.
    IEventParameter2 param2( strChar.upperCase()[0],
                             event.parameter2().number2() );
               // Only change the character to uppercase.
    event.window()->sendEvent( IWindow::character,
                               event.parameter1(),
                               param2);
    event.setResult( true );                   /* Mark key as processed.*/
    dontPassOn = true;                  /* Don't pass on original event.*/
  }

  return dontPassOn;
}
```

Figure 83.   UpperCaseKBDHandler Definition

Creating a Class Interface Part from Your Event Handler Class

To create the UpperCaseKbdHandler class interface part, you must create the definition of that part in Visual Builder. Actually, creating a keyboard handler part in Visual Builder is very simple, because a keyboard handler does not have any features. Visual Builder must have the following information to use a keyboard handler:

❑ Name of the header file where the keyboard handler class is declared, namely, kbdhdr.hpp

❑ Macro defined in the header file to avoid multiple inclusions, namely, _KBDHDR_

❑ Name of the library where the definition of the keyboard handler definition is stored. The library name is used at link time. The simplest way of handling the library is to declare it in the source code with the #pragma library statement:

```
#ifndef __NO_DEFAULT_LIBS__
   #pragma library("kbdhdr.lib")
#endif
```

The linker uses this information to retrieve the name of the library it needs to build the application.

If you do not use the #pragma library statement, you can specify the name of the library in the linking options of the project where you are using the keyboard handler.

The simplest and fastest way of creating the UpperCaseKbdHandler class interface part is to write a Visual Builder export file (or VBE file) and import it in Visual Builder. A VBE file is a flat file that you use to describe a part and its interface. Use your favorite editor to create the KBDHDR.VBE file with the following contents:

```
//VBBeginPartInfo: UpperCaseKbdHandler
//VBParent: IKeyboardHandler
//VBIncludes: "kbdhdr.hpp" _KBDHDR_
//VBPartDataFile: KBDHDR.VBB
//VBComposerInfo: class,204,dde4vr30
//VBPreferredFeatures: this
//VBEndPartInfo: UpperCaseKbdHandler
```

To import the KBDHDR.VBE file in Visual Builder, start Visual Builder and select the *File→Import Part Information...* menu item. Enter the information as shown in Figure 84.

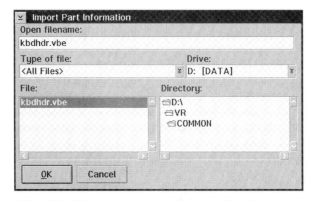

Figure 84. Visual Builder: Importing kbdhdr.vbe Part Information File

Visual Builder creates a VBB file (kbdhdr.vbb) from the information stored in the VBE file. You are now ready to use the UpperCase-KbdHandler event handler.

Using Your Keyboard Handler

Before using the event handler, you must import it as a nonvisual part in Visual Builder and open the settings of the part to which you want to attach the handler. Select the Handlers page and enter the name of the handler you want to attach to the part. If several handlers already have been attached to this part, you can choose the order in which you want your handler to be added to the handler list with the **Add before** or **Add after** push buttons (see Figure 60 on page 160). The handlers are activated according to the order in the list.

You can use the nonvisual part, IHandler, to control the activation and deactivation of the handler.

Visual Builder provides you with an IHandler part to process a specific event of a part. The IHandler part attributes and actions are:

❑ **Attribute**

➤ **enabled**: indicates whether or not the handler is enabled

❑ **Actions**

➤ **disable**: disables the handler so that it does not process window events

➤ **start**: attaches the handler to the IWindow object

➤ **stop**: detaches the handler from the IWindow object

As an example, suppose you want to attach an event handler to an entry field or detach an event handler from an entry field when clicking on a specific push button (Figure 85):

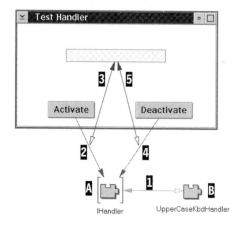

Figure 85. Simple Application with Handler

1. Add an IHandler variable part to the free-form surface, **A**.

2. Add the event handler part you built to the free-form surface, **B**.

3. Connect the *this* of the event handler to the *this* of the variable, **1**.

4. Connect the **buttonClickEvent** event of the *Activate* push button to the **start** action of the IHandler variable part, **2**, and pass the *this* of the entry field to the connection as a parameter, **3**. In this way, when the push button is clicked, the event handler is attached to the entry field.

5. Connect the **buttonClickEvent** event of the *Deactivate* push button to the **stop** action of the IHandler variable part, ▟, and pass the ***this*** of the entry field to the connection as a parameter, ▐. In this way, when the push button is clicked, the event handler is detached from the entry field.

So far, you have built all of the parts that you need to make up the Property subsystem; that is, the parts that constitute the static structure of the subsystem. Now, you need some "glue," so that the parts can communicate with each other; that is, you must build the dynamic structure of the subsystem by connecting the parts. That is what you do in Chapter 9, "Connecting the Parts," on page 227.

9

Connecting the Parts

Before you begin this chapter we suggest that you refer to "Using Visual Builder" on page 27 for a complete description of connections. From now on, we assume that you have enough knowledge to distinguish one connection from another.

To help you implement the connections between parts, we use the CRC cards, the static and the dynamic model refined at the design level (see Chapter 4, "Designers at Work," on page 83).

In this chapter, we show you how to connect the parts, and we explain the various connections. You refine each view in a bottom-up order according to the view hierarchy (Figure 53 on page 145). For each view we provide step-by-step guidelines to help you add the necessary subparts and build the connections to implement the part's logic. We strongly recommend that you name your subparts with the names that are shown in the figures in this chapter.

> **Attention**
>
> For every part to be refined, you must locate the corresponding Work-
> Frame/2 project and open the associated VBB file—by double-clicking with
> your left mouse button—to start Visual Builder.

APropertyView

Four groups of connections are built in APropertyView:

❑ A group that enables the user to select a video file (Figure 86 on page 229)

❑ A group that enables the user to play a video file (Figure 86 on page 229)

❑ A group that enables the user to edit within the multiple-line edit (MLE) control of the description page (Figure 87 on page 232)

❑ A group that updates the marketing page according to the business logic stored in the AMarketingInfo nonvisual part (Figure 88 on page 234)

We explain these connections below.

Selecting a Video File

In the Visual Realty application, the user selects a video file by clicking on the *Find...* push button (see Figure 86). Notice that, in "APropertyView" on page 156, the *FileName* entry field is set to read-only, so the user must click on *Find...* to select a file. This limiting condition prevents the user from mistyping the video file name, path name, or both.

Visual Builder provides the IVBFileDialog part for selecting files. It is a "wrapper" of the standard file dialog window available in PM.

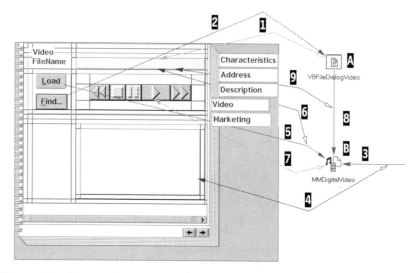

Figure 86. Connections for Selecting a Video File

Follow the step-by-step instructions in Table 27 to implement the selection of a video file.

Table 27. (Part 1 of 2) Implementing a Video File Selection

Step	Action
1	Open the APropertyView part.
2	Switch to the Video page.
3	Add an IVBFileDialog* part on the free-form surface, **A** (IVBFile-Dialog part is located in the *Other* category).
4	Open the settings notebook of IVBFileDialog and set the values as follows: **Field** **Value** Title Digital Video File name *.AVI These values tailor the file dialog box and allow filtering of the files for the selection.

Table 27. (Part 2 of 2) Implementing a Video File Selection

Step	Action
5	Connect the *filename* attribute of the IVBFileDialog* part to the *text* attribute of the *VideoFileName* entry field, **1**. This attribute-to-attribute connection guarantees that whenever the user selects a file, the content of the *VideoFileName* entry field is changed accordingly.
6	Connect the **buttonClickEvent** event of the *Find...* push button to the **ShowModally** action of the IVBFileDialog* part, **2**. Use the **ShowModally** action to force the user to select a file name before returning to the Video page of the notebook.

Note: Reverse highlighted numbers and letters are keyed to Figure 86 on page 229.

Adding Multimedia Features

To enable the user to play digital video files, use the IMMDigitalVideo part from the \IBMCPP\DDE4VB\VBMM.VBB file. Among other nifty features, this part enables users to load a video file (extension .AVI) on a different thread and play it in the window of their choice.

Follow the step-by-step instructions in Table 28 to add multimedia features to your part.

Table 28. (Part 1 of 2) Implementing Multimedia Features

Step	Action
1	Add an IMMDigitalVideo* part, on the free-form surface, **3**. (IMMDigitalVideo part is located in the VBMM.VBB file. Use the *Option → Add part...* from the Composition Editor pull-down menu to add it to the free-form surface.)
2	Connect the **ready** event of the APropertyView part to the **setWindow** action of the IMMDigitalVideo* part, **3**. This connection requires a parameter: the window where the video is played.
3	Connect (see **4**) the *handle* attribute of the **ICanvas*** part to the connection **3**. This connection enables the video to be played on the canvas. This connection is not necessary if you do not want to specify a window for the video. If you do not specify a window for the video, the video is played in a default window created by the part.

Table 28. (Part 2 of 2) Implementing Multimedia Features

Step	Action
4	Connect the **buttonClickEvent** event of the *Load* push button to the **loadOnThread** action of the IMMDigitalVideo* part, **5**. The connection requires a video file name as a parameter (notice that the connection is dashed).
5	Connect (see **6**) the ***text*** attribute of the *VideoFileName* entry field to the ***filename*** attribute of the connection **5**.
6	Connect the ***playableDevice*** attribute of the IMMPlayerPanel* part to the **this** attribute of the IMMDigitalVideo* part, **7**. This connection associates each behavior feature of IMMDigital-Video with the corresponding animated button of the IMMPlayer-Panel.
7	Connect the **pressedOKEvent** event of the IVBFileDialog* part to the **loadOnThread** action of the IMMDigitalVideo* part, **8**. This connection loads the video file name so that the video can be played.
8	Connect (see **9**) the ***text*** attribute of the *VideoFileName* entry field to the **filename** parameter of the connection **8**.

Note: Reverse highlighted numbers and letters are keyed to Figure 86 on page 229.

Tip!

If you have trouble accessing the controls located in the video group box, you can move the group box on the free-form surface, make your connections, and move the group box back to the video page. To move the group box back to the video page, follow these steps:

1. Resize it down on the free-form surface.
2. Drop it on one of the upper-left cells of the multicell canvas.
3. Resize it up with the mouse while holding the **ALT** key.

The **ALT** key lets you resize a control to make it span multiple cells of a multicell canvas.

You can also access the Tabbing and Depth Order dialog box of the canvas where the group box is located and move the group box above the controls it surrounds.

Adding a Pop-up Menu

To facilitate editing the description page, add a pop-up menu to the MLE control so that the user can use its copy, cut, paste, and undo functions (see Figure 87). For more information about how to build a menu, refer to the *Visual Builder User's Guide*.

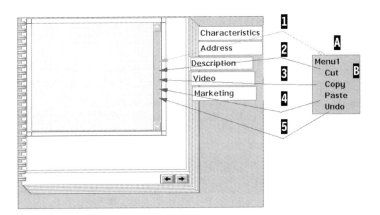

Figure 87. Building a Pop-up Menu for the Multiple-Line Edit Control

To implement these connections, follow the step-by-step instructions in Table 29.

Table 29. (Part 1 of 2) Building a Pop-up Menu	
Step	**Action**
1	Switch to the Description page.
2	Add an IMenu* part on the free-form surface, **A**. (The IMenu part is located in the *Frame extensions* category.)
3	Click on the **Sticky** check box at the bottom of the palette. When you select *Sticky*, the mouse remains loaded with the part you last selected. This makes it easy to drop several copies of the same part.
4	Add four IMenuItem* parts on the part, **A** (see **B** for the first menu item). Because the *Sticky* check box is selected, you do not have to reselect the IMenuItem* part from the parts palette.
5	Deselect the **Sticky** check box.
6	Add an IMenuSeparator* part between the third and fourth menu item.

Table 29. (Part 2 of 2) Building a Pop-up Menu

Step	Action
7	Change the label of each menu item to match those in Figure 87.
8	Connect the ***menu*** attribute of MultiLineEditDescription to the ***this*** attribute of the IMenu* part, **1**. The menu is associated with the MLE control.
9	Connect the **commandEvent** event of the *Cut* menu item to the **cut** action of MultiLineEditDescription, **2**.
10	Connect the **commandEvent** event of the *Copy* menu item to the **copy** action of MultiLineEditDescription, **3**.
11	Connect the **commandEvent** event of the *Paste* menu item to the **paste** action of MultiLineEditDescription, **4**.
12	Connect the **commandEvent** event of the *Undo* menu item to the **undo** action of MultiLineEditDescription, **5**. You can access the **undo** action from a dialog box, which is displayed when you select the *More...* option in the MultiLineEditDescription pop-up menu.

Note: Reverse highlighted numbers and letters are keyed to Figure 87 on page 232.

Connecting a Nonvisual Part to a Visual Part

To update the value of its different static text controls, the Marketing page must be able to access the services of the AMarketingInfo nonvisual part (refer to "AMarketingInfo" on page 214).

The entry fields of APropertyView provide AMarketingInfo with the values for the price, size, commission rate, and down payment rate. In return, the AMarketingInfo part provides APropertyView with the values for the price/sqft, commission, and down payment (Figure 88).

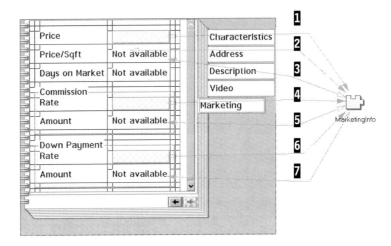

Figure 88. Connections between AMarketingInfo and Marketing Page

To implement these connections, follow the step-by-step instructions in Table 30.

Table 30. (Part 1 of 2) Using AMarketingInfo Part	
Step	**Action**
1	Switch to the Marketing page.
2	Add a AMarketingInfo* part on the free-form surface, **A** (use the *Option → Add part...* from the Composition Editor pull-down menu).
3	Connect the ***valueAsDouble*** attribute of EntryFieldPrice to the ***price*** attribute of AMarketingInfo*, **1**. Use the *valueAsDouble* attribute instead of the *text* attribute because the AMarketingInfo part expects a double value.
4	Connect the ***valueAsDouble*** attribute of EntryFieldSize to the ***size*** attribute of AMarketingInfo*, **2**. Note that the *size* attribute is located on the Characteristics page.
5	Connect the ***pricePerSqft*** attribute of AMarketingInfo* to the ***text*** attribute of staticTextPriceSqft, **3**.
6	Connect the ***valueAsDouble*** attribute of EntryFieldCommission-Rate to the ***commissionRate*** attribute of AMarketingInfo*, **4**.

Table 30. (Part 2 of 2) Using AMarketingInfo Part

Step	Action
7	Connect the **_commissionValue_** attribute of AMarketingInfo to the **_text_** attribute of staticTextCommissionValue, **5**.
8	Connect the **_valueAsDouble_** attribute of EntryFieldDown-PaymentRate to the **_downPaymentRate_** attribute of AMarketing-Info, **6**.
9	Connect the **_downPayment_** attribute of AMarketingInfo to the **_text_** attribute of staticTextDownPaymentValue, **7**.

Note: Reverse highlighted numbers and letters are keyed to Figure 88. The static text control, *StaticTextDaysOnMarket*, is not updated in this view. It will be connected in another view.

You can now save your part and generate its code. From the Visual Builder window, select *Save and generate → Part source* in the *File* pull-down menu.

Design Considerations

In most cases, it is worthwhile to encapsulate service parts in other parts. Such encapsulation enhances reusability while reducing complexity. In APropertyView, you embed the multimedia features, file dialog window, and AMarketingInfo part to hide the complexity of the view and make it a self-contained part that is easily reusable. It is possible to build separate parts for the different pages and embed the nonvisual parts in the pages. However, because the pages are simple and will not be reused, they are directly implemented at the notebook level (see "Using a Notebook Control" on page 157).

At this point, you may wonder why you do not embed the Data Access Builder nonvisual parts and the database services parts in APropertyView. The reason is simple: You reuse APropertyView for the property creation and property update. Moreover, the type of Data Access Builder part used in each case is quite different:

❑ In the property creation process, the data flows from the view, where the user enters the property information, to the Data Access Builder parts (APropertyCreateView—see Figure 90 on page 239 and Figure 91 on page 241). The Data Access Builder parts are embedded in APropertyCreateView to represent the new records that are added to the database.

❑ In the property update process, the data flows from the Data Access Builder part variables to the view where the user can update the property information (APropertyUpdateView—see

Figure 97 on page 252). The Data Access Builder part variables are embedded in APropertyUpdateView to represent the records that already exist in the database.

Both APropertyCreateView and APropertyUpdateView reuse APropertyView to collect the user information. However, you cannot embed Data Access Builder parts or Data Access Builder part variables in APropertyView because:

❑ In the first case, you could reuse APropertyView for APropertyCreateView but not for APropertyUpdateView.

❑ In the second case, you could reuse APropertyView for APropertyUpdateView but not for APropertyCreateView.

The above example reveals the kind of trade-off you must make if you want a part to be truly reusable.

APropertyCreateView

From the CRC card, we know that APropertyCreateView part is responsible for creating a new property. From the design object model of the Property subsystem, we know that to create a property we must create each of its components: PropertyLog, AMarketingInfo, Multidoc, and Address. Each component has a corresponding class generated by Data Access Builder, namely, Property_log, Marketing_info, Multidoc, and Prop_address (see Figure 89). These parts are the collaborators of APropertyCreateView.

The event-trace diagram for the creation of a property provides the information for connecting the different parts involved in the creation process. A first group of connections initializes each component (Address, Marketing_info, Property_log, Multidoc, and Property itself) as the user enters the property information from the view. These connections are attribute-to-attribute connections from the promoted attributes of APropertyView to the corresponding attributes in the Data Access Builder parts.

The second group of connections is triggered as soon as the user clicks on the *Create* push button and adds the contents of each Data Access Builder part to its respective table. These connections are event-to-action connections from the *Create* push button of APropertyCreateView to each Data Access Builder part.

In the sections that follow, you build the part in three steps:

1. You add the parts required to implement the part logic.
2. You build the attribute-to-attribute connections.
3. You build the event-to-action connections.

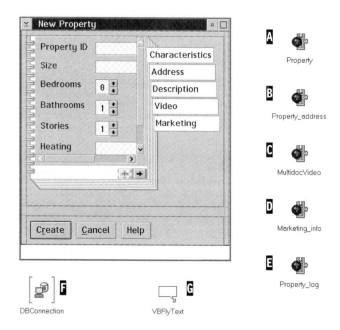

Figure 89. APropertyCreateView and Its Subparts

To add the parts required to implement the part logic, follow the step-by-step instructions in Table 31. Be sure your Data Access Builder parts are loaded in the Visual Builder Window.

Table 31. (Part 1 of 2) Adding Parts in APropertyCreateView

Step	Action
1	Open the APropertyCreateView part.
2	Add a Property* part, **A**, on the free-form surface (*Option → Add Part...* from the Composition Editor). This part is initialized with the information on the Characteristics and Description pages.
3	Add a Property_address* part, **B**, on the free-form surface (*Option → Add Part...* from the Composition Editor). This part is initialized with the information on the Address page.
4	Add a Multidoc* part, **C**, on the free-form surface (*Option → Add Part...* from the Composition Editor). This part is initialized with the information on the Video page.

Table 31. (Part 2 of 2) Adding Parts in APropertyCreateView

Step	Action
5	Add a Marketing_info* part, **D**, on the free-form surface (*Option →* *Add Part...* from the Composition Editor). This part is initialized with the information on the Marketing page.
6	Add a Property_log* part, **E**, on the free-form surface (*Option → Add Part...* from the Composition Editor). This part is set up automatically with a custom logic connection.
7	Add an IDatastore* variable part, **F** on the free-form surface (*Option → Add Part...* from the Composition Editor). This variable part holds the database connection. The connection is established when the application starts (see "Managing Database Connection" on page 246 and "Using Variable Parts" on page 243).

Note: You can also add a variable part from the *Models* category. If you do, you must change the type of the variable to **IDatastore*** (option *Change Type...* in the variable part pop-up menu). Notice that the IVBVariablePart* part is called the IVBVariable* part in the parts palette. In the rest of this book, we call a variable from its reference name: IVBVariablePart.

Step	Action
8	Promote the IDatastore* variable part so that it can get its contents from other parts (see "Managing Database Connection" on page 246).
9	Add an IVBFlyText* part, **G**, on the free-form surface (located in the *Other* category). This part is used to display contextual help text in the window info area (see "Adding Fly-over Help to a Control" on page 247).

Note: Reverse highlighted letters are keyed to Figure 89 on page 237.

Once you have placed the parts on the free-form surface, you can build the connections. First, build the group of attribute-to-attribute connections that associate the contents of each entry field of the view with the corresponding Data Access Builder part's attribute (see Figure 90). Then, connect the IVBFlyText part to the window info area.

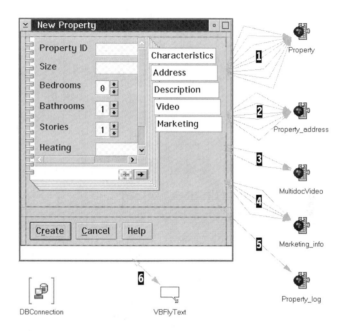

Figure 90. Attribute-to-Attribute Connections in APropertyCreateView

Make the attribute-to-attribute connections as shown in Table 32.

Key	Connection	Description
1	❏ property_id → propertyID ❏ propertySize → size ❏ propertyBedrooms → bed-rooms ❏ propertyBathrooms → bath-rooms ❏ propertyStories → stories ❏ propertyHeating → heating ❏ propertyCooling → cooling ❏ multiLineEditDescription-Text → description	Synchronize the value of each attribute (Property part).

Table 32. (Part 1 of 2) Making Attribute-to-Attribute Connections in APropertyCreateView

Table 32. (Part 2 of 2) Making Attribute-to-Attribute Connections in
APropertyCreateView

Key	Connection	Description
2	❑ address_id → propertyID ❑ addressViewEntryFieldAreaText → area ❑ addressViewEntryFieldCityText → city ❑ addressViewEntryFieldStreetText → street ❑ addressViewEntryFieldZipCodeText → zip_code ❑ addressViewComboBoxStateText → state	Synchronize the value of each attribute (Property_address part). The address_id → propertyID connection enables the Property and Address tables to be joined.
3	❑ propertyID → multidoc_id ❑ filename → VideoFileName	Synchronize the value of each attribute (MultidocVideo part). The propertyID → multidoc_id connection enables the Property and Multidoc tables to be joined.
4	❑ propertyID → property_id ❑ commissionRate → commission_rate ❑ downPaymentRate → down_payment_rate ❑ price → price	Synchronize the value of each attribute (Marketing_info part). The propertyID → property_id connection enables the Property and Marketing_info tables to be joined.
5	propertyID → property_id	For joining the Property and Property_log tables.

Note: Fly-over help is detailed in "Adding Fly-over Help to a Control" on page 247.

6	this → longTextControl	Display the long text of fly-over help in the window area.

Note: Reverse highlighted numbers are keyed to Figure 90 on page 239. To keep the drawings simple, we do not key all connections.

If you look closely at the event-trace diagram of the property creation scenario (Figure 38 on page 98), you can see that all of the attribute-to-attribute connections refer to the *initialize* arrows between the APropertyCreateView and each Data Access Builder class. Of course in the event-trace diagram, we do not represent all of the arrows. Rather, we draw one *initialize* arrow for several attribute-to-attribute connections

---

Tip!

To browse a set of connections all at once (either to see the connection order or to display the list of all connections without having to select connections one by one and look at the status line), select the reorder connection feature. From a selected part, click on the right mouse button and select the *Reorder Connections From* option from the part's pop-up menu. You will get a list of all connections issued from that part. You can change the order of the connections by dragging and dropping the connections within the list (see Figure 92 on page 243)

Now you can build the event-to-action connections, which refer to the *add* arrows drawn from APropertyCreateView to each Data Access Builder class (see Figure 91 and Table 33).

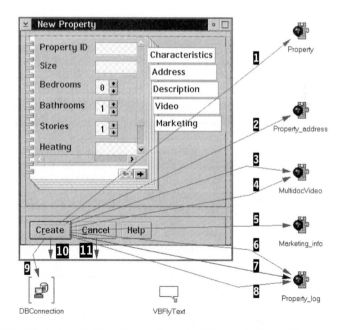

Figure 91. Event-to-Action Connections in APropertyCreateView

Table 33. Making Event-to-Action Connections in APropertyCreateView

Key	Connection	Description
1	buttonClickEvent → add	Add a row in the Property table.
2	buttonClickEvent → add	Add a row in the Property_address table.
Note: The order of the next two connections is crucial!		
3	buttonClickEvent → type	Set the document type. VIDEO is the only type implemented (see "Passing a Parameter to a Connection" on page 248).
4	buttonClickEvent → add	Add a row in the Multidoc table.
5	buttonClickEvent → add	Add a row in the Marketing_info table.
Note: In the next three connections buttonClickEvent → add must be the last connection!		
6	buttonClickEvent → status	Set the property status to AVAILABLE at creation time (see "Passing a Parameter to a Connection" on page 248).
7	buttonClickEvent → customLogic	Set the time stamp creation (see "Using Custom Logic" on page 249).
8	buttonClickEvent → add	Add a row in the Property_log table.
9	buttonClickEvent → commit	Commit the transaction in the database.
10	buttonClickEvent → close	Close the window.
11	buttonClickEvent → close	Close the window.
Note: Reverse highlighted numbers are keyed to Figure 91 on page 241.		

Ensure that the event-to-action connections from the *Create* push button are in the proper order. To check the order of connections drawn from a part, use the *Reorder Connections From...* option from the part's pop-up menu (see Figure 92).

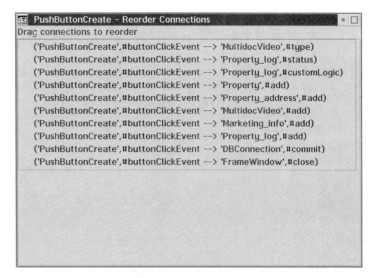

Figure 92. Connection Order for the Create Push Button

You can now save your part and generate its code. From the Visual Builder window, select *Save and generate → Part source* in the *File* pull-down menu.

Using Variable Parts

Variable parts play an important role in applications. You use variable parts primarily in two situations:

❑ To act as a placeholder inside a composite part for parts that cannot be found in the composite part. Using variable parts in nonvisual parts enables you to pass data or functions between parts. Using variable parts in visual parts enables you to pass data across different visual parts. For example, you use an IDatastore* variable part to transmit the connection from one visual part of the application to another (see "Managing Database Connection" on page 246). You will also use variable parts in the APropertySearchResultView and APropertyUpdateView to pass the record selected in the first view to the second view.

❑ To represent part instances created with factory parts (see "Using an Object Factory to Update the Database" on page 271).

You can add a variable part on the free-form surface in three different ways:

❑ Select a variable part from the *Models* category. Once the variable part is on the free-form surface, you must change its type to the type of the part it represents.

❑ From the *Composition Editor* menu, use *Options* → *Add part...* to add a part. Instead of selecting *Part* in the *Add as* radio button, you select *Variable*. In this case the type of the variable part is automatically set according to the part class you have entered.

❑ Use the tear-off feature to expose a subpart of a part (see "Tearing Off an Attribute" on page 316). In this case the type of the variable part is automatically set according to the class of the attribute exposed.

It is often better to use a variable part to update a set of entry fields than it is to promote text attributes of entry fields and then update the entry field contents one by one from another part by using attribute-to-attribute connections. For example, suppose you build a simple property view to display some property information (Figure 93). You would use the Data Access Builder Property part to hold the property information.

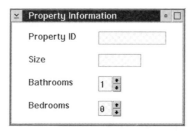

Figure 93. Simple View to Display Property Information

Each time you want to reuse the Property view from another part and update the contents of each entry field with the property information, you must connect each attribute from the Property part to the text attribute of each entry field. In this case, you must promote the text attribute of each entry field of the Property view (Figure 94).

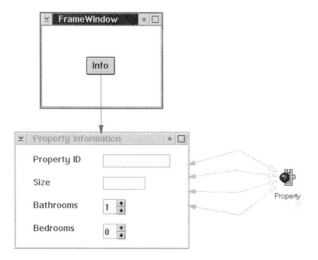

Figure 94. Reusing the Property View from Another Part: First Try

A better design would be to use a Property variable part in the Property view and promote only the variable part itself (Figure 95).

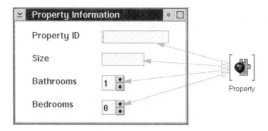

Figure 95. Simple Property View with Its Associated Variables

In this way, when you use the Property view from another part, you draw only one connection to update the view (Figure 96).

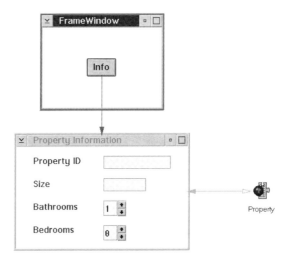

Figure 96. Reusing the Property View from Another Part: Second Try

In our application, you use variable parts in APropertyUpdateView to set the contents of entry fields in each notebook page. You set the variable contents from APropertySearchResultView, using only one connection (see "APropertySearchResultView" on page 265).

Managing Database Connection

Before the user can access a subsystem, a database connection must be established (see Chapter 6, "Mapping Relational Tables Using Data Access Builder," on page 127). A problem arises when the application accesses the database from several views. In that case, each view must hold an IDatastore* part to connect to the database, and the application ends up with some overhead each time the user switches from one view to another, chaining database connections all along. To avoid this problem, use only one IDatastore* part in your application primary view and pass it to the other views through variable parts. This is a convenient and efficient way of managing a unique connection shared among several application views.

Each part using the database must contain a variable part of type IDatastore*. This variable part must be promoted to receive a reference of IDatastore* from the parts that use it.

Now, let us suppose that your application consists of several parts that are organized in a five-level hierarchy. If some parts of the last level must access the database, you must add and promote an IDatastore* variable part in all intermediate levels from the second level up to the fifth. This action is necessary because the promote feature cannot jump a hierarchy level.

In our case, you add an IDatastore* part in the primary view, AReal-MainView, to establish one database connection at startup. Then, because this database connection must be used in APropertyUpdate-View, you have to add and promote an IDatastore* variable part in each view that belongs to the hierarchy branch: APropertySearchPa-rameterView, APropertySearchResultView, and APropertyUpdate-View (see the view hierarchy in Figure 53 on page 145).

Adding Fly-over Help to a Control

To provide instant help to the novice user, you can use *fly-over help*, which consists of a text string that is displayed when the user positions the mouse pointer over a control, such as an entry field or a push button. The text should be short and should indicate the purpose of the control.

The application can provide two kinds of fly-over help:

❑ A short text string that your application displays in a bubble (it is also called *bubble help*) next to the subpart on which you have your mouse pointer

❑ A long text string (more explanatory) that your application displays in a text control (such as an entry field or an info area)

To provide fly-over help for a subpart:

1. Drop an IVBFlyText* part on the free-form surface (IVBFlyText* part is located in the *Other* category).

2. Open the settings of the subpart and, on the control page, enter the fly-over short text, fly-over long text, or both.

Text entered in fly-over short text is displayed as a bubble help for this subpart, and you do not need any connections to make it work!

Text entered in fly-over long text can be displayed in a window info area: Connect the ***this*** of the info area to the longTextControl of the IVBFlyText* part (for more information refer to the *Visual Builder User's Guide*).

To add fly-over help to the *Create* push button, follow these steps:

1. Open the settings notebook of the *Create* push button.

2. Switch to the Control page.

3. In the *Fly over short text* entry field, type in the following text: **Create a new property**. This text will display in a bubble when the user positions the mouse on the *Create* push button.

4. In the *Fly over long text* entry field, type in the following text: **Fill in each entry field before creating a property in the database**. This text will display in the frame window info area added for this purpose.

These few steps are all you have to do to give your application slick contextual help! Save the part again and regenerate its source code to register the changes.

In the next sections, feel free to add your own fly-over short and long texts for your parts.

Passing a Parameter to a Connection

Sometimes an event-to-action connection needs one or several parameters to execute. In such cases, the connection displays as a dashed line. You can provide the connection with the parameters in two ways:

❑ Open the settings of the connection and click on the **Set Parameters...** push button. A dialog box is displayed and you are prompted to give the parameter's value. If the parameter is a text string and the type of the parameter is an IString, you can enter the string without double quotes. Otherwise, you must surround the string with double quotes. In this case the parameters are set *statically*: Each time the connection fires, it uses the same parameter values.

❑ Connect an attribute of the matching type to the parameter of the connection. This parameter is shown in the connection pop-up menu. The parameter connection is a kind of attribute-to-attribute connection, but it is unidirectional (see "Using Visual Builder" on page 27). In this case, the parameters are set *dynamically*: Each time the connection fires, it uses the parameter values according to the parameter connection.

In connection **3** (see Table 33 on page 242), you provide the string, VIDEO, as the type of medium to which the file name refers. Double-click with the mouse on this connection to get the connection settings dialog box. Then click on the **Set Parameters...** push button. You can see VIDEO in the type entry field (notice that there are no quotes). Do the same for the property status, setting the *status* attribute of the Property_log* part to AVAILABLE (other property statuses are PENDING and SOLD).

Using Custom Logic

A custom logic connection is an easy way of calling your own custom-ized C or C++ code whenever an attribute's value changes or an event occurs. When you connect an attribute to a custom logic, the attribute event identifier is used to notify the custom logic connection and call your code when the attribute's value changes. You can use this connec-tion for small code that you do not plan to reuse. For more information about custom logic connections, refer to the *Visual Builder User's Guide*.

In APropertyCreateView, you use a custom logic connection to set the *download_timestamp* and *last_update* attributes of the Property_log table.

A *download_timestamp* is associated with the creation time and date of each property record in the database. A *last_update* attribute is associated with the date and time of the update of each property record in the database. It contains the date and time when the record is created or updated in the database. In DB2/2 the *creation-time-stamp* attribute is a string of 26 characters with the following format:

yyyy-mm-dd-hh.mm.ss.xxxx

where

❏ yyyy represents the year (for example, 1995)
❏ mm represents the month (for example, 06 for June)
❏ dd represents the day (for example, 23 for the twenty-third)
❏ hh.mm.ss.xxxx represents the time (format: hour.minute.sec-ond.millisecond)

IDate and ITime parts are combined to make up the time stamp as fol-lows:

Code to Store Current Time Stamp
```
target → setDownload_timestamp(
      IString(IDate::today().asString("%Y-%m-%d"))+"-"+
      IString(ITime::now().asString("%H.%M.%S")));
target → setLast_Update(
      IString(IDate::today().asString("%Y-%m-%d"))+"-"+
      IString(ITime::now().asString("%H.%M.%S")));
```

IDate::today() returns the current date. The asString() method is used to translate the current date in the yyyy-mm-dd format that is com-patible with the DATE type of DB2/2 tables (for more information, see the *IBM Open Class Library Reference*).

ITime::now() returns the current time, and the asString() method is used to translate it into the correct DB2/2 time format, hh-mm-ss. The same code is applied to the *last_update* attribute because at creation time, the creation_time stamp and last_update time stamp are the same.

Info

The IDate and ITime parts are class interface parts. As mentioned in "AMarketingInfo" on page 214, class interface parts are nonvisual parts that have no notification ability. In other words, they cannot send events to other parts. But, you can trigger their action from your application events. Visual Builder provides many class interface parts that conveniently wrap standard classes from the IBM Open Class Library to enable you to use the classes in the Composition Editor. In the same way, you can use your own C++ classes in Visual Builder as class interface parts (refer to Chapter 8, "Creating Nonvisual Parts," on page 213 and Chapter 10, "If You Want to Know More about Visual Builder...," on page 323).

Notice that you must use the set methods to change the attribute value of Property_log. Otherwise, the target part will never be notified that the attribute has changed.

Tip!

The target of the custom logic connection is the Property_log* part. Therefore you call its methods by using the `target →` `function(parm1,...)` expression. Sometimes your custom logic code may require that you use more than one part. To access the parts, you must select the free-form surface as the target connection. The free-form surface represents the composite part itself, and each of its subparts is known as a pointer within the part. In the code generated by Visual Builder, the identifier of a pointer to a subpart is the name of the subpart with the letter **i** as a prefix. For example, in APropertyCreateView, if you had used the free-form surface (which represents APropertyCreateView* itself) as the target for the custom logic connection, you would have written the snippet code as follows:

```
target → iProperty_log → setDownload_timestamp(
    IString(IDate::today().asString("%Y-%m-%d"))+"-"+
    IString(ITime::now().asString("%H.%M.%S")));
target → iProperty_log → setLast_Update(
    IString(IDate::today().asString("%Y-%m-%d"))+"-"+
    IString(ITime::now().asString("%H.%M.%S")));
```

Because you use the IDate and ITime parts in your visual part, you must include their corresponding header files in the code generated by Visual Builder.

1. Switch to the Class Editor of APropertyCreateView.

2. In the *User files included in generation* group box fill in the *Required include files* list box as follows:

<idate.hpp> _IDATE_
<itime.hpp> _ITIME_

The idate.hpp and itime.hpp header files will be included in the APropertyCreateView header file. The preprocessor uses the _IDATE_ and _ITIME_ variables to avoid including the headers if they already have been included by other subparts of the view.

You can now save your part and generate its code. From the Visual Builder window, select *Save and generate* → *Part source* in the *File* pull-down menu.

APropertyUpdateView

APropertyUpdateView is used to update the property information. In many ways, APropertyUpdateView is similar to APropertyCreate-View. However, unlike APropertyCreateView, the property records of APropertyUpdateView are not created across the five relational tables. They are updated across the same tables.

An instance of APropertyUpdateView is created when the user has already selected a property from the container. (This container displays the result of a search in APropertySearchResultView.) The significant difference in the update process is that the property and its components already exist. For this reason, when you add the Data Access Builder parts on the free-form surface, you must add them as variable parts, not as parts (Figure 97). The contents of the variable are set by parameter connections in APropertySearchResultView (see "Using Variable Parts" on page 243).

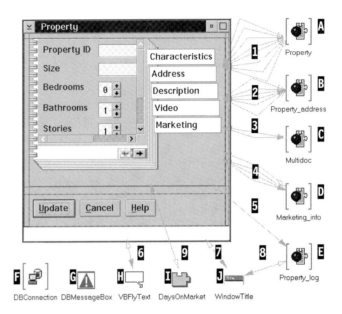

Figure 97. Attribute-to-Attribute Connections in APropertyUpdateView.

To add the different subparts to the free-form surface, follow the step-by-step instructions in Table 34. (Numbers refer to Figure 97).

Table 34. (Part 1 of 3) Adding Subparts in APropertyUpdateView	
Step	**Action**
1	Open the APropertyUpdateView part.
2	Add a Property* variable part, **A**, to the free-form surface (*Option → Add Part...* from the Composition Editor). This variable receives its contents from APropertySearchResultView and sets the Characteristics and Description page information.
3	Add a Property_address* variable part, **B**, to the free-form surface (*Option → Add Part...* from the Composition Editor). This variable gets its contents from APropertySearchResultView and sets the Address page information.
4	Add a Multidoc* variable part, **C**, to the free-form surface (*Option → Add Part...* from the Composition Editor). This variable gets its contents from APropertySearchResultView and sets the Video page information.

Table 34. (Part 2 of 3) Adding Subparts in APropertyUpdateView

Step	Action
5	Add a Marketing_info* variable part, ◨, to the free-form surface (*Option → Add Part...* from the Composition Editor). This variable gets its contents from APropertySearchResultView and sets the Marketing page information.
6	Add a Property_log* variable part, ◨, to the free-form surface (*Option → Add Part...* from the Composition Editor). This part is automatically updated with a custom logic connection.
7	Add an IDatastore* variable part, ◨ to the free-form surface (*Option → Add Part...* from the Composition Editor). This variable holds the database connection that established when the application starts (see "Using Variable Parts" on page 243 and "Managing Database Connection" on page 246).

Note: You can also add a variable part from the *Models* category. If you do so, you must change the type of the variable to the type of the part it represents (use the *Change Type...* option in the variable part pop-up menu).

Step	Action
9	Promote the Property* variable part.
10	Promote the Property_address* variable part.
11	Promote the Multidoc* variable part.
12	Promote the Marketing_info* variable part.
13	Promote the Property_log* variable part.
14	Promote the IDatastore* variable part.

Note: Each variable part is promoted to be accessible from other parts and to receive its contents from these parts (see "Using Variable Parts" on page 243).

Step	Action
15	Add an IMessageBox* part, ◨, on the free-form surface (located in the *Other* category). This message box is used to display an exception if the transaction cannot be committed (see "Showing Exception in a Message Box" on page 259).
16	Add an IVBFlyText* part, ◨, on the free-form surface (located in the *Other* category) and add some fly-over short and long texts to the different push buttons (see "Adding Fly-over Help to a Control" on page 247).

Table 34. (Part 3 of 3) Adding Subparts in APropertyUpdateView

Step	Action
17	Add an IVBLongPart* part, **I**, on the free-form surface (*Option* → *Add Part...* from the Composition Editor). This part contains the number of days since the property was created in the database (see "Using Sample Parts" on page 259).
18	Add an ITitle* part, **J**, on the free-form surface (located in the *Frame Extensions* category). This part represents the frame window title. Its *objectText* attribute is updated by the *last_update* attribute of Property_log (see "Updating a Window Title Dynamically" on page 264).

Note: Reverse highlighted letters are keyed to Figure 97 on page 252.

Because APropertyUpdateView is similar to APropertyCreateView, we use the same mode of presentation: First we describe the attribute-to-attribute connections, then we describe the event-to-action, parameter, and custom logic connections.

Connect the parts with the attribute-to-attribute connections shown in Table 35.

Table 35. (Part 1 of 2) Making Attribute-to-Attribute Connections in APropertyUpdateView

Key	Connection	Description
I	❏ propertyID → property_id ❏ size → propertySize ❏ bedrooms → propertyBedrooms ❏ bathrooms → propertyBathrooms ❏ stories → propertyStories ❏ heating → propertyHeating ❏ cooling → propertyCooling ❏ description → multiLineEditDescriptionText	Synchronize the value of each attribute of Property part with the Characteristics page entry fields.

Table 35. (Part 2 of 2) Making Attribute-to-Attribute Connections in APropertyUpdateView

Key	Connection	Description
2	❏ propertyID → address_id ❏ area → addressViewEntry-FieldAreaText ❏ city → addressViewEntry-FieldCityText ❏ street → addressViewEn-tryFieldStreetText ❏ zip_code → addressViewEn-tryFieldZipCodeText ❏ state → addressViewCom-boBoxStateText	Synchronize the value of each attribute of Property_address part with the Address page entry fields. The propertyID → property_id connection enables the Property and Address tables to be joined.
3	❏ multidoc_id → propertyID ❏ VideoFileName → filename	Synchronize the value of each attribute of MultidocVideo part with the Video page entry fields. The propertyID → property_id connection enables the Property and Multidoc tables to be joined.
4	❏ property_id → propertyID ❏ commission_rate→ commissionRate ❏ down_payment_rate → downPaymentRate ❏ price → price	Synchronize the value of each attribute of Marketing_info part with the Video page entry fields. The propertyID → property_id connection enables the Property and Marketing_info to be joined.
5	property_id → propertyID	Join the Property and Property_log tables.
6	this → longTextControl	Display the long text of fly-over help in the window area.
7	this → owner	Associate the window title control with the main window.
8	last_update → viewText	Synchronize the value of last_update with the contents of the window title.
9	valueAsText → DaysOnMarket	Synchronize the value of the DaysOnMarket part with the DaysOnMarket feature promoted from PropertyView.

Note: Reverse highlighted numbers are keyed to Figure 97 on page 252. To keep the drawings simple, we do not key all of the connections.

Because the event-trace diagram of the property update scenario is not detailed enough, you cannot see the attribute-to-attribute connections (Figure 40 on page 101). Rather, you see a connection from APropertySearchResultView and APropertyUpdateView with the *send info* label. This connection is the representation of the data which flows from one view to another by means of the variable parts (see "Using Variable Parts" on page 243).

Using event-to-action, parameter, custom logic and event-to-member function connections, connect the subparts as shown in Figure 98 and Table 36.

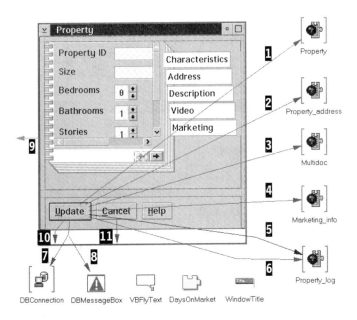

Figure 98. Event-to-Action Connections in APropertyUpdateView

Table 36. (Part 1 of 2) Making Event-to-Action Connections in APropertyUpdateView		
Key	**Connection**	**Description**
1	buttonClickEvent → update	Update the row in the Property table.
2	buttonClickEvent → update	Update the row in the Property_address table.

Table 36. (Part 2 of 2) Making Event-to-Action Connections in
APropertyUpdateView

Key	Connection	Description
3	buttonClickEvent → update	Update the row in the Multidoc table. Notice that you do not have to set the type to VIDEO because it already has been set up, and it cannot be changed from the view.
4	buttonClickEvent → update	Update the row in the Marketing_info table.

Note: For the next two connections, buttonClickEvent → update must be the last connection!

Key	Connection	Description
5	buttonClickEvent → custom-Logic	Set the last update time stamp (see "Using Custom Logic" on page 249).
6	buttonClickEvent → update	Update the row in the Property_log table.
7	buttonClickEvent → commit	Commit the transaction in the database.
8	exceptionOccurred → showException	Show the commit exception in the message box when it occurs.
9	visible → daysOnMarket()	Compute the number of days the property is on the market when the window is displayed (see "Using the Member Function Connection" on page 260).
10	buttonClickEvent → close	Close the window.
11	buttonClickEvent → close	Close the window.

Note: Reverse highlighted numbers are keyed to Figure 98 on page 256.

Ensure that the event-to-action connections from the *Update* push button are in the proper order. To check the order of connections drawn from a part, use the *Reorder Connections From...* option from the part's pop-up menu (see Figure 99).

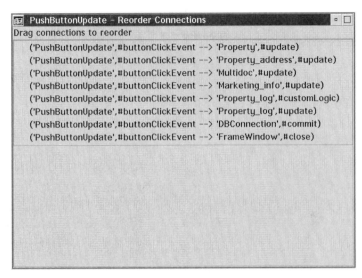

Figure 99. Connection Order for the Update Push Button

Because IDate, ITime, IString, and the IString parser parts are used through connection **10**, to calculate the number of days the property is on the market, you must include their corresponding header files in the code generated by Visual Builder:

1. Switch to the Class Editor of APropertyUpdateView.

2. In the group box entitled *User files included in generation*, fill in the *Required include files* list box as follows:

> **<idate.hpp>   _IDATE_**
> **<itime.hpp>   _ITIME_**
> **<istring.hpp> _ISTRING_**
> **<istparse.hpp> _ISTPARSE_**

These header files are included in the APropertyUpdateView header file. The processor uses _IDATE_, _ITIME_, _ISTRING_, and _ISTPARSE_ variables to avoid including these headers if they already have been included by other subparts of the view.

You can now save your part and generate its code. From the Visual Builder window, select *Save and generate → Part source* in the *File* pull-down menu.

As with APropertyCreateView, you can see the correspondence of the event-to-action *update* in the view and its representation in the event-trace diagram of the property update scenario (Figure 40 on page 101).

Showing Exception in a Message Box

To trigger the display of a message box when a part throws an exception, follow these steps:

1. Add an IMessageBox* part to the free-form surface.

2. Open the message box settings and set the title to your liking.

3. Connect the **exceptionOccurred** event of the event-to-action connection that throws the exception to the **showException** action of the message box.

When the connection is triggered, the action is executed in a *try* block. If the action fails, a *catch* block allows the connection to execute an alternative action, such as showing the message box (for more information on the C++ exception handling framework, refer to the *C/C++ Language Reference*). This facility is used in AProperty UpdateView to catch a commit exception on the database. In the same way, the application can display a message box when an exception occurs during the update of the database.

You can also tailor the message box to your needs, using the **show** action. Open the settings of the exceptionOccurred → show connection and set the message and the severity of the exception (see "Using a Message Box to Display the Clause" on page 292).

Tip!

You can use the message box to trace the flow of your program and display some variable contents or some attribute values during the execution of the program. For example, suppose you want to trigger an **A** action when a push button is clicked. To check the contents of the variable on which the action depends, you connect the **buttonClickEvent** event of the push button to the **show** action of a message box and send the contents of the variable as a parameter to this connection. This event-to-action connection must be triggered before action **A** is executed (see "Using a Message Box to Display the Clause" on page 292 and Figure 116 on page 293).

Using Sample Parts

Along with the basic part library (VBBase.VBB), the database access part library (VBDAX.VBB), and the multimedia part library (VBMM.VBB) provided with Visual Builder, comes another useful part library: VBSAMPLE.VBB. This library deserves to be called the *programmer toolbox* of Visual Builder. It includes parts that enhance the basic types of the C++ language, such as String, Long, or Boolean. It also includes some general parts that you can reuse for basic file input/output or mathematical computation (see also "AUpLoadView" on page 298).

In this view, you use the IVBLongPart part to hold the number of days the property is on the market. This part contains many methods that you might find useful for your future applications. In the rest of the application you will use two other parts from VBSAMPLE.VBB:

❑ **IVBStringPart** is the equivalent version, for the Visual Builder, of the standard IString class. Unlike the class interface IString, IVBStringPart is a fully enabled part that can notify your own parts. You will use it, for example, to hold the SQL clause from which the agent selects a list of properties in APropertySearchParameterView (see "Building the Clause" on page 285).

❑ **IVBBooleanPart** is the equivalent version, for the Visual Builder, of the standard IBoolean class. You will use it to build the SQL clause from check box controls in APropertySearchParameterView (see "Managing the User Input" on page 284).

Using the Member Function Connection

The number of days the property is on the market is calculated by an *event-to-member function* connection. This connection can be a valuable alternative to a custom logic connection when you have to reuse your own C++ code within the same part or when the code is more than a few lines. There are two types of member function connections: the event-to-member function connection and the attribute-to-member function connection. Both types enable you to call a member function of your part that you declare and define in the specific hpv and cpv user files.

The member function connection may reveal some advantages over the custom logic connection:

❑ The code is written in cpv and hpv files, which are separated from the actual cpp and hpp files part that generates Visual Builder for the part. Thus, each time the visual part code is generated, it does not impact your member function code.

❑ In addition to a *public* access specifier, you can choose to declare the member functions with *private* or *protected* access specifiers. You may find this facility useful in the context of derivation in controlling the access of such "implementation functions" to inherited members.

In our example, you add a public method, void DaysOnMarket() (Figure 100), to APropertyUpdateView to calculate the number of days a property is on the market. This number is calculated from the current date and the creation time stamp of the property.

```
/********************************************************************/
/*                                                                *
/*    Declaration of the daysOnMarket member function             *
/*                                                                *
/*    Description:                                                 *
/*             This method calculates the time difference between *
/*             the system date and the property creation date.    *
/*                                                                *
/********************************************************************/

public:
      void APropertyUpdateView::daysOnMarket();
```

Figure 100. DaysOnMarket Public Method Declaration

The public method converts the database time stamp to an IDate format and calculates the difference from the current date by using the *dateToday* function, which returns the system date (see Figure 101). Then, the method sets the contents of the *DaysOnMarket* part.

```
IDate dateToday;
IString day, month, year, temp;
iProperty_log
      ->target()
      ->download_timestamp() >> year
                            >> '_'
                            >> month
                            >> '_'
                            >> day
                            >> '_'
                            >> temp;

IDate::Month monthYear;

switch (month.asInt()) {
        case 1:
           monthYear = IDate::January;
           break;
        case 2:
           monthYear = IDate::February;
           break;
        case 3:
           monthYear = IDate::March;
           break;
        case 4:
           monthYear = IDate::April;
           break;
        case 5:
           monthYear = IDate::May;
           break;
        case 6:
           monthYear = IDate::June;
           break;
        case 7:
           monthYear = IDate::July;
           break;
        case 8:
           monthYear = IDate::August;
           break;
        case 9:
           monthYear = IDate::September;
           break;
        case 10:
           monthYear = IDate::October;
           break;
        case 11:
           monthYear = IDate::November;
           break;
        case 12:
           monthYear = IDate::December;
           break;
} /* end switch */

IDate creationDate = IDate(monthYear, day.asInt(), year.asInt());
iDaysOnMarket->setValue(dateToday - creationDate);
```

Figure 101. DaysOnMarket Public Method Definition

To build the event-to-member function action (see **10** in Table 36 on page 256), follow these instructions:

1. Select the *Connect* option from the IFrameWindow* part pop-up menu and select the **visible** event. The pointer becomes a spider.

2. Move the pointer to the free-form surface and click with the left mouse button. Then choose the **More...** option from the pop-up menu. In the dialog box (Figure 102), you are prompted to select the access specifier and enter the member function prototype.

3. In the *Access* drop-down list, select **public** as the access specifier.

4. In the line below, enter the member function prototype: **void DaysOnMarket()**.

5. Click on the **OK** push button. A light green connection is drawn from the IFrameWindow* part to the free-form surface.

6. Switch to the Class Interface Editor. In the *User files included in generation* group box, fill in the hpv and cpv entry fields with the respective values, **vrpupdv.hpv** and **vrpupdv.cpv**.

7. With your favorite editor, edit the hpv and cpv files as shown in Figure 100 on page 261 and Figure 101 on page 262.

Figure 102. Member Function Dialog Box

In Chapter 10, "If You Want to Know More about Visual Builder...," on page 323, we show you how to use the browser provided with Visual-Age for C++ to avoid entering the prototype of your methods in the member function dialog box.

Updating a Window Title Dynamically

The frame window extension category of the parts palette enables you to tailor your frame window. You have been shown how to add an info area or a menu to your frame window. Using an ITitle* part, you can change the title of the window after the window is created:

1. Add an ITitle* part to the free-form surface.

2. Specify the frame window to which the ITitle* part is related. You can consider two options:

   - Draw an attribute-to-attribute connection from the *this* attribute of the frame window to the *owner* attribute of the ITitle* part.

   - Open the ITitle* part settings and set the *owner* attribute to the name of the related window (do not forget to prefix the name with *i*; see "Using Custom Logic" on page 249).

3. Use the ITitle* part as follows:

   - If you want to change the title when an event occurs, connect the event to the **setTitleText** action of the ITitle* part and set the parameters required by the connection. (Click on the **Set Parameters...** push button in the connection settings and enter the title in the objectName parameter. You can optionally specify the view name and the view number.)

   - If you want to set the title from one or more attributes of other parts, connect a text attribute to the *objectText* or *viewText* attributes of the ITitle* part. You can optionally connect a numeric attribute to the *viewNumber* attribute of the ITitle* part.

In our case, you display the time stamp of the property creation by using an attribute-to-attribute connection from the *last_update* attribute of Property_log to the *viewText* attribute of the Title part (see connection 8 in Figure 97 on page 252). The objectText attribute of the IFrameWindow* part is directly set in the Composition Editor to "Property."

ADeleteDialogView

ADeleteDialogView visual part is used by each subsystem to warn users before they delete a record in the database. This view is so simple that we do not provide you with step-by-step instructions.

In fact, there is only one connection to draw! To complete the view:

1. Open ADeleteDialogView.
2. Connect the **buttonClickEvent** event of the *Cancel* push button to the **close** action of the frame window.

You can now save your part and generate its code. From the Visual Builder window, select *Save and generate → Part source* in the *File* pull-down menu.

Even this simple view gives us a good opportunity to point out that you should always close your frame window part by using an event-to-action connection within the part. This approach makes your part easier to reuse because it behaves independently of other parts. However, sometimes you need to draw the part's connections within a composite part that reuses your part. This is the case for the event-to action connection: **buttonClickEvent** event of the *OK* push button to the **close** action of the frame window. Indeed, when the user clicks the *OK* push button, an event-to-action connection must delete the records in the database before closing the window. Once the records are deleted, the **close** action must be triggered from an event-to-action drawn in the part that manages the record deletion. These two event-to-actions are executed sequentially. Therefore, you must promote the **buttonClickEvent** event of the *OK* push button to access it from another part.

Of course, you could decide to include the parts involved in the deletion process of a property in ADeleteDialogView—such as the Data Access Builder parts—but, in this case, ADeleteDialogView would not have been reusable by the other subsystems. In effect, the parts involved in the deletion process vary from one subsystem to another.

APropertySearchResultView

APropertySearchResultView displays properties according to a buyer's preferences. This view is relatively complex. Therefore, we introduce a useful approach that will help you aggregate several nonvisual parts into one nonvisual part.

APropertySearchResultView is responsible for executing a query against the REAL database. The query is performed according to the clause transmitted by APropertySearchParameterView.

A PropertyManager manages the extraction from the database and interacts with a container to display each matching property as a PropertyContainerObject (see Figure 41 on page 102).

The user can execute several actions from the container:

Update a property: APropertyUpdateView can be called to update the property selected in the container.

Delete a property: ADeleteDialogView can be called to delete the property selected in the container.

View the property video: The property video can be played using an IMMDigitalVideo* part.

Access the Sale transaction subsystem: The status of the property can be changed from AVAILABLE to PENDING.

Display the interested buyers: Buyers whose preferences match the characteristics of the selected property can be displayed.

In the description that follows, we do not cover the interaction of the Property subsystem with the Buyer subsystem and the Sale transaction subsystem. (Look at the application provided with the book to see how the Property subsystem interacts with the other subsystems.) Also, we do not cover the multimedia facility because it does not provide additional information (see "Adding Multimedia Features" on page 230). Rather, we divide the building of APropertySearchResultView into three sections:

1. We show you how to display a selection of properties in a container, using the PropertyManager part ("Selecting Properties from the Database" on page 267).

2. We explain how to simultaneously retrieve the property information from five tables ("Retrieving Information Across Multiple Tables" on page 268).

3. We describe how to use an Object Factory to update property information that has been retrieved ("Using an Object Factory to Update the Database" on page 271).

Each section brings more and more parts and connections onto the free-form surface. Thus, to complete this view, ensure that you follow the instructions in the correct order.

Selecting Properties from the Database

At the design level (Figure 41 on page 102), PropertyManager is responsible for interacting with the database and retrieving properties according to a specific clause. PropertyManager collaborates with PropertyCnr to display the list of properties extracted from the database.

At the implementation level, you decide the type of information you have to display in the container. Indeed, to display information from separate tables in the same container, you have to build a view that gathers information from each table. As mentioned in Chapter 6, "Mapping Relational Tables Using Data Access Builder," on page 127 we choose to display three types of information from three different tables:

❑ Property characteristics from the PROPERTY table
❑ Property address from the PROPERTY_ADDRESS table
❑ Property status from the PROPERTY_LOG table

Thus, you are provided with the PROP_AD_LOG view that joins the PROPERTY PROPERTY_ADDRESS, and PROPERTY_LOG tables. You then map the view, using Data Access Builder, into two parts: Prop_ad_logManager and Property_ad_log.

You use the select method of Property_ad_logManager to run the query against the database. The clause is given as a parameter of the action. The select action is triggered when APropertySearchResultView is ready (Figure 103).

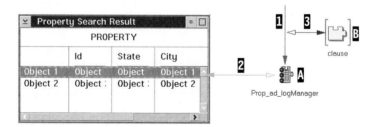

Figure 103. Querying the Database

To implement the database query, follow the step-by-step instructions in Table 37.

Step	Action
Table 37. (Part 1 of 2) Adding Parts to Query the Database	
Step	**Action**
1	Open APropertySearchResultView part.

Table 37. (Part 2 of 2) Adding Parts to Query the Database

Step	Action
2	Add a Prop_ad_logManager* part, **A**, on the free-form surface.
3	Add an IVBStringPart* variable part, **B**, on the free-form surface. This part contains the clause transmitted by APropertySearchPa-rameterView.
4	Promote the ***this*** attribute of the variable to ensure that the clause is accessible from APropertySearchParameterView.
5	Connect the **ready** event of APropertySearchResultView to the **select** action of Prop_ad_logManager, **1**.
6	Connect the ***items*** attribute of the Property_ad_logManager* part to the ***items*** attribute of the container, **2**. This attribute-to-attribute connection keeps the contents of the container synchronized with the set of rows extracted from the database.
7	Connect (**3**) the ***text*** attribute of the clause to the **clause** parameter of the connection **1**. This connection transmits the contents of the clause to the select method of Prop_ad_logManager.

Note: Reverse highlighted letters and numbers are keyed to Figure 103 on page 267.

Retrieving Information Across Multiple Tables

From the container, the user can perform the following actions on a selected property:

Open   Displays a property and allows the user to update its information

Delete   Removes a property from the database

To associate actions with an object selected in the container, you attach a pop-up menu to the container (see "Adding a Pop-up Menu" on page 232).

Each action involves a lot of information. Indeed, updating or deleting a property encompasses updating or deleting records on every table that makes up the property information; that is, PROPERTY, PROPERTY_ADDRESS, MULTI_DOC, MARKETING_INFO, and PROPERTY_LOG.

To access these tables, you use their associated Data Access Builder parts: Property, Property_address, Multidoc, Marketing_info, and Property_log.

When the user selects a property in the container, its identifier can be propagated to each Data Access Builder part by attribute-to-attribute connections, and the *retrieve* method of each Data Access Builder part can be triggered to retrieve the corresponding record in each table (Figure 104).

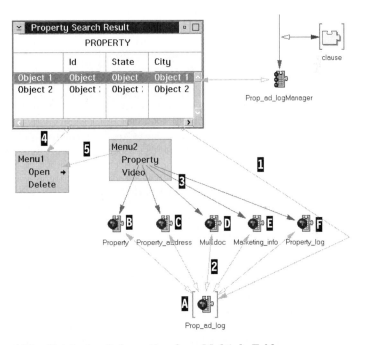

Figure 104. Retrieving Information from Multiple Tables

To retrieve the property information, follow the step-by-step instructions in Table 38.

Table 38. (Part 1 of 2) Adding Parts to Retrieve Information from Multiple Tables	
Step	**Action**
1	Add an IVBVariablePart* part, **A**, on the free-form surface and change its type to Prop_ad_log*. This variable part references the property selected in the container.

Table 38. (Part 2 of 2) Adding Parts to Retrieve Information from Multiple Tables

Step	Action
2	Add a Property* part, **B**, on the free-form surface. This part is used to retrieve the Property (characteristics) information of the selected property.
3	Add a Property_address* part, **C**, on the free-form surface. This part is used to retrieve the Property_address information of the selected property.
4	Add a Multidoc* part, **D**, on the free-form surface. This part is used to retrieve the Multi_doc information of the selected property.
5	Add a Marketing_info* part, **E**, on the free-form surface. This part is used to retrieve the Marketing_info information of the selected property.
6	Add a Property_log* part, **F** on the free-form surface. This part is used to retrieve the Property_log information of the selected property.
7	Add two IMenu* parts on the free-form surface.
8	Add three IMenuItem* parts on each IMenu* and change their labels as shown in Figure 104 on page 269.

Note: Reverse highlighted letters are keyed to Figure 104 on page 269.

Once you have placed the parts on the free-form surface, connect them as in Table 39.

Table 39. (Part 1 of 2) Connecting Parts to Retrieve Property Information

Key	Connection	Description
1	selectedElement → this	Property_ad_log is a placeholder for the property selected in the container.

Table 39. (Part 2 of 2) Connecting Parts to Retrieve Property Information

Key	Connection	Description
2	❑ property_id → property_id (from Property) ❑ property_id → address_id (from Property_address) ❑ property_id → multidoc_id (from Multidoc) ❑ property_id → property_id (from Marketing_info) ❑ property_id → property_id (from Property_log)	Synchronize the value of each identifier for the retrieve. These identifiers are selected as **Data identifiers** in the notebook settings of each relational table (see Chapter 6, "Mapping Relational Tables Using Data Access Builder," on page 127).
Note: You must draw the connections of step 2 before drawing the connection of step 3.		
3	❑ commandEvent → retrieve (from Property) ❑ commandEvent → retrieve (from Property_address) ❑ commandEvent → retrieve (from Multidoc) ❑ commandEvent → retrieve (from Marketing_info) ❑ commandEvent → retrieve (from Property_log)	Retrieve each row according to the identifier value.
4	menu → this	Attach Menu1 to the container
5	menu → this	Attach Menu2 as a submenu of the Open menu item.
Note: Reverse highlighted numbers are keyed to Figure 104 on page 269. To keep the drawings simple, we do not key all connections.		

Using an Object Factory to Update the Database

Once the information is retrieved, it can be updated. To update the property selected in the container, APropertySearchResultView collaborates with APropertySearchUpdateView. The collaboration is based on a "use" relationship: APropertySearchResultView uses the APropertyUpdateView part to provide an updating function from its container. APropertySearchResultView activates the collaboration by creating an instance of APropertyUpdateView. The property information is the link attribute between the two parts. It is transmitted during the instance creation (Figure 105).

To create an instance of a part, use an IVBFactory part (this part is available from the palette in the *Models* category). Factory parts enable your application to dynamically create a visual or a nonvisual part. This differs from parts that are added to the free-form surface and created statically when the application starts.

Like variable parts, factory parts are placeholders for other parts. Each factory part must be set to the type of the class it represents. The factory part works in tandem with a variable part that represents the instance created. You have to use variable parts with factory parts each time you access the attributes or activate a method of the instance created. Unlike variable parts, factory parts run a *create* method, which in turn runs the corresponding part class constructor, creating a new instance.

You can set up the instance attributes during the create call in two ways:

❑ You provide the factory part with the required attribute values, using parameter connections. In this case, the connections are triggered within the *create* method but after executing the part constructor. The factory creates as many different instances as the attribute values supplied by the parameter connections (see connection **2** in Table 40 on page 273).

❑ You set the attribute values in the settings notebook of the factory. In this case the parameters are passed to the class constructor. The factory creates a *clone* of the same class each time the **new** action is triggered.

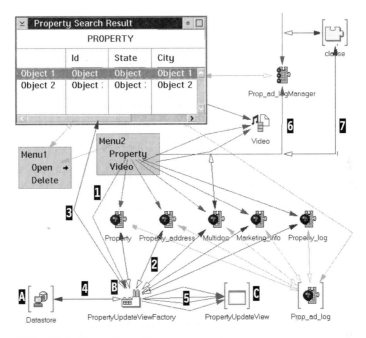

Figure 105. Updating a Property

Using factory parts involves the following steps:

1. Adding and setting the factory part
2. Adding and setting the variable part
3. Connecting the event to the factory part
4. Connecting the factory part to its variable part

Table 40 presents step-by-step instructions for using a factory of APropertyUpdateView to update the property information.

Table 40. Updating the Database	
Step	**Action**
1	Add an IVBVariablePart* part, **A**, to the free-form surface and change its type to IDatastore*. This variable represents the database connection. It is transmitted to APropertyUpdateView to commit the database transaction.
2	Add an IVBFactory* part, **B**, to the free-form surface and change its type to APropertyUpdateView*. This factory object enables creation of an instance of APropertyUpdateView dynamically.

Table 40. Updating the Database

Step	Action
3	Add an IVBVariablePart* part, **C**, to the free-form surface and change its type to APropertyUpdateView*. This variable represents the APropertyUpdateView instance.

Note: Reverse highlighted letters are keyed to Figure 105 on page 273.

Once you have placed the parts on the free-form surface, connect them as in Table 41.

Table 41. (Part 1 of 2) Connecting Parts to Update Property Information

Key	Connection	Description
1	commandEvent → new	Create an instance of APropertyUpdateView.
2	❑ property → this ❑ property_address → this ❑ multidoc → this ❑ marketing_info → this ❑ property_log → this	Transmit each part as a parameter to the factory for update.
3	owner → this	APropertyUpdateView is shown modally, and the frame window is its owner.
4	this → dBConnection	Transmit the database connection to APropertyUpdateView. dBConnection is a variable promoted in APropertyUpdateView.

Note: The order of the next five connections is crucial!

Key	Connection	Description
5	❑ newEvent → this ❑ newEvent → setFocus ❑ newEvent → showModally ❑ newEvent → deleteTarget	Associate the instance with the factory. APropertyUpdateView is shown modally. The window instance is deleted when it closes.
6	commandEvent → select	Refreshes the container after the update.
7	Connect the **this** attribute of the variable to the **clause** parameter of the connection **6**.	Clause is given as the parameter for the connection.

Table 41. (Part 2 of 2) Connecting Parts to Update Property Information		
Key	**Connection**	**Description**
Note: Reverse highlighted letters and numbers are keyed to Figure 105 on page 273. To keep the drawings simple, we do not key all connections.		

Ensure that the event-to-action connections from the menu item and APropertyUpdateView instance are in the proper order. To check the order of connections drawn from a part, use the *Reorder Connections...* option from its pop-up menu.

Deleting a Property

In this section we describe how to implement the delete option of the container pop-up menu (see Figure 106). First we list the parts involved, then we list all of the connections between the parts. For clarity, we do not represent all of the parts and connections that have been added and drawn in the preceding figures.

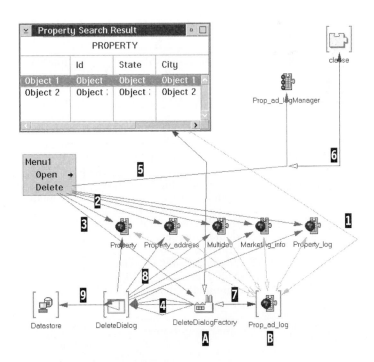

Figure 106. Deleting a Property

Add the subparts to APropertySearchResultView as shown in Table 42.

Step	Action
	Table 42. Adding Parts to Delete a Property from the Database
1	Add an IVBFactory* part, **A**, to the free-form surface and change its type to ADeleteDialog*. This factory creates an instance of ADelete-Dialog dynamically.
2	Add an IVBVariablePart* part, **B**, to the free-form surface and change its type to ADeleteDialog*. This variable represents the ADeleteDialog instance.

Note: Reverse highlighted letters are keyed to Figure 106. To keep the drawings simple, we do not key all connections.

When the subparts are in place, connect them to implement the logic of the delete option (see Table 43).

Key	Connection	Description
	Table 43. (Part 1 of 2) Connecting Parts to Delete a Property from the Database	
1	selectedElement → this	PropertyUpdateView is a place-holder for the property selected in the container. Note that this connection already has been drawn in Table 38 on page 269 (see connection **1**).
	Note: The order of the next two steps is crucial!	
2	❑ commandEvent → retrieve (from Property) ❑ commandEvent → retrieve (from Property_address) ❑ commandEvent → retrieve (from Multidoc) ❑ commandEvent → retrieve (from Marketing_info) ❑ commandEvent → retrieve (from Property_log)	Retrieve each row according to the identifier value.
3	commandEvent → new	Create an instance of ADelete-Dialog.
	Note: The order of the next two steps is crucial!	

Table 43. (Part 2 of 2) Connecting Parts to Delete a Property from the Database

Key	Connection	Description
4	❏ newEvent → this ❏ newEvent → setFocus ❏ newEvent → showModally ❏ newEvent → deleteTarget	Associate the instance with the factory. ADeleteDialog is shown modally. The window instance is deleted when it closes.
5	newEvent → select	Select action is run to refresh the container after the delete.
6	this → clause	The clause is given as the parameter for the connection.
7	property_id → recordIDText	Transmit the record identifier to the delete dialog window.
Note: The order of the next two steps is crucial!		
8	❏ PushButtonOKButtonClick-Event → delete (from Property) ❏ PushButttonOKButton-ClickEvent → delete (from Property_address) ❏ PushButtonOKButtonClick-Event → delete (from Multidoc) ❏ PushButtonOKButtonClick-Event → delete (from Marketing_info) ❏ PushButtonOKButtonClick-Event → delete (from Property_log)	Delete each record in each table.
9	PushButtonOKButtonClick-Event → commit	Commit the transaction when done.

Note: Reverse highlighted letters and numbers are keyed to Figure 106 on page 275. To keep the drawings simple, we do not key all connections.

Ensure that the event-to-action connections from the menu item and the push button of APropertyUpdateView are in the proper order. To check the order, use the *Reorder Connections...* option from the part selected.

You can now save your part and generate its code. From the Visual Builder window, select *Save and generate → Part source* in the *File* pull-down menu.

As you may notice, the view is getting a bit confusing, and the parts are cluttered with too many connections. You can hide connections between parts by using the *Browse Connections* option from every part's menu. With this option, you can control the visibility of connections from and to the selected part. If you use the Browse Connections option from the free-form surface, you can hide all of the connections of the Composition Editor.

In our view, it is quite easy to identify some nonvisual parts that work exclusively together and could be gathered into one part. In the next section, we show you how to aggregate several nonvisual parts to simplify the view.

APropertyDelete

APropertyDelete is a nonvisual part created to encapsulate the operations necessary to delete a property from the database. To create this aggregate part, use the Composition Editor and build its logic visually (see Figure 107).

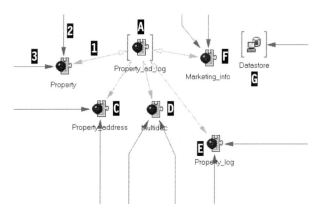

Figure 107. Building APropertyDelete

Using the Composition Editor to Build a Nonvisual Part

Follow the step-by-step instructions in Table 44 to build the nonvisual part and its components.

Step	Action
	Table 44. (Part 1 of 2) Adding Parts to Build APropertyDelete
1	From the Visual Builder window, create a nonvisual part as follows: **Field** **Value** Class name APropertyDelete Description Nonvisual part to delete properties File name VRPROP.VBB Part type Nonvisual part Base class IStandardNotifier The Part Interface Editor is displayed.
2	From the Event page of the Part Interface Editor, create a new event, **deleteEvent**, using the default settings. This event triggers the **delete** action over the five tables. To send this event to the subparts that make up APropertyDelete, you create, in step 3, an action that sends a deleteEvent notification to each subpart. When notified, each subpart executes the **delete** action.
3	From the action page of the Part Interface Editor, create a new action, **delete**, using the default settings. This action will be called from the commandEvent of APropertySearchResultView.
4	Switch to the Composition Editor.
5	Add an IVBVariablePart* part to the free-form surface and change its type to Prop_ad_log*, **A**. This variable receives its value from the Prop_ad_log variable part of APropertySearchResultView and must be promoted.
6	Promote the *this* attribute of the Prop_ad_log* variable part.
7	Add a Property* part to the free-form surface, **B**.
8	Add a Property_address* part to the free-form surface, **C**.
9	Add a Multidoc* part to the free-form surface, **D**.
10	Add a Property_log* part to the free-form surface, **E**.
11	Add a Marketing_info* part to the free-form surface, **F**

Table 44. (Part 2 of 2) Adding Parts to Build APropertyDelete

Step	Action
12	Add an IVBVariablePart* part to the free-form surface, **C**, and change its type to IDatastore*. This variable receives the database connection from APropertySearchResultView and must be promoted.
13	Promote the *this* attribute of the **IDatastore*** variable part.

Note: Reverse highlighted letters are keyed to Figure 107 on page 278.

To connect the parts to each other, refer to the original view, APropertySearchResultView, and to Table 45.

Table 45. (Part 1 of 2) Connecting Parts to Build APropertyDelete

Key	Connection	Description
1	❏ property_id → property_id (from Property) ❏ property_id → address_id (from Property_address) ❏ property_id → multidoc_id (from Multidoc) ❏ property_id → property_id (from Marketing_info) ❏ property_id → property_id (from Property_log)	Synchronize the value of each identifier for the retrieve (only the first connection is keyed in Figure 107 on page 278).
2	❏ deleteEvent → retrieve (from Property) ❏ deleteEvent → retrieve (from Property_address) ❏ deleteEvent → retrieve (from Multidoc) ❏ deleteEvent → retrieve (from Marketing_info) ❏ deleteEvent → retrieve (from Property_log)	Retrieve each record from each table (only the first connection is keyed in Figure 107 on page 278).

Table 45. (Part 2 of 2) Connecting Parts to Build APropertyDelete

Key	Connection	Description
3	❑ deleteEvent → del (from Property) ❑ deleteEvent → del (from Property_address) ❑ deleteEvent → del (from Multidoc) ❑ deleteEvent → del (from Marketing_info) ❑ deleteEvent → del (from Property_log)	Delete the property across the five tables (only the first connection is keyed in Figure 107 on page 278).
4	deleteEvent → commit	Commit the transaction in the database.

Note: Reverse highlighted numbers are keyed to Figure 107 on page 278.

Ensure that the event-to-action connections used in APropertyDelete are in the proper order. To check the order, use the *Reorder Connections...* option from the free-form surface (see Figure 108).

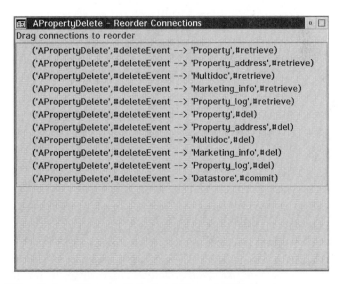

Figure 108. Order of Connections for APropertyDelete

Notice that the sequence of the part's logic is directly expressed in this window. You can follow, line by line, which statement is executed to delete each part of the property information in the five relational tables.

Before saving and generating the code, switch to the Class Editor. In the *User files included in generation* group box, type in the following file names (see Figure 109):

❏ User .hpv file: **vrppdel.hpv**
❏ User .cpv file: **vrppdel.hpv**

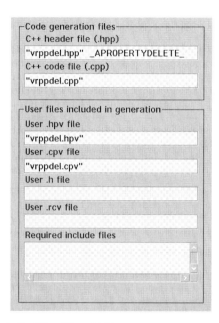

Figure 109. Detail of the Class Editor

You can save and generate the part's source and the part's features. Then, from your favorite editor, edit the vrppdel.cpv file and add the code in Figure 110 to the delete method:

```
notifyObservers(INotificationEvent(APropertyDelete::deleteEventId, *this))
```

Figure 110. Code to Generate deleteEventId

When notifyObservers is called, it notifies the event-to-action connections of APropertyDelete, which in turn triggers the **retrieve**, **delete**, and **commit** actions on the database.

To use APropertyDelete, just drop it on the free-form surface of APropertySearchResultView and connect the parts as follows (see Figure 111):

1. Connect the ***this*** attribute of the Prop_ad_log variable to the propAdLog promoted variable part of APropertyDelete, **1**.

2. Connect the ***this*** attribute of the DBConnection variable part to the dbConnection promoted variable part of APropertyDelete, **2**.

3. Connect the **pushButtonOKButtonClickEvent** event of the ADeleteDialog variable to the **del** action of APropertyDelete, **3**.

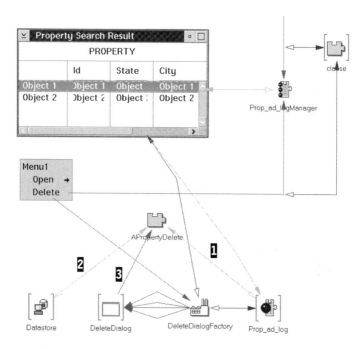

Figure 111. Using APropertyDelete Part

Notice that the Data Access Builder parts have been removed (they are still necessary for the update function). You can embed ADelete-DialogView factory and its instance in APropertyDelete part to encapsulate the entire process. You just need a connection from the commandEvent of the delete menu item to the **delete** action of APropertyDelete.

APropertySearchParameterView

APropertySearchParameterView is used to build a query on property criteria. The query is then sent to APropertySearchResultView to be executed against the database.

The query is the link attribute between APropertySearchParameter-View and APropertySearchResultView and can be traced in the design object model of the application (see Figure 41 on page 102).

When the user clicks on the *Search* push button in APropertySearch-ParameterView, the query is sent as a clause to APropertySearch-ResultView. APropertySearchResultView collaborates with a Data Access Builder part, PropertyManager, to execute the query against the database. Upon completion, the container held by AProperty-SearchResultView is updated with the matching properties.

The query is built according to the following property criteria:

❏ Area
❏ Price range
❏ Size range
❏ Number of bedrooms
❏ Number of bathrooms

The user can choose to search a property by using all or some of the criteria. The user can choose each criterion involved in the query by selecting its corresponding check box. After selecting a check box, the user can specify a value for the criterion.

Because APropertySearchParameterView includes many connections, let us build it in two phases:

❏ In the first phase ("Managing the User Input" on page 284), we show you how to use a check box control and an IVBBooleanPart to control the user input.

❏ In the second phase ("Building the Clause" on page 285), we explain how to build the clause from the user input by using an event-to-member function connection.

Managing the User Input

You manage the user input by using a check box control as a switch. This switch enables or disables user access to the criteria entry fields. To react to the selection of the check box, you use an IVBBooleanPart part that can be found in the VBSAMPLE.VBB. file. This parts holds a Boolean value and can react according to its value (for more information, consult the *Visual Builder Parts Reference*).

Two events are relevant:

valueFalseEvent   Enables the part to notify other parts as soon as its value is set to FALSE

valueTrueEvent   Enables the part to notify other parts as soon as its value is set to TRUE

The check box, in turn, is a two-status control that can be either selected or unselected. If it is selected, its *selected* attribute holds a TRUE value. If it is not selected, it holds a FALSE value.

The idea is now quite simple. We use the number of bedrooms criterion to illustrate the description (see Figure 112). The same building process applies to the other criteria. Here are the steps:

1. Connect the **selected** attribute of the check box (**A**) to the **value** attribute of IVBBooleanPart (**B**) with an attribute-to-attribute connection (**1**).

2. Connect the **valueFalseEvent** event of IVBBooleanPart to the **disable** action of the entry field (**C**) to prevent the user from typing in a value (**2**).

3. Connect the **valueTrueEvent** event of IVBBooleanPart to the **enable** action of the entry field to enable the user to enter the number of bedrooms (**3**).

4. Connect the **valueTrueEvent** event of IVBBooleanPart to the **setFocus** action of the entry field to position the cursor (**4**).

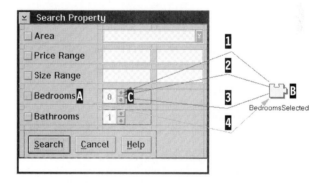

Figure 112. *Number of Bedrooms Selection*

When the application starts, the input controls (entry fields, dropdown list box, and spin buttons) are disabled because their *enabled* check box is deselected on the Control page of their settings notebook (see "APropertySearchParameterView" on page 188).

Building the Clause

The clause is built from the contents of the input controls whose corresponding check box is selected.

You use an IVBStringPart part to represent the clause. This part can be found in the VBSAMPLE.VBB file. The part is initialized with an event-to-member function connection (see "Using the Member Function Connection" on page 260 and connection **6** in Figure 115 on page 290), which triggers a member function of APropertySearchParameterView: *BuildClause*. The member function accesses:

❏ The check boxes to verify that they are selected
❏ The entry fields related to the check boxes that are selected
❏ The Clause part to set its contents

Because BuildClause is a member function of APropertySearchParameterView, each subpart can be accessed from BuildClause by its name prefixed with an *i* (see Figure 113).

```
Boolean addAnd = false;
target → iClause → assignTextToEmpty();

/* area is selected */
if( iAreaSelected → value() ) {
    iClause → appendText("area = '" + iArea → text() + "'");
    addAnd = true;
}

/* bedrooms is selected */
if( iBedroomsSelected → value() )
  if( addAnd )
    iClause → appendText(" and bedrooms = " +
            IString(iBedrooms → value()));
  else {
    iClause → appendText("bedrooms = " +
            IString(iBedrooms → value()));
    addAnd = true;
}

/* price is selected */
.....
if (addAnd)
    iClause → appendText(" and status = 'AVAILABLE'");
else
    iClause → appendText("status = 'AVAILABLE'");

return addAnd;
```

Figure 113. Code Fragment of BuildClause Member Function

The BuildClause member function is declared as a public member function with the following prototype: Boolean BuildClause(). The return code enables you to check whether the clause is empty (see "Using a Message Box to Display the Clause" on page 292). Notice that we could have declared the member function with input parameters, such as the price range or the size range, and transmitted the parameter values through parameter connections from the entry controls to the event-to-member function connection. The member function is declared in the vrpsrcv.hpv file and defined in the vrpsrcv.cpv file. These two files must be added to the definition of APropertySearchParameterView by filling in the corresponding entry fields in the *User files included in generation* group box (see "Using the Member Function Connection" on page 260).

The complete code of the BuildClause member function is given in Appendix E on page 357.

Notice that the code remains simple and does not include all controls that would be necessary for a real application.

APropertySearchParameterView collaborates with APropertySearchResultView to execute the query against the database. Similarly to the relationship between APropertySearchResultView and APropertyUpdateView or APropertyDeleteView, the collaboration is based on a use relationship: APropertySearchParameterView uses the SELECT properties service of APropertySearchResultView. APropertySearchParameterView activates the collaboration by creating an instance of APropertySearchResultView. The clause is the link attribute between these two parts. It is transmitted during the instance creation (see connection **12** in Figure 115 on page 290).

To create an instance of APropertySearchResultView, use an IVBFactory part (see "Using an Object Factory to Update the Database" on page 271).

To refine the view, add the subparts required as shown in Figure 114 and the step-by-step instructions in Table 46.

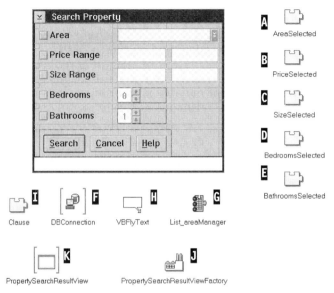

Figure 114. Subparts of APropertySearchParameterView

Table 46. Adding Parts to Build APropertySearchParameterView	
Step	**Action**
1	Open the APropertySearchParameterView part.
2	Add five IVBBooleanPart* parts on the free-form surface and change their names as follows: ❑ **A**, AreaSelected ❑ **B**, PriceSelected ❑ **C**, SizeSelected ❑ **D**, BedroomsSelected ❑ **E**, BathroomsSelected
3	Add an IDatastore* variable part, **F** to the free-form surface. This variable is transmitted to the factory of APropertySearchResult-View.
4	Add a List_areaManager* part, **G**. This part is used to list the area available from the database, in the area drop-down list box (use *Option → Add Part...* from the Composition Editor).
5	Add an IVBFlyText* part, **H**, to the free-form surface. This part is used to display the fly-over long-text help in the window info area.

Table 46.	Adding Parts to Build APropertySearchParameterView
Step	**Action**
6	Add short and long fly-over texts to the check boxes, entry fields, and push buttons.
7	Add an IVBStringPart* part, **I**, to the free-form surface. This part holds the clause built by the custom logic connection.
8	Add an IVBFactory* part, **J**, to the free-form surface. This part creates an instance of APropertySearchResultView.
9	Change the factory type to **APropertySearchResultView***.
10	Check the **Auto delete** mark on the General page of the factory notebook settings. The window instance of APropertySearchResult-View is deleted automatically when it closes. The Auto delete check mark must be checked only for visual part instances that are shown modelessly.
11	Add an APropertySearchResultView* variable part, **K**, to the free-form surface. This part represents the instance created by the factory.
Note: Reverse highlighted letters are keyed to Figure 114 on page 288.	

Once you have placed the subparts on the free-form surface, you can draw the connections as shown in Figure 115 and Table 47.

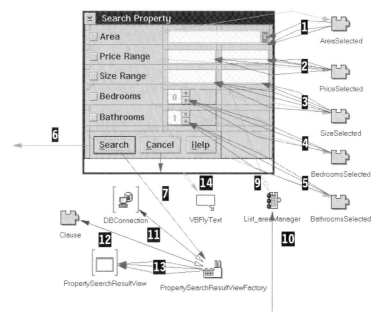

Figure 115. APropertySearchParameterView: The Big Picture

Table 47. (Part 1 of 3) Connecting Parts to Build APropertySearchParameterView	

Key	Connection	Description
1	❑ selected (checkBoxArea) → value (AreaSelected) ❑ valueTrueEvent → enable ❑ valueTrueEvent → setFocus ❑ valueFalseEvent → disable	Control the input for the area.
2	❑ selected (CheckBoxPrice) → value (PriceSelected) ❑ valueTrueEvent → enable (MinimumPrice) ❑ valueTrueEvent → enable (MaximumPrice) ❑ valueTrueEvent → setFocus (MinimumPrice) ❑ valueFalseEvent → disable (MinimumPrice) ❑ valueFalseEvent → disable (MaximumPrice)	Control the input for the price range.

Table 47. (Part 2 of 3) Connecting Parts to Build
APropertySearchParameterView

Key	Connection	Description
3	❏ selected (CheckBoxSize) → value (SizeSelected) ❏ valueTrueEvent → enable (MinimumSize) ❏ valueTrueEvent → enable (MaximumSize) ❏ valueTrueEvent → setFocus (MinimumSize) ❏ valueFalseEvent → disable (MinimumSize) ❏ valueFalseEvent → disable (MaximumSize)	Control the input for the size range.
4	❏ selected(CheckBoxBedrooms) → value (Bedrooms-Selected) ❏ valueTrueEvent → enable ❏ valueTrueEvent → setFocus ❏ valueFalseEvent → disable	Control the input for the number of bedrooms.
5	❏ selected (CheckBoxBathrooms) → value (Bathrooms-Selected) ❏ valueTrueEvent → enable ❏ valueTrueEvent → setFocus ❏ valueFalseEvent → disable	Control the input for the number of bathrooms.
Note: The order of the next two connections is crucial!		
6	buttonClickEvent → BuildClause()	Build the clause and initialize the IVBStringPart.
7	buttonClickEvent → new	Create an instance of APropertySearchResultView.
8	buttonClickEvent → close	Close the window if user selects the Cancel option.
9	items → items	Synchronize the records of the relational view with the contents of the drop-down list box.
10	ready → refresh	Load the rows of the List_area table into the IVSequence held by the List_areaManager* part.

Table 47. (Part 3 of 3) Connecting Parts to Build
APropertySearchParameterView

Key	Connection	Description
11	DBConnection → this	Transmit the database connection to APropertySearchResultView. DBConnection is a variable promoted in APropertySearchResultView.
12	Clause → this	Transmit the clause to APropertySearchResultView. Clause is a variable promoted in APropertySearchResultView.
Note: The order of the next three connections is crucial!		
13	❑ newEvent → this ❑ newEvent → setFocus ❑ newEvent → visible	Associate the instance with the factory. APropertySearchResultView is shown modelessly.
14	this → longTextControl	Set the target of the fly-over help to the window info area.
Note: Reverse highlighted numbers are keyed to Figure 115 on page 290. To keep the drawings simple, we do not key all connections.		

For additional practice, you may want to build a nonvisual part to generate the clause. For example, you can consider a part made of five attributes (area, price, size, bedrooms, bathrooms, and clause). The *clause* attribute is updated dynamically according to the value of the other attributes (see Chapter 8, "Creating Nonvisual Parts," on page 213 for a similar nonvisual part). To use the part in APropertySearchResultView, connect each *text* attribute from the drop-down list box, entry fields, and numeric spin buttons to their corresponding attribute in the nonvisual part and connect the *clause* attribute of the nonvisual part to the Clause parameter of PropertySearchResultViewFactory.

You can display the clause before it is used by PropertySearchResultViewFactory. In the next section, we show you how to use a message box to display the clause.

Using a Message Box to Display the Clause

A message box can be a useful tool for debugging your program when things go wrong (see Figure 116). You can use a message box as a substitute for the standard *printf* function to display variable or parameter values at run time. Using the message box and the Boolean part, you can manage the behavior of the box to display all types of messages ranging from informative to critical.

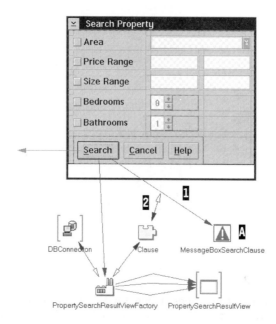

Figure 116. Using a Message Box to Display the Clause

To display the SELECT clause in a simple message box, follow the step-by-step instructions in Table 48.

Table 48. Using a Message Box to Display the Clause

Step	Action
1	Add an IMessageBox* part, **A**, to the free-form surface.
2	Connect the **buttonClickEvent** event of the *Search* push button to the **show** action of the message box, **1**.
3	Connect (see **2**) the **text** attribute of the Clause part to the **message** parameter of the connection, **1**.
4	Open the settings of the connection **2** and click on the ***Set Parameters...*** push button. In the dialog box, select ***information*** in the severity list box (see Figure 117). The severity parameter associates an icon type with the message box.

Note: Reverse highlighted numbers are keyed to Figure 116.

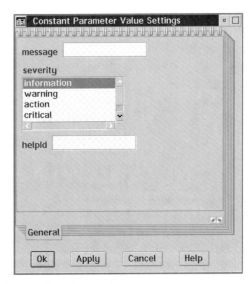

Figure 117. Message Box Parameter

Let us improve our part to display a warning message each time the clause is empty. In the following example, you use the same message box to display an information message when the clause is not empty and a warning message when the clause is empty (Figure 118).

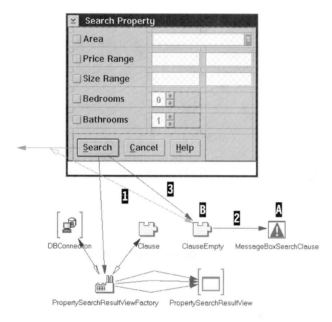

Figure 118. Using Message Box to Display a Warning Message

You use the return code (see Figure 113 on page 286) of the member function connection to decide whether or not the clause is empty:

❏ The clause is empty if the return code is equal to FALSE.
❏ The clause is not empty if the return code is equal to TRUE.

The IVBBooleanPart part provides you with the means to trigger the **show** action of the message box. Use an IVBBooleanPart part to display the warning message, as shown in the step-by-step instructions in Table 49.

Table 49. (Part 1 of 2) Using Message Box to Display a Warning Message

Step	Action
1	Add an IMessageBox* part, **A**, to the free-form surface.
2	Add an IVBBooleanPart* part, **B**, to the free-form surface.
3	Open the IVBBooleanPart* part settings and set its value to **TRUE** in selecting the *value* check box.
4	Connect the ***actionResult*** attribute of the member function connection to the ***value*** attribute of the IVBBooleanPart* part, **1**.

Table 49. (Part 2 of 2) Using Message Box to Display a Warning Message

Step	Action
5	Connect the **valueFalseEvent** event of the IVBBooleanPart* part to the **show** action of the message box, **2**.
6	Open the settings of the connection **2** and set the values as follows:

Parameter	Value
message	Clause is empty! All records will be retrieved.
severity	Warning

When the clause is empty, the IVBBooleanPart* part value is set to FALSE and triggers the display of the warning message.

Step	Action
7	Connect the **buttonClickEvent** event of the *Search* push button to the **assignValueToTrue** action of the IVBBooleanPart* part, **3**. This connection is necessary to reset the IVBBooleanPart* part so that it can notify connection **2** when the clause is empty. In effect, if the IVBBooleanPart* part value is already FALSE and the **Search** push button is clicked, connection **1** does not change the IVB-BooleanPart* part value when it triggers because it is already set to FALSE. Thus, the Boolean part does not notify connection **2**, and the warning message box does not show again.

Note: Reverse highlighted letters and numbers are keyed to Figure 118 on page 295.

Let us now use the same message box to display the clause when it is not empty. The first idea that comes to mind is to reuse the IVB-BooleanPart part to trigger the **show** action of the message box whenever the clause is not empty. In effect, you could connect the **valueTrueEvent** event of the IVBBooleanPart part to the **show** action of the message box. Unfortunately, you must reset the IVB-BooleanPart part to the FALSE value if you want the message box to show when the clause is not empty two consecutive times. Thus, you need another IVBBooleanPart part to activate the message box action (Figure 119).

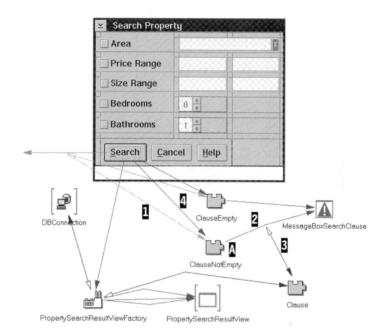

Figure 119. Message Box Displaying a Warning or Information Message

To display the clause in a message box when it is not empty, refine the part as shown in Table 50.

Table 50. (Part 1 of 2) Using Message Box to Display a Warning or Information Message	
Step	**Action**
1	Add another IVBBooleanPart* part, **A**, to the free-form surface.
2	Open the IVBBooleanPart* part settings and set its value to **FALSE** in selecting and deselecting the *value* check box. In effect, to ensure that initial part values are set the way you expect, always explicitly set them. When you drop the IVBBooleanPart* part on the free-form surface, its value is undefined. When you open the settings from the part, the check box for the value is not selected. The deselected check box indicates only that the value has never been set. To set it to **FALSE**, you must select and deselect the check box.
3	Connect the ***actionResult*** attribute of the member function connection to the **value** attribute of the IVBBooleanPart* part, **1**.

Table 50. (Part 2 of 2) Using Message Box to Display a Warning or
Information Message

Step	Action
4	Connect the **valueTrueEvent** event of the IVBBooleanPart* part to the **show** action of the message box, **2**.
5	Open the settings of connection **2** and set the severity parameter to **information**. When the clause is not empty, the IVBBooleanPart* part value is set to TRUE and triggers the display of the information message.
6	Connect (see **3**) the *text* attribute of the Clause part to the **message** parameter of connection **2**.
7	Connect the **buttonClickEvent** event of the *Search* push button to the **assignFalseToFalse** action of the IVBBooleanPart* part, **4**. This connection is necessary to reset the IVBBooleanPart* part so that it can notify connection **2** when the clause is not empty.

Note: Reverse highlighted letter and numbers are keyed to Figure 119 on page 297.

You can now save your part and generate its code. From the Visual
Builder window, select *Save and generate → Part source* in the *File*
pull-down menu.

AUpLoadView

AUpLoadView is a generic view that enables the user to export tables
in a specific directory. A command file is called for this purpose. There
is one command file per subsystem:

- ❏ BUYER.CMD command file generates export files for the tables related to the buyer information.

- ❏ PROPERTY.CMD command file generates export files for the tables related to the property information.

- ❏ SALE.CMD command file generates export files for the tables related to the sale transaction information.

In addition, the UPLOAD.CMD command file generates the export
files of all relational tables.

The export files are generated in the upload directory. The user sets the directory in two ways:

❏ By selecting the settings option from the menu bar of the Visual Realty application main window

❏ By selecting the settings option from the menu bar of the service subsystem window

AUpLoadView is reused in all subsystems. Because a different command file is used for each subsystem, it is the responsibility of each subsystem to provide AUpLoadView with the correct command file when required. A string part, **B**, is used to hold the command file name for this purpose. The text attribute of this part is promoted. Each subsystem which calls AUpLoadView initialized this attribute by providing the factory of type AUpLoadView* with the corresponding value.

The upload directory is retrieved from the application profile setup in ARealSettingsView (see "ARealSettingsView" on page 206 and Figure 120).

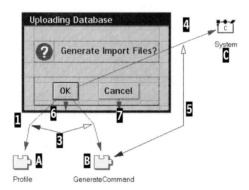

Figure 120. AUpLoadView

To build the AUpLoadView part, add the necessary subparts to the free-form surface and make the connections as shown in Table 51.

Table 51. (Part 1 of 3) Building AUpLoadView Part	
Step	**Action**
1	Open the AUpLoadView part.
2	Add an IProfile* part to the free-form surface, **A**. This part retrieves the upload directory from the application profile.

Table 51. (Part 2 of 3) Building AUpLoadView Part

Step	Action
3	Open the settings notebook of the IProfile* part and set the fields as follows: **Field** — **Value** defaultApplicationName — REAL name — REAL.INI The application profile is set to REAL.INI, and its default application name is REAL.
4	Add an IVBStringPart* variable part to the free-form surface, **B**, and promote its *text* attribute. This variable part holds the specific command file name that is to be executed. The file name is transmitted by the calling view.
5	Add an stdlibSamples* part on the free-form surface, **C**. This part is located in the VBSAMPLE.VBB file. It provides a wrapper to call your own external functions, such as a command file or external C routines.
6	Connect the **buttonClickEvent** event from the *OK* push button to the action **elementWithKey** action of the profile part, **1**. This action retrieves the data associated with a corresponding key for a specific application.
7	Open the settings of the connection **1** and set the fields as follows: **Field** — **Value** key — UPLOADPATH applName — REAL The upload directory associated with the key UPLOADPATH is retrieved from the REAL application name in the REAL.INI profile.
8	Connect the **buttonClickEvent** event from the *OK* push button to the **appendText** action of the IVBStringPart* part, **2**. This connection appends the upload path, given as a parameter, to the command file string.
9	Connect the ***actionResult*** attribute from connection **1** to the ***appendText*** attribute of connection **2** (see connection **3**). The upload directory is given as a parameter to the connection to be appended to the upload command.
10	Connect the **buttonClickEvent** event from the *OK* push button to the **system** action from the systemCommand part **4**. This connection triggers the execution of the command file.

Table 51. (Part 3 of 3) Building AUpLoadView Part

Step	Action
11	Connect the ***string*** attribute from the variable to the *text* attribute from the connection **4** (see connection **5**). The whole command line is passed to the connection as a parameter for the system command.
12	Connect the **buttonClickEvent** event from the *OK* push button to the **close** action of the frame window, **6**.
13	Connect the **buttonClickEvent** event from the *Cancel* push button to the **close** action of the frame window, **7**.

Note: The order of connections **1**, **2**, **4**, and **6** is crucial! Reverse highlighted letters and numbers are keyed to Figure 120 on page 299.

You can now save your part and generate its code. From the Visual Builder window, select *Save and generate* → *Part source* in the *File* pull-down menu.

Building this part gives us the opportunity to introduce the stdlibSamples part from VBSAMPLE.VBB. This part provides you with many actions that correspond to the functions of the standard C library. You can think of this part as a wrapper of the standard C library. To use the part, just drop it on the free-form surface and connect an event of your application to one of its actions. You may have to draw some extra connections to provide the action with the necessary parameters. If you look in VBSAMPLE.VBB, you will find other useful parts, such as stdioSamples or mathSamples. The stdioSamples part is a wrapper of the standard C input/output library; the mathSamples part provides you with a convenient way of calling general-purpose mathematic functions.

You can do your "shopping" in this file, selecting the part that suits your needs. You can browse the features of a part by using the *Browse Part Features* option from the part's pop-up menu (see Figure 121).

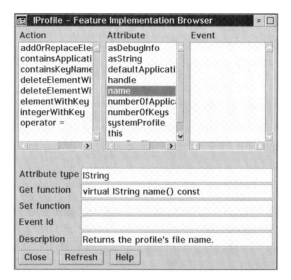

Figure 121. Browsing the IProfile Part's Features

You can, for example, check whether a part has some specific attributes that might be relevant in the context of your application and whether these attributes can be updated by some set member functions.

You cannot modify a part's feature from the browser. To modify a part's feature, use the Part Interface Editor.

APropertyManagementView

APropertyManagementView is the primary view of the Property subsystem. From this view, the user can access the main functions of the subsystem: create a property, search a property, and generate export files. Each option is associated with a graphic push button that triggers the creation of an instance of APropertyCreateView, APropertySearchResultView, or AUpLoadView according to the option selected. You use three factory parts to build this view. The visual part instances created by each factory part are shown modally to the user (Figure 122).

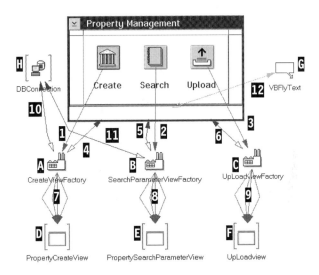

Figure 122. APropertyManagementView

To build APropertyManagementView, follow the instructions in Table 52.

Table 52. (Part 1 of 2) Building APropertyManagementView Part	
Step	**Action**
1	Open the APropertyManagementView part.
2	Add three Factory* parts to the free-form surface, **A**, **B**, **C**, and change their respective type to APropertyCreateView*, AProperty-SearchParameterView*, and AUpLoadView*.
3	Add three IVBVariablePart* parts to the free-form surface, **D**, **E**, **F**, and change their respective type to APropertyCreateView*, AProp-ertySearchParameterView*, and AUpLoadView*. Double click on F and initialize *generateCommandText* with **PROPERTY.CMD** (add one trailing blank to prevent from concatenate the upload path parameter when the **appendText** action is called in AUpLoad-View).
4	Add an IVBFlyText* part to the free-form surface, **G**.

Table 52. (Part 2 of 2) Building APropertyManagementView Part

Step	Action
5	Add an IDatastore* variable part to the free-form surface, ▇. This variable part represents the database connection established when the application starts. As explained in "Managing Database Connection" on page 246, this database connection must be propagated, through variable parts, to the view that requires it.
6	Connect the **buttonClickEvent** event of the *Create* graphic push button to the **new** action of CreateViewFactory, ▇.
7	Connect the **buttonClickEvent** event of the *Search* graphic push button to the **new** action of SearchParameterViewFactory, ▇.
8	Connect the **buttonClickEvent** event of the *Upload* graphic push button to the **new** action of UpLoadViewFactory, ▇.
9	Connect the *this* attribute of the IFrameWindow* part to the *owner* attribute of each factory part, ▇, ▇, ▇.
10	Connect each factory part to its corresponding variable with the following connections in the proper order, ▇, ▇, ▇: ❑ newEvent → this ❑ newEvent → setFocus ❑ newEvent → showModally ❑ newEvent → deleteTarget Notice that the **deleteTarget** action is necessary to clean the memory because the view instances are shown modally.
11	Connect the *this* of the DBConnection variable to the *dBConnection* attribute of CreateViewFactory, ▇. This attribute is an IDatastore* variable that is promoted in APropertyCreateView. With this connection, the database connection is transmitted to APropertyCreateView.
12	Connect the *this* of the DBConnection variable to the *dBConnection* attribute of SearchParameterViewFactory, ▇. This attribute is an IDatastore* variable that is promoted in APropertySearchParameterView. With this connection, the database connection is transmitted to APropertySearchParameterView.
13	Connect the *this* attribute of the IInfoArea* part to the *longTextControl* attribute of the IVBFlyText* part, ▇. The long fly-over help texts are displayed in the info area. You can add your own long and short fly-over help texts to the controls of your choice.

Note: Reverse highlighted letters and numbers are keyed to Figure 122.

You can now save your part and generate its code. From the Visual

Builder window, select *Save and generate → Part source* in the *File* pull-down menu.

ALogonView

When the application starts, ALogonView enables the user to connect to the database. As with ADeleteDialogView, this view is so simple that we do not provide you with step-by-step instructions. In fact, there is only one connection to draw! To complete the view:

1. Open ALogonView.

2. Connect the **buttonClickEvent** event of the *Cancel* push button to the **close** action of the frame window.

You can now save your part and generate its code. From the Visual Builder window, select *Save and generate → Part source* in the *File* pull-down menu.

ARealSettingsView

OS/2 provides the programmer with a set of functions to organize, query, read, and write pieces of data in special OS/2 files called *profiles*. Applications can use profiles to store specific information, such as the window position or font choice. The system itself uses profiles to store system configuration information. We distinguish between *system profiles*, which are used to hold operating system configuration information, and *user profiles*, which users use to store information related to their applications.

The structure of a profile is simple (Figure 123). Each piece of data is identified by a key. Collections of data are combined into groups identified by an application name. The application name must be unique in the profile. The key must be unique within a given application. To access data within a profile, you specify its application name and its key.

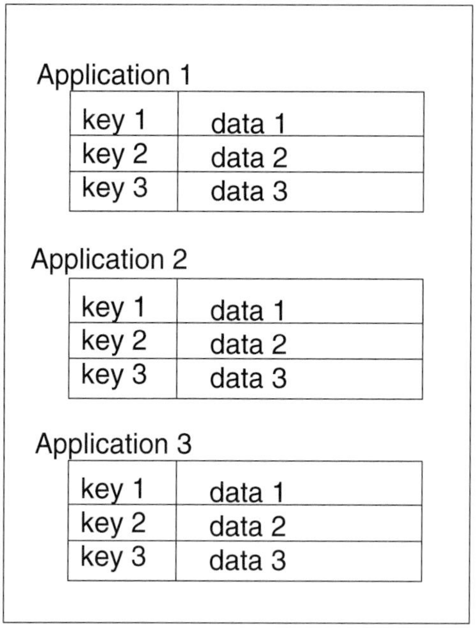

```
Application 1
  key 1    data 1
  key 2    data 2
  key 3    data 3

Application 2
  key 1    data 1
  key 2    data 2
  key 3    data 3

Application 3
  key 1    data 1
  key 2    data 2
  key 3    data 3
```

Figure 123. Structure of a Profile

ARealSettingsView is responsible for maintaining the settings of our application in such a profile. In this profile, you store information about the different directories that are accessed during database upload and download (see "ARealSettingsView" on page 206):

❑ Movie path
❑ Upload path
❑ Download path

The information is stored in the *REAL.INI* profile under the application name *REAL*. The following keys are associated with the directories:

❑ MOVIEPATH, for the movie directory
❑ UPLOADPATH, for the upload directory
❑ DOWNLOADPATH, for the download directory

To maintain a profile, ARealSettings uses the services of an IProfile part (see Figure 124). IProfile part, like IDate part, is a class interface part that has no notification ability (see "Connecting a Nonvisual Part to a Visual Part" on page 233).

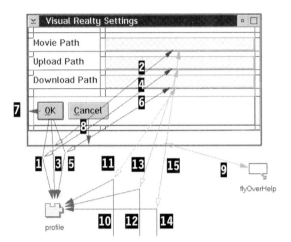

Figure 124. ARealSettings Part

Because ARealSettingsView is simple, we provide you with only one instruction table. To build this part, add the necessary subparts and make the connections as indicated in Table 53.

Table 53. (Part 1 of 3) Building ARealSettingsView Part	
Step	**Action**
1	Open the ARealSettingsView part.
2	Add an IVBFlytext* part on the free-form surface, **A**.
3	Add short and long fly-over texts to the entry fields and the push buttons.
4	Add an IProfile* part on the free-form surface, **B**. Open its settings and set up the part as follows: **Field** **Value** defaultApplicationName REAL name REAL.INI REAL.INI holds the REAL application settings.

Step	Action
	Table 53. (Part 2 of 3) Building ARealSettingsView Part
5	Connect the **buttonClickEvent** event of the *OK* push button to the **addOrReplaceElementWithKey** action of the IProfile part **1**. Then, set the connection parameters as follows: **Field** **Value** key MOVIEPATH applName REAL The data parameter is retrieved from the corresponding entry field.
6	Connect the ***text*** attribute of the movie path entry field to the *data* attribute of the connection **1** (see **2**).
7	Connect the **buttonClickEvent** event of the *OK* push button to the **addOrReplaceElementWithKey** action of the IProfile* part **3**. Then, set the connection parameters as follows: **Parameter** **Value** key UPLOADPATH applName REAL The data parameter is retrieved from the corresponding entry field.
8	Connect the ***text*** attribute of the upload path entry field to the ***data*** attribute of the connection **3** (see **4**).
9	Connect the **buttonClickEvent** event of the *OK* push button to the **addOrReplaceElementWithKey** action of the IProfile* part **5**. Then, set the connection parameters as follows: **Parameter** **Value** key DOWNLOADPATH applName REAL The data parameter is retrieved from the corresponding entry field.
10	Connect the ***text*** attribute of the download path entry field to the ***data*** attribute of the connection **5** (see **6**).
11	Connect the **buttonClickEvent** event from the *OK* push button to the **close** action of the frame window, **7**.
12	Connect the **buttonClickEvent** event from the *Cancel* push button to the **close** action of the frame window, **8**.
13	Connect the ***this*** attribute from the window info area to the ***longTextControl*** attribute of the fly-over help, **9**.

Table 53. (Part 3 of 3) Building ARealSettingsView Part

Step	Action
14	Connect the **ready** event from the free-form surface to the **elementWithKey** action of the IProfile* part, **10**. Then, set the connection parameters as follows: **Parameter** **Value** key DOWNLOADPATH applName REAL The data parameter is retrieved from the profile at startup.
15	Connect the *actionResult* attribute of connection **10** to the *text* attribute of the download path entry field, **11**.
16	Connect the **ready** event from the free-form surface to the **elementWithKey** action of the IProfile* part, **12**. Then, set the connection parameters as follows: **Parameter** **Value** key UPLOADPATH applName REAL The data parameter is retrieved from the profile at startup.
17	Connect the *actionResult* attribute of connection **12** to the *text* attribute of the upload path entry field, **13**.
18	Connect the **ready** event from the free-form surface to the **elementWithKey** of the IProfile* part, **14**. Then, set the connection parameters as follows: **Parameter** **Value** key MOVIEPATH applName REAL The data parameter is retrieved from the profile at startup.
19	Connect the *actionResult* attribute of connection **14** to the *text* attribute of the movie path entry field, **15**.

Note: The order of connections **1**, **3**, **5**, and **7** is crucial! Reverse highlighted letters and numbers are keyed to Figure 124 on page 307.

You can now save your part and generate its code. From the Visual Builder window, select *Save and generate → Part source* in the *File* pull-down menu.

ARealMainView

When the application starts, ARealMainView is displayed. From this view, the user can log on to the database, change the application settings, or access one subsystem. To access one of the subsystems, the user must establish a connection to the database. In the sections that follow, you build the ARealMainView part in four steps:

1. Implement the logon function that enables the user to connect to the database.

2. Build the access to the settings of the application and to the Property subsystem.

3. Tailor the fly-over help feature, using the attribute tear-off facility.

4. Add help to the application.

Logging on to the Database

The logon push button enables the user to access the logon view. From this view, the user can enter a user ID and a password to get connected to the REAL database. ARealMainView uses the ALogonView services to collect the logon information (Figure 125). ALogonView, in turn, uses the IDatastore services to connect to the database. If an exception occurs during the logon procedure (wrong user ID or password), a message box warns the user and prompts for the user ID and password to be reentered.

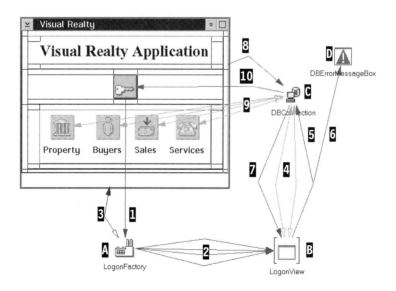

Figure 125. Logon to the Database

To implement the logon function, follow the step-by-step instructions in Table 54.

Table 54. Adding Parts for the Logon Function

Step	Action
1	Open the ARealMainView part.
2	Add an IVBFactory* part, **A**, on the free-form surface and change its type to ALogonView*. This part creates the instance of ALogonView to get the user ID and password.
3	Add an IVBVariablePart* part, **B**, to the free-form surface and change its type to ALogonView*. This part represents the ALogon-View instance created by the factory.
4	Add an IDatastore* part to the free-form surface, **C**. Open its settings and fill in the *datastoreName* attribute with the name of the database: **REAL**. This part represents the connection to the database. This part is transmitted to each subsystem to allow each to access the different tables (see "Managing Database Connection" on page 246).
5	Add an IMessageBox* part, **D**, to the free-form surface. This message box displays a warning message if the connection fails (because of incorrect authentication, for example).

Note: Reverse highlighted letters are keyed to Figure 125 on page 310.

Once you have placed the parts on the free-form surface, make the connections as shown in Table 55.

Table 55. (Part 1 of 2) Connecting Parts for the Logon Function

Key	Connection	Description
1	buttonClickEvent → new	Create an instance of ALogon-View to get the user authentication.

Note: The order of the next four connections is crucial!

Key	Connection	Description
2	❑ newEvent → this ❑ newEvent → setFocus ❑ newEvent → showModally ❑ newEvent → deleteTarget	Associate the ALogonView variable with the instance created by the factory. ALogonView is displayed as a modal window.

Table 55. (Part 2 of 2) Connecting Parts for the Logon Function

Key	Connection	Description
3	owner → this	The frame window is the owner of the instance created by the factory (ALogonView is shown modally).
4	❑ EntryFieldUserIDText → userName ❑ EntryFieldPasswordText → authentication	Transmit the userid and the password to IDatastore.
5	PushButtonOKClickEvent → connect	Connect to the database when the user validates his or her user ID and password.
6	exceptionOccurred → showException	The exception is returned by the message box, and the user can try to log on again.
7	connected → close	If the connection is established, the logon window is closed.
8	close → disconnect	Close the connection when the main window is closed.
9	❑ isConnected → enabled (Properties graphic push button) ❑ isConnected → enabled (Buyers graphic push button) ❑ isConnected → enabled (Sales graphic push button) ❑ isConnected → enabled (Services graphic push button)	Enable the different graphic push buttons to let the user access the subsystems when the database connection is established. Notice that the graphic push buttons are initially disabled at startup (see "ARealMainView" on page 208).
10	isConnected → disable	Disable the logon graphic push button to prevent the user from connecting again to the database when the connection is established.

Note: Reverse highlighted numbers are keyed to Figure 125 on page 310. To keep the drawings simple, we do not key all connections, and we do not show ARealMainView with its multicell canvases.

Notice that connection 10 is fired whenever the connection status of the IDatastore* part changes. Here you do not have to use another

Boolean part to ensure that the value is changed to TRUE. In effect, at startup, this value is set to FALSE. Thus, you can be sure that the first time it changes, it is set to TRUE.

Accessing the Application Settings and the Property Subsystem

Once the database connection is established, the user can access the Property subsystem. From the menu bar, the user can also access the settings of the application and provide the directories required, to upload or download the database to or from the server. In both cases, you use a factory to dynamically create an instance of the corresponding view (see Figure 126).

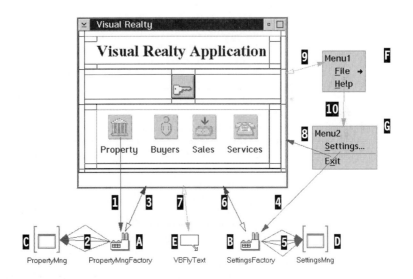

Figure 126. Application Settings and Property Subsystem Access

To complete the ARealMainView part, follow the step-by-step instructions in Table 56.

Table 56. (Part 1 of 2) Adding Parts to Access the Application Settings and Property Subsystem	
Step	**Action**
1	Add two IVBFactory* parts, **A** and **B**, to the free-form surface and change their respective types to APropertyManagementView* and ARealSettingsView*. These parts create the instances of APropertyManagementView and ARealSettingsView.

Table 56. (Part 2 of 2) Adding Parts to Access the Application Settings and
Property Subsystem

Step	Action
2	Add two IVBVariablePart* parts, **C** and **D**, to the free-form surface and change their respective types to APropertyManagementView* and ARealSettingsView*. These part represent the APropertyManagementView and ARealSettingsView instances created by each factory.
3	Add an IVBFlyText* part to the free-form surface, **E**. This part enables the fly-over help to be displayed. The short help text is displayed as a bubble help and the long help text is displayed in the window info area (see "Adding Fly-over Help to a Control" on page 247).
4	Add an IMenu* part, **F** to the free-form surface.
5	Add an IMenu* part to the first menu and change its label to **~File** (this is a shortcut to build a cascade menu). The cascade menu, **G**, enables the user to access the application settings or exit the application.
6	Add an IMenuItem* part to the first menu part and change its label to **~Help**. Open the menu item settings notebook and select **helpCommand** in the *Command type* list box. From this option, the user accesses the application general help.
7	Add an IMenuItem* part to the second menu part and change its label to **~Settings....** Open the notebook settings of the menu item and add **ALT+S** as the accelerator key: Check the **ALT** check box in the *Accelerator* group box and select the **S** key in the key drop-down list. From this option, the user accesses the application settings.
8	Add an IMenuSeparator* part to the second menu part.
9	Add an IMenuItem* part to the second menu part and change its label to **E~xit**. Open the notebook settings of the menu item and add **F3** as the accelerator key: Select the **F3** key in the key drop-down list. From this option, the user can exit the application.
10	Add short and long fly-over texts to every graphical push button and menu item.

Note: Reverse highlighted letters are keyed to Figure 126 on page 313.

Once you have placed the parts on the free-form surface, make the connections as shown in Table 57.

Table 57. (Part 1 of 2) Connecting Parts for Property Subsystem and Settings Access

Key	Connection	Description
1	buttonClickEvent → new	Create an instance of APropertyManagementView.
	Note: The order of the connections from the factory is crucial (see "Using an Object Factory to Update the Database" on page 271).	
2	❏ newEvent → this ❏ newEvent → setFocus ❏ newEvent → showModally ❏ newEvent → deleteTarget	Associate the AProperty-ManagementView variable part with the instance created by the factory. APropertyManagement-View is displayed as a modal window.
3	owner → this	The frame window is the owner of the instance created by the factory (APropertyManagement-View is shown modally).
4	commandEvent → new	Create an instance of AReal-SettingsView.
	Note: The order of the connections from the factory is crucial (see "Using an Object Factory to Update the Database" on page 271).	
5	❏ newEvent → this ❏ newEvent → setFocus ❏ newEvent → showModally ❏ newEvent → deleteTarget	Associate the ARealSettings-View variable part with the instance created by the factory. ARealSettingsView is displayed as a modal window.
6	owner → this	The frame window is the owner of the instance created by the factory (ARealSettingsView is shown modally).
7	this → longTextControl	Display the long fly-over help in the window info area.
8	commandEvent → close	Close the window when this option is selected.
9	menu → this	The menu is associated with the main window.

<table>
<tr><td colspan="3">Table 57. (Part 2 of 2) Connecting Parts for Property Subsystem and Settings Access</td></tr>
</table>

Key	Connection	Description
10	menu → this	The submenu is associated with the first menu item. This connection is built automatically when you drop a menu part on another menu part.

Note: Reverse highlighted numbers are keyed to Figure 126 on page 313. To keep the drawings simple, we do not key all connections, and we do not show ARealMainView with its multicell canvases.

To transmit the database connection to APropertyManagementView, you must connect the ***this*** attribute of the IDatastore part, DBConnection, to the ***dBConnection*** promoted variable of APropertyManagementView (this connection is not shown on Figure 126 to avoid overloading the figure.)

Tearing Off an Attribute

Fly-over help is a great feature for a novice user, but it can become a nightmare when the user gains experience. It is actually rather irritating to have a bubble help display each time you position the mouse pointer on a control with which you are already familiar. To tailor the fly-over help behavior, you can set up the delay between the time the pointer has stopped on a control and the time the bubble help is displayed. To do so, access the event handler of the fly-over help part and set its *delayTime* attribute to the value of your choice (the value is given in milliseconds).

It is not possible to access directly the *delayTime* attribute from an IVBFlyText* part. Rather, you can *tear off* its *flyOverHelpHandler* attribute and from it access the *delayTime* attribute. The torn-off attribute is not a separate part, but a variable that represents the attribute itself (Figure 127). Tearing off an attribute is like peeling an onion: From a part, you can tear off one of its attributes; then from that attribute, you can tear off another attribute, and so on.

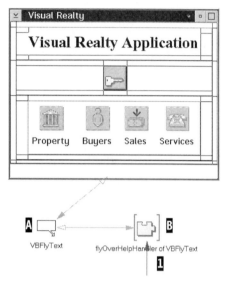

Figure 127. Tearing Off an Attribute

To tailor the fly-over help behavior of ARealMainView, follow these step-by-step instructions:

1. Select the viewText* part on the free-form surface, **A**.

2. Select the ***Tear-Off Attribute*** option from its pop-up menu. A list of the IVBFlyText* part's attributes is displayed.

3. Select ***flyOverHelpHandler*** from the list. The torn-off attribute, **B**, is created on the free-form surface as a variable that points to the flyOverHelpHandler attribute of the IVBFlyText* part.

4. Connect the **ready** event from the free-form surface to the **delay-Time** action of the torn-off attribute, **1**.

5. Double-click on the connection and click on the ***Set parameters...*** push button to set the delay time.

6. Type in the delay time in milliseconds. One thousand milliseconds is a good value.

> **Tip!**
>
>
>
> Tearing off an attribute is quite different from promoting an attribute. When you tear off an attribute, you create a reference that points to the attribute and an attribute-to-attribute connection that associates the attribute with the reference. Because most of the time the attribute is a part itself (as opposed to a primitive type such as integer or real), you can access its attributes and methods. When you promote an attribute, you generate an extra member function, which enables a composite part to access its promoted attribute. When you use the tear-off facility, you must not forget that each torn-off attribute involves creation of an attribute-to-attribute connection and its associated class. This requirement can introduce overhead in your application if the torn-off attribute is not justified.

Adding Help to Your Application

You can provide your application with two basic help types:

General help   Provides general information for a specific window, explaining its purpose and how it operates.

Context-sensitive help   Provides help information for the current choice, object, or group of choices or objects. The user can display the context-sensitive help by tabbing or moving the cursor to an object and either:

- Pressing the **F1** key (this is automatically handled by PM

or

- Selecting the *Help* push button or menu option if you have provided one

In our application we used both types of help.

Before connecting any help files to the application, you must first create them. For convenience we have provided two help sources:

- ❏ MAIN.IPF, the general help
- ❏ SETTINGS.IPF, the application settings help

Use the IPF compiler (the IPF compiler comes with the OS/2 2.1 toolkit and the OS/2 Warp toolkit) to generate a binary help file (these files have an HLP extension) for each source file by issuing the `ipfc IPF_file` command.

Then, place your HLP files in the `D:\VR\HELP` directory to make them accessible to your application. Do not forget to add the `D:\VR\HELP` directory in the HELP variable of your CONFIG.SYS system file.

To connect the help to the application, add an IHelpWindow* part on the free-form surface and set its *Help libraries* attribute to the associated help file name (this attribute is accessible from the settings notebook of the IHelpWindow* part).

To provide general help to your application, open the settings notebook of your main window and, on the Control page, enter the resource number for the general information help panel in the *Help panel id* entry field.

To provide a context-sensitive help to a subpart, open the subpart settings notebook and, on the Control page, enter the resource number for the specific information help panel in the *Help panel id* entry field.

You can associate a different help file for each application subsystem in two ways:

❑ You can add an IHelpWindow* part to the free-form surface where the main window subsystem is located and set the *Help libraries* attribute to the corresponding help file. In this way you, statically associate the help window with the main window subsystem. Use this solution when you have created multiple help library files for your application. You will use this method to connect the MAIN.HLP file to our main window (see the GeneralHelp part in Figure 128).

❑ You can dynamically associate a help window with a window that is generated by an object factory. In this case, you add an IHelpWindow* part to the free-form surface of the view that holds the factory and set the *Help libraries* attribute to the help file of the child window. Then, connect the **newEvent** event from the object factory to the **setAssociatedWindow** action of the help window. You will use this method to connect the SETTINGS.HLP help file to ARealSettings (see the SettingsHelp part in Figure 128). This solution can be used when you have one help library file for all of the panels of one subapplication. This solution enables you to gather all of the IHelpWindow* parts in the same view, thus facilitating the maintenance of several help library files.

If you have several IHelpWindow* parts in one view, you must explicitly use the **setAssociatedWindow** action to associate a window with its corresponding help library file.

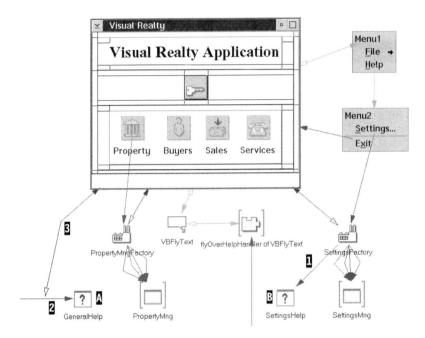

Figure 128. Adding Help to the Application

To add a help facility to the application, follow the instructions in Table 58.

Table 58. (Part 1 of 2) Adding Help to the Application	
Step	**Action**
1	Add two IHelpWindow* parts, **A** and **B**, to the free-form surface. (The IHelpWindow* part is located in the *Other* category.)
2	Open the settings window of each IHelpWindow* part and fill in the *Help libraries* entry fields as follows: **Part**　　　　　**Help libraries** GeneralHelp　　　REAL.HLP SettingsHelp　　　SETTINGS.HLP The corresponding help files are associated with their corresponding IHelpWindow* part.
3	Connect the **newEvent** event of ARealSettings factory to the **setAssociatedWindow** action of SettingsHelp,**1**.
4	Connect the **ready** event of ARealMainView to the **setAssociatedWindow** action of GeneralHelp, **2**.

Table 58. (Part 2 of 2) Adding Help to the Application

Step	Action
5	Connect the *this* attribute of the IFrameWindow* to the **associatedWindow** parameter of connection **2**, (see **3**).

You must now add the resource numbers to the settings of ARealMain-View (Table 59) and ARealSettingsView (Table 60) to access the specific help information.

Table 59. Adding Help Resource Numbers for ARealMainView

Step	Action
1	Open the settings notebook of the IFrameWindow* part.
2	Switch to the Control page and enter **100** in the *Help panel id* entry field.
3	Open the notebook settings of the graphical push button and, on the Control page, set the *Help panel id* as follows: **Button** **Help panel id** Logon 110 Properties 120 Buyers 130 Sales 140 Services 150
4	Open the notebook settings of the menu items and, on the Control page, set the *Help panel id* as follows: **Menu item** **Help panel id** File 160 Help 170 Settings 180 Exit 190
5	Save the part and regenerate its source code.

Table 60. Adding Help Resource Numbers for ARealSettingsView

Step	Action
1	Open the ARealSettingsView part.
2	Open the settings notebook of the IFrameWindow* part.

Table 60. Adding Help Resource Numbers for ARealSettingsView

Step	Action
3	Switch to the Control page and enter **200** in the *Help panel id* entry field.
4	Open the notebook settings of each entry field and, on the Control page, set the *Help panel id* as follows: **Entry field** **Help panel id** EntryFieldMovie 210 EntryFieldUpLoad 220 EntryFieldDownLoad 230
5	Save the part and regenerate its source code.

— **Tip!** —

When you generate the code for your application, Visual Builder creates a help table in the resource file (.rc) that it generates. It inserts in the help table the resource number that you specify on the Control page of each subpart. From the resource file, you can translate your help file without recompiling the entire application.

Congratulations! You have built your first subsystem. Now we suggest that you compile your code and run it in the WorkFrame/2 environment. You are now ready to take the plunge and explore other subsystems to discover new tricks for your future applications. In the next chapter, we go a step further and reveal the magic of Visual Builder: the notification framework.

10

If You Want to Know More about Visual Builder...

This chapter takes you behind the scenes of Visual Builder. After reading this chapter, you will be able to understand how drawing a connection between two parts makes them cooperate and how the code is generated. You must understand those concepts if you want to import your existing C++ code as parts in Visual Builder or build your own parts.

Notification Framework Concepts

The world of Visual Builder is ruled by notifiers and observers. A *notifier* enables other objects to register themselves as dependent on any change in the properties of the notifier. In other words, an object can tell a notifier: *I have a value that depends on one of your attributes. Could you notify me when the attribute value changes?*

Each notifier maintains a list of objects that are interested in a certain event. To register itself to a notifier, an object adds an *observer* to that list. Notifiers are responsible for publishing their supported notification events, managing the list of observers, and notifying observers when an event occurs.

Notifier objects indicate the notification events that they support by providing a series of unique identifiers in their interface. In Visual Builder, a notification ID is a unique string built from the class name and the attribute or event name, for example, IPushButton::text.

Whenever an event occurs, the notifier object sends out its notifications to all of its dependent observers. The observer can choose to either handle or ignore a notification by checking the event notification ID.

Observers and notifiers are defined in the IBM Open Class Library notification framework, respectively, as the *IObserver* and *INotifier* abstract classes.

How Visual Builder Uses the Notification Framework

Let us take a simple example. With the Composition Editor, create two visual parts: a static text and an entry field. Then, draw an attribute-to-attribute connection between the *text* attribute of the static text and the *text* attribute of the entry field so that both values always remain the same (Figure 129).

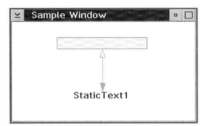

Figure 129. Sample Window: Using an Attribute-to-Attribute Connection

Visual Builder generates two default names for the parts you created: StaticText1 and EntryField1. Visual parts, such as IEntryField, generally inherit from the IWindow class, whereas nonvisual parts derive from the IStandardNotifier class. Both IWindow and IStandardNotifier provide a concrete implementation of the notifier protocol.

In Visual Builder all parts are notifiers. From there, you can deduce that drawing a connection between two parts is equivalent to creating an observer for the *source* of the connection. The connection is then responsible for updating its *target* part whenever the source undergoes any state change.

Technical Information!

The way in which you draw a connection between two parts is not innocent: The direction of the arrow determines which is the source and which is the target. The only exception to this rule is the attribute-to-attribute connection, where the connected parts play both the source and target roles (two-way arrow). However, the way in which you draw an attribute-to-attribute connection determines which attribute value will be used at initialization.

Scenario for a Connection

Let us define who the actors are in our scenario. We have two visual parts, IEntryField and IStaticText, and the connection. To simplify the scenario, we deliberately omit the IFramewindow and ICanvas parts, which are also used in our example.

Connection Class Definition

For the connection, Visual Builder generates a child class of the IObserver class as follows:

```
class sampleViewConn0 : public IObserver {
public:
    virtual  ~sampleViewConn0(){};

    //-----------------------
    // public member functions
    //-----------------------
    void initialize(IEntryField * aSource, IStaticText * aTarget)
        {source = aSource; target = aTarget;};
    ...
protected:...

private:
    //-----------------------
    // private member data
    //-----------------------
    IEntryField * source;
    IStaticText * target;
};
```

Parts and Connection Initialization

The instances of our main actors are created:

```
iEntryField1 = new IEntryField(...);
iStaticText1 = new IStaticText(...);
conn0 = new sampleViewConn0();
```

Hackers!

When generating the code, Visual Builder always prefixes any variable name with an *i*, creating names such as *iEntryField1*.

Notifiers are created disabled and must be enabled before they can notify any event. Therefore, Visual Builder parts can initialize themselves before the support for notification is effectively enabled. Notification enabling is provided by the *enableNotification* method defined in the INotifier abstract class. For our example, the entry field and static text objects are enabled as follows:

```
iEntryField1->enableNotification()
iStaticText1->enableNotification();
```

The next step is to initialize the connection with its source and target attributes and register the connection as an observer for the source part and the target part. Note that bidirectional initialization is particular to attribute-to-attribute connections; for any other connection, such as an event-to-action connection, the connection is registered only to the source part. Registration is performed through the handle-NotificationFor() method defined in the IObserver class:

```
conn0->initialize(iEntryField1, iStaticText1)
conn0->handleNotificationsFor(*iEntryField1);
conn0->handleNotificationsFor(*iStaticText1);
```

The connection is now ready to handle any event data that a notifier sends. Figure 130 summarizes the initialization process.

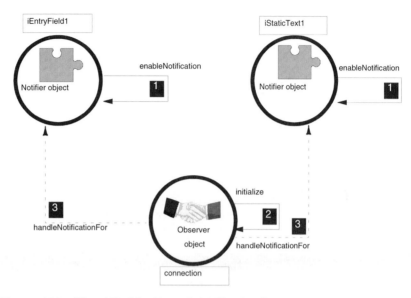

Figure 130. Visual Builder Parts Initialization Process

Notification Flow

Let us now update the text in the entry field and try to understand the sequence of events in the system. The text attribute has a unique notification ID, namely, *EntryField::textID*. The IEntryField class defines a setText() method, which is called each time the value of the text attribute must be updated. It is the responsibility of the setText() method to use the *notifyObservers()* method to indicate that the text attribute has changed. The setText() method could be implemented as follows:

```
IEntryField& IEntryField::setText(const IString& aText)
{
  if (!(iText == aText))
  {
    iText = aText;
    notifyObservers(INotificationEvent(IEntryField::textId, *this));
  } // endif
  return *this;
}
```

Whenever the notifyObservers() method is called, each observer applies the dispatchNotificationEvent() method to its list of observers. It is the responsibility of each observer to override the dispatchNotificationEvent() method according to its own needs. Usually, the first step is to check whether the corresponding event should be handled or ignored and then perform the necessary updates.

In our example, the sampleViewConn0 class redefines the dispatchNotificationEvent() method as follows:

```
protected:
    //-------------------------------
    // protected member functions
    //-------------------------------
    IObserver&
    dispatchNotificationEvent(const INotificationEvent& anEvent)
        {
          /* Initialization of target part */
          if (anEvent.notificationId() == VBINITIALIZEID) setTarget();
          if ((anEvent.notificationId() == IEntryField::textId)
              && (source == &anEvent.notifier()))
                setTarget();  /* set target to source value */
          else
          if ((anEvent.notificationId() == IStaticText::textId)
              && (target == &anEvent.notifier()))
                setSource();  /* set source to target value */
          return(*this);
        };
```

Because the conn0 instance is registered to the IEntryField observers list, the connection is said to be fired, and the setTarget() function is called, updating the value of the staticText text attribute.

Figure 131 summarizes the notification flow.

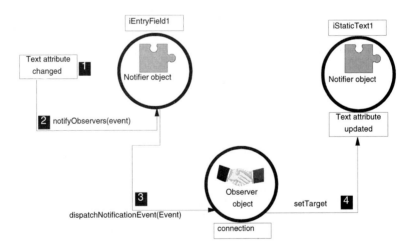

Figure 131. Visual Builder Notification Flow

Using Connections as Notifiers

Let us now modify our example: We want to bring up a message box whenever the connection cannot be fired and display the exception. We add an IMessageBox* part (see the Exceptions part in Figure 132) to our example, and we draw an event-to-action connection (connection1) between the exceptionOccurred event of the first connection (connection0) to the showException action of the Exceptions part.

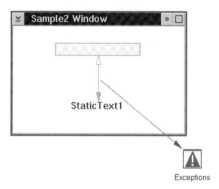

Figure 132. Sample2 Window: Using a Message Box for Exception Handling

The code generated for the connection0 definition is now different. The attribute-to-attribute connection0 plays two roles: the role of observer to perform the text attributes update and the role of notifier to send the exceptionOccurred event to connection1. The class definition generated for connection0 is now:

```
class sample2viewConn0 : public IObserver, public IStandardNotifier {
public:
    virtual  ~sample2viewConn0(){};
    //----------------------------
    // public member functions
    //----------------------------
    void initialize(IEntryField * aSource, IStaticText * aTarget)
    {
        source = aSource;
        target = aTarget;
        enableNotification();
    };
protected:

private:
    //------------------------
```

```
// private member data
//-----------------------
IEntryField * source;
IStaticText * target;
};
```

The main difference between this sample and the previous sample in "Parts and Connection Initialization" on page 326 is that connection1 has to register itself as an observer to a connection instead of a visual or nonvisual part. In addition, connection0 must enable itself for notification in the initialize function call. The parts and connections initialization is declared as follows in the generated code:

```
conn0->initialize(iEntryField1, iStaticText1)
conn0->handleNotificationsFor(*iEntryField1);
conn0->handleNotificationsFor(*iStaticText1);
conn1->initialize(conn0, iExceptions);
conn1->handleNotificationsFor(*conn0);
```

As a notifier, connection1 must call the notifyObservers() function if an exception occurs while updating the target text attribute. This notification is sent in the setTarget() function and defined as follows:

```
setTarget()
{
    try {target->setText(source->text());}
    catch (IException& exc) {
    notifyObservers(INotificationEvent(exceptionId,
                                       *this,
                                       true,
                                       IEventData((void *)&exc)));
    };
}
```

With all of the above in mind, you are ready to take your existing C++ classes and transform them into parts. The next section provides you with some guidelines to achieve that goal.

From Classes to Nonvisual Parts in Visual Builder

In this section, we convert a generic flat file class to a fully enabled nonvisual part that can be used in Visual Builder. (See Appendix E on page 357 for the source code for the flat file class.) We provide step-by-step instructions for performing this task. We focus on nonvisual parts, but the method of creating your own visual parts is exactly the same, provided that you use the IWindow class as a parent for your visual part. Another solution would be to create a child class from any visual part, such as IFrameWindow, and modify it to suit your requirements.

To achieve the transition from a C++ class to a nonvisual part, you must enable your C++ class as a notifier and declare the part interface used in Visual Builder. First, modify the class definition so that your class inherits from IStandardNotifier. Then, create a unique notification ID for all events that your part might send. Finally, modify the code to call the notifyObservers() function each time an attribute is modified (if you want the change to be public, of course). You can describe the part interface by either writing a part information file or using the Part Interface Editor in Visual Builder.

Technical Information!

If you want to use a part as the *source* for a connection, it must be able to send notifications to other parts. Thus, you must complete all modifications as described in this section. However, if you only want to use a part as the *target* of a connection, only the creation of the part interface is mandatory, and the part does not have to be enabled as a notifier. Such a part is called a *class interface* part. An example of a class interface part is provided in Chapter 8, "Creating Nonvisual Parts," on page 213.

The flatFile class has the following interface:

❑ Member data

➢ fileName (IString)
➢ currentLine (IString)
➢ fileHandler (fstream)
➢ FileIsOpened (Boolean)
➢ eofReached (Boolean)

❑ Member functions

➢ getFileName (get accessor method for the fileName attribute)
➢ setFileName (set accessor method for the fileName attribute)
➢ getCurrentLine (get accessor method for the currentLine attribute)
➢ setCurrentLine (set accessor method for the currentLine attribute)
➢ readLine
➢ readFile
➢ writeLine
➢ open
➢ close

Before you actually transform a class into a part, ask yourself the following questions:

1. Which member functions should I include in the part interface?

2. Which attributes should I include in the interface, and do I have to send an event whenever the attributes undergo a state change?

3. Do I have to create additional events that would be useful when using this part in Visual Builder?

Typically, the fileHandler, fileIsOpened, and eofReached data members are internal to the behavior of the class and should not be used from Visual Builder. Rather, you want to signal when the fileIsOpened and eofReached Booleans are TRUE. Therefore, you add the fileIsOpened and eofReached events to the part interface.

The only attributes that you have to modify or retrieve through their get and set member functions are fileName and currentLine.

Finally, you must convert the open, close, readFile, readLine, and writeLine member functions as actions.

With all of the above in mind, you can begin to write the part interface.

Describing the Part Interface

You can describe a part interface in two ways. The technique you use depends on how much code you have and how complex it is:

❏ Using the class browser, import the methods definitions of your C++ class into the Visual Builder Part Interface Editor and then create a VBB file.

❏ Write a part information file (a VBE file) and import it in Visual Builder to produce a VBB file.

Using the Part Interface Editor

The first step is to generate browser database files for your existing code. The usual method is to compile the code with the /Fb option. You might also use the browser QuickBrowse facility directly from Visual Builder. This facility is available from the Part Interface Editor *only* if you started Visual Builder from a WorkFrame/2 project in which the BrsMon action is defined.

To create the nonvisual part interface, start Visual Builder and select *Part→New*. Figure 133 shows the information to enter for the flatFile part.

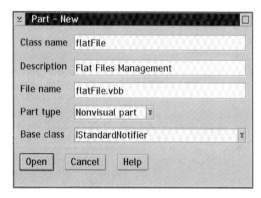

Figure 133. Part-New Window: Creating a FlatFile Nonvisual Part

In our example, the flatFile class definition is stored in the flatfile.hpp file and the implementation is in the flatfile.cpp file. You must specify this information in the *Code Generation Files* group box of the Class Editor. You also must specify user-defined file names, such as flatfile.hpv and flatfile.cpv.

To import the methods definition, switch to the Part Interface Editor and select *Browser→Open Browser Data...* from the *File* menu item. The Part Interface Editor looks for a flatfile.pdb file in the working directory (it actually builds this name from the nonvisual part name and the .pdb extension) and provides you with a list of available functions. Thus, you can avoid the long, boring task of manually entering the definition of the functions by using the Part Interface Editor (and probably introducing a few errors).

Tip!

Browser data analysis is case-sensitive. In other words, if you call your part *flatFile* and your class name is *FlatFile*, Visual Builder will not be able to import the methods definition. To avoid any naming problems, a good rule is to give the same name to your class, the corresponding nonvisual part, and the files where you store your class definition.

You can now create your attributes, actions, and events in the same way as explained in Chapter 8, "Creating Nonvisual Parts," on page 213. For example, the fileName attribute is defined as described in Figure 134. The easiest way to create the attribute definition is to enter the name for the attribute **1**, select its type **2**, click on the **Add with defaults** button **3** so that the notification ID is generated for you, and select the **get** **4** and **set** **5** methods.

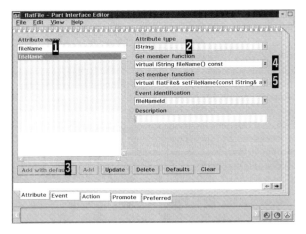

Figure 134. Part Interface Editor Window: Creating an Attribute Definition

Once you have described all of your part features, the next step is to generate the code that you have to add to your legacy code. You already have the methods definition as well as the attributes definition, so all you need is the events declaration and definition. Visual Builder appends this code to the user-defined generation files you defined in the Class Editor, namely, flatfile.hpv and flatfile.cpv.

Attention!

Be careful when saving. When you choose *Save* from any Visual Builder editor, you create a flatfile.vbb file. This is safe and highly recommended! But, if you choose *Save* then *Generate→Part Source*, you are actually creating the part, that is, you are *erasing* the flatfile.cpp and flat-file.hpp files.

To generate the code corresponding to events, select *Save and Generate→Feature source...* from the *File* menu item and select only the items from the events data members list. Then click on the **Generate selected** push button to generate the source code of the selected items. If the flatfile.cpv and flatfile.hpv files do not exist, they are automatically created. If the files exist, Visual Builder appends the generated code to them. The events definition and declaration are as follows:

```
// Definition in the flatfile.cpv file
```

```
INotificationId FlatFile::fileIsOpenedId = "FlatFile::fileIsOpened";
INotificationId FlatFile::eofReachedId = "FlatFile::eofReached";
INotificationId FlatFile::fileNameId = "FlatFile::fileName";
INotificationId FlatFile::currentLineId = "FlatFile::currentLine";
```

```
// Definition in the flatfile.hpv file
```

```
static INotificationId fileIsOpenedId;
static INotificationId eofReachedId;
static INotificationId fileNameId;
static INotificationId currentLineId;
```

Writing a Part Information File

A part information file (or VBE file) is a flat file that describes a part interface. It contains the definition of the part itself, as well as its actions, attributes, and events. Visual Builder can import a VBE file to create the corresponding VBB file. For details on the syntax of the statements you use to write such a file, see *Building VisualAge C++ Parts for Fun and Profit*.

Here is an extract of the export file that you must create to import the flatFile part in Visual Builder.

```
//VBBeginPartInfo: FlatFile,"A Flat File Management Class"
//VBParent: IStandardNotifier
//VBIncludes: "FlatFile.hpp" _FLATFILE_
//VBPartDataFile: FlatFile.vbb
//VBComposerInfo: nonvisual
//VBEvent: fileName, "fileName",fileNameId
//VBAttribute: fileName,
//VB:          "The file Name",
//VB:          IString,
//VB:          IString fileName() const,
//VB:          FlatFile& setFileName(const IString& aFileName),
//VB:          fileNameId
//VBAction: close
//VB:       "Close the flat file",,
//VB:       FlatFile& close()
   ...
//VBEndPartInfo: FlatFile
```

This method is quite efficient in terms of time and simplicity if you have a class with few methods and few attributes. You can also use REXX, for example, to write templates for part information files and develop a script that would generate the export file for you from the class information.

Modifying Your Code

To use your part as a *source* for a connection, you must modify it to become a notifier. Modify its definition as follows:

```
class FlatFile: public IStandardNotifier {
  public:...
};
```

Because your part uses the IBM Open Class Library notification framework, you must include the corresponding definition files as well as the files generated from the Part Interface Editor. Include the following files in the flatfile.cpp file:

- ❑ inotifev.hpp
- ❑ iobservr.hpp
- ❑ istdntfy.hpp
- ❑ ivbdefs.h
- ❑ flatfile.hpp
- ❑ flatfile.cpv

The flatfile.hpp file must include the flatfile.hpv file within the private (or protected) section of the class definition:

```
class FlatFile: public IStandardNotifier {
public:
    ...
protected:
    ...
private:
#include "FlatFile.hpv"
};   //FlatFile
```

Now your part must send a list of events to the "external world." Therefore, you must call the notifyObservers() method each time an attribute of your part is modified or whenever you want to signal a particular event. For example, whenever the fileName attribute of your FlatFile class changes, you call the notifyObservers() method by modifying the setFileName() method as follows:

```
FlatFile& FlatFile::setFileName(const IString& aFileName)
{
  if ( fileName != aFileName ) {
     fileName = aFileName;
     notifyObservers(INotificationEvent(FlatFile::fileNameId, *this));
  }
  return *this;
}
```

Attention!

To avoid unnecessary overhead, we highly recommend testing the new value to be assigned to an attribute *before* calling the notifyObservers() function.

Congratulations! Your class is now a part and you can fully exploit its power from Visual Builder.

When Parts Become Observers...

Let us take a simple example of a part becoming an observer. With the Composition Editor, create a defaultButtons visual part from an ICanvas* part and three IPushButton* subparts as depicted in Figure 135.

Figure 135. The defaultButtons Composite Visual Part

The defaultButtons visual part can be reused in other visual parts to provide a standard look and feel in your applications. For this purpose, you must be able to access the defaultButtons subparts' features from any of the parts where you reuse the defaultButtons part. You know by now that this is not possible unless you promote the features of the subparts, that is, the features of the three push buttons. Let us promote the buttonClickEvent event feature of each push button and examine the generated code.

The first thing you notice when you look at the code is that the defaultButtons part inherits from both the ICanvas and IObserver classes:

```
class defaultButtons : public ICanvas, public IObserver {
public:
   ...
};
```

In fact, the defaultButtons part must be able to observe the subparts whose features are promoted and catch the notification events corresponding to the promoted features. To publish those events, Visual Builder generates the defaultButtons source code so that one notification event ID is created for each promoted feature, and each promoted feature is added to the defaultButtons public interface:

// Declaration in the defaultb.hpp file

```
static const INotificationId pBOkButtonClickEvent;
static const INotificationId pBCancelButtonClickEvent;
static const INotificationId pBHelpButtonClickEvent;
```

// Definition in the defaultb.cpp file

```
const INotificationId defaultButtons::pBOkButtonClickEvent =
            "defaultButtons::pBOkButtonClickEvent";

const INotificationId defaultButtons::pBCancelButtonClickEvent =
            "defaultButtons::pBCancelButtonClickEvent";

const INotificationId defaultButtons::pBHelpButtonClickEvent =
            "defaultButtons::pBHelpButtonClickEvent";
```

To observe its subparts, the defaultButtons part must register itself to the list of observers of each subpart that has a promoted feature. For this purpose, Visual Builder generates a call to the handleNotificationFor() method in the initializePart() method of the defaultButtons part for each subpart that has a promoted feature:

```
defaultButtons & defaultButtons::initializePart()
{
   this->handleNotificationsFor(*iPBOk);
   this->handleNotificationsFor(*iPBCancel);
   this->handleNotificationsFor(*iPBHelp);
   makeConnections();
   notifyObservers(INotificationEvent(readyId, *this));
   return *this;
}
```

Visual Builder also generates one member function for each subpart that has at least one promoted feature. This member's feature returns the subpart itself and is used when the defaultButton is reused in another part to access the subpart features:

```
IPushButton *  getPBOk() const { return iPBOk };
IPushButton *  getPBCancel() const { return iPBCancel; };
IPushButton *  getPBHelp() const { return iPBHelp; };
```

As an observer, the defaultButtons part must override the dispatchNo-tificationEvent() virtual method. Basically, the defaultButtonsPart maps the notification event published by its subparts to the new notification events created for each promoted feature. As an example, the following piece of code captures the buttonClickId from the *OK* push button and publishes it under its new name:

```
IObserver&
defaultButtons::dispatchNotificationEvent(const INotificationEvent & anE
vent)
{
  if ((anEvent.notificationId() == IPushButton::buttonClickId)
      &&
      (iPBOk == &anEvent.notifier()))
      notifyObservers(INotificationEvent(pBOkButtonClickEvent,
                              *this,
                              anEvent.hasNotifierAttrChanged(),
                              IEventData((void *)anEvent.eventData()),
                              anEvent.observerData()));
    else
      ...
}
```

Congratulations! You are now experts on the IBM notification framework and its application in Visual Builder.

Chapter 10. If You Want to Know More about Visual Builder...

339

Installing the Application

All of the files that you need to run the sample application are stored
in the CD-ROM that accompanies this book. If you do not have the
required products, the CD-ROM provides you with a trial version of
DB2™ Version 2 (DB2 Software Developer's Kit included) and Visual-
Age for C++ for OS/2.

To make it easy for you to install the Visual Realty application, we have included an installation program on the CD-ROM itself. This program copies all the files you need to the correct locations on your hard disk and creates the WorkFrame/2™ projects.

Follow these steps to install the Visual Realty application:

1. Insert the CD-ROM into your CD-ROM drive.
2. Open the CD-ROM drive from the drive folder.
3. Double-click on the **install.exe** program to start the installation.
4. Follow the on-screen directions in the install program.

Consult the READ.ME file located on your CD-ROM for the latest information regarding the sample application and the installation procedure.

B

OMT Notation

In this appendix we show the schema representation of the object model (see Figure 136) and the state diagram (see Figure 137) for the Object Modeling Technique method.

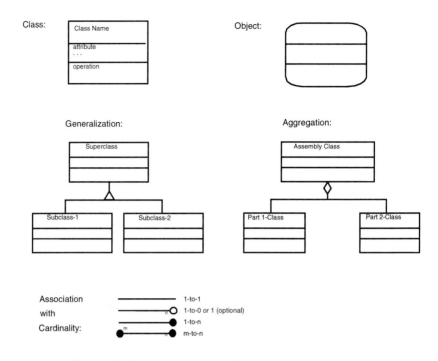

Source: Object-Oriented Modeling and Design - James Rumbaugh et al.

Figure 136. OMT Notation: Object Model

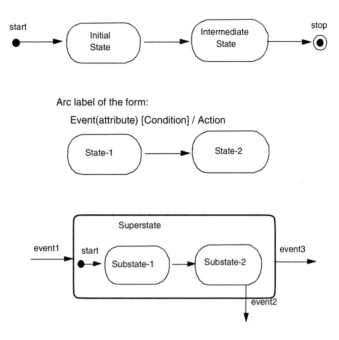

Arc label of the form:

Event(attribute) [Condition] / Action

Figure 137. OMT Notation: State Diagram

C

Database Definition

This appendix lists the data definition language that defines the layout of the relational tables used in the Visual Realty application.

BUYER_ADDRESS TABLE

```
CREATE TABLE USERID.BUYER_ADDRESS
       ( ADDRESS_ID CHAR(11) NOT NULL,
         STREET CHAR(40),
         AREA CHAR(40) NOT NULL,
         CITY CHAR(40),
         STATE CHAR(2),
         ZIP_CODE CHAR(5) FOR BIT DATA,
         PRIMARY KEY ( ADDRESS_ID ) )
```

BUYER TABLE

```
CREATE TABLE USERID.BUYER
       ( BUYER_ID CHAR(11) NOT NULL,
         FIRST_NAME CHAR(20) NOT NULL,
         LAST_NAME CHAR(20) NOT NULL,
         MARITAL_STATUS CHAR(1),
```

```
                              GENDER CHAR(1),
                              INCOME DECIMAL(15,2),
                              WORK_PHONE CHAR(12) FOR BIT DATA,
                              HOME_PHONE CHAR(12) FOR BIT DATA,
                              PRIMARY KEY ( BUYER_ID ) )
```

BUYER_LOG TABLE
```
            CREATE TABLE USERID.BUYER_LOG
                    ( BUYER_ID CHAR(11) NOT NULL,
                      CREATION_TIMESTAMP TIMESTAMP,
                      LAST_UPDATE TIMESTAMP,
                      PRIMARY KEY ( BUYER_ID ) )
```

MARKETING_INFO TABLE
```
            CREATE TABLE USERID.MARKETING_INFO
                    ( PROPERTY_ID CHAR(5) NOT NULL,
                      PRICE DECIMAL(7,0) NOT NULL,
                      DAYS_ON_MARKET SMALLINT,
                      COMMISSION_RATE DECIMAL(5,2),
                      DOWN_PAYMENT_RATE DECIMAL(5,2),
                      PRIMARY KEY ( PROPERTY_ID ) )
```

MULTIDOC TABLE
```
            CREATE TABLE USERID.MULTIDOC
                    ( MULTIDOC_ID CHAR(5) NOT NULL,
                      FILENAME VARCHAR(254) NOT NULL,
                      TYPE CHAR(20) NOT NULL,
                      PRIMARY KEY ( MULTIDOC_ID ) )
```

PREFERENCE TABLE
```
            CREATE TABLE USERID.PREFERENCE
                    ( BUYER_ID CHAR(11) NOT NULL,
                      MAX_PRICE DECIMAL(15,2),
                      MIN_PRICE DECIMAL(15,2),
                      MAX_SIZE DECIMAL(15,2),
                      MIN_SIZE DECIMAL(15,2),
                      BEDROOMS SMALLINT,
                      BATHROOMS SMALLINT,
                      STORIES SMALLINT,
                      HEATING CHAR(30),
                      COOLING CHAR(30),
                      PRIMARY KEY ( BUYER_ID ) )
```

PROPERTY TABLE
```
            CREATE TABLE USERID.PROPERTY
                    ( PROPERTY_ID CHAR(5) NOT NULL,
                      SIZE DECIMAL(5,0) NOT NULL,
                      BEDROOMS SMALLINT NOT NULL,
                      BATHROOMS SMALLINT NOT NULL,
                      STORIES SMALLINT NOT NULL,
```

```
                    COOLING CHAR(30) NOT NULL,
                    HEATING CHAR(30) NOT NULL,
                    DESCRIPTION VARCHAR(512),
                    PRIMARY KEY ( ( PROPERTY_ID ) )
```

PROPERTY_ADDRESS TABLE

```
          CREATE TABLE USERID.PROPERTY_ADDRESS
                    ( ADDRESS_ID CHAR(5) NOT NULL,
                    STREET CHAR(40) NOT NULL,
                    AREA CHAR(40),
                    CITY CHAR(40) NOT NULL,
                    STATE CHAR(2),
                    ZIP_CODE CHAR(5) FOR BIT DATA,
                    PRIMARY KEY ( ( ADDRESS_ID ) )
```

PROPERTY_LOG TABLE

```
          CREATE TABLE USERID.PROPERTY_LOG
                    ( PROPERTY_ID CHAR(5) NOT NULL,
                    DOWNLOAD_TIMESTAMP TIMESTAMP NOT NULL,
                    LAST_UPDATE TIMESTAMP NOT NULL,
                    STATUS CHAR(15) NOT NULL,
                    PRIMARY KEY ( PROPERTY_ID ) )
```

SALE_TRANSACTION TABLE

```
          CREATE TABLE USERID.SALE_TRANSACTION
                    ( TRANSACTION_ID TIMESTAMP NOT NULL,
                    LAST_UPDATE TIMESTAMP NOT NULL,
                    AGREEMENT_FORM_ID INTEGER NOT NULL,
                    STATUS CHAR(10) NOT NULL,
                    BUYER_ID CHAR(11) NOT NULL,
                    PROPERTY_ID CHAR(5) NOT NULL,
                    PRIMARY KEY ( TRANSACTION_ID ) )
```

PROP_AD_LOG VIEW

```
          CREATE VIEW USERID.PROP_AD_LOG
                    ( PROPERTY_ID,
                    SIZE,
                    BEDROOMS,
                    BATHROOMS,
                    AREA,
                    CITY,
                    STATE,
                    STATUS,
                    PRICE,
                    COMMISSION_RATE,
                    DOWN_PAYMENT_RATE) AS
          SELECT A.PROPERTY_ID,
                    SIZE,
                    BEDROOMS,
                    BATHROOMS,
```

```
                        AREA,
                        CITY,
                        STATE,
                        STATUS,
                        PRICE,
                        COMMISSION_RATE,
                        DOWN_PAYMENT_RATE
            FROM USERID.PROPERTY A,
                USERID.PROPERTY_ADDRESS B,
                USERID.PROPERTY_LOG C
                USERID.MARKETING_INFO D
            WHERE ( A.PROPERTY_ID=ADDRESS_ID AND
                    A.PROPERTY_ID=C.PROPERTY_ID AND
                    A.PROPERTY_ID=D.PROPERTY_ID )
```

BUYER_INFO VIEW

```
            CREATE VIEW USERID.BUYER_INFO
                    ( BUYER_ID,
                      FIRST_NAME,
                      LAST_NAME,
                      INCOME,
                      WORK_PHONE,
                      HOME_PHONE,
                      STREET,
                      AREA
                      CITY,
                      STATE,
                      ZIP_CODE) AS
            SELECT  BUYER_ID,
                      FIRST_NAME,
                      LAST_NAME,
                      INCOME,
                      WORK_PHONE,
                      HOME_PHONE,
                      STREET,
                      AREA,
                      CITY,
                      STATE,
                      ZIP_CODE
              FROM USERID.BUYER A,
                  USERID.BUYER_ADDRESS B,
              WHERE ( BUYER_ID=ADDRESS_ID )
```

LIST_AREA VIEW

```
            CREATE VIEW USERID.LIST_AREA
                    ( AREA ) AS
            SELECT DISTINCT AREA FROM
                    USERID.PROPERTY_ADDRESS A,
```

```
                    USERID.PROPERTY_LOG B
       WHERE ( ADDRESS_ID=PROPERTY_ID ) AND
              ( STATUS='AVAILABLE') )
```

D Class Dictionary

In this appendix we list the parts that you need to build the sample application.

Visual Parts

Part Name	VBB File	File Stem	Description
AAddressView	VRCOMM	vrcadrv	Address view of buyer and property
ADeleteDialogView	VRCOMM	vrcdel	Warning delete dialog view
ALogonView	VRCOMM	vrclogv	Logon view to connect to the database
ARealSettingsView	VRCOMM	vrcrsetnv	Application settings view
APropertyCreateView	VRPROP	vrpcrtv	View for recording property
APropertyManagement-View	VRPROP	vrpmngv	Primary view of the property subsystem
APropertySearchParam-eterView	VRPROP	vrpsrcv	Search criteria view for property
APropertySearchResult-View	VRPROP	vrpsrrsv	Tabular view of properties
APropertyUpdateView	VRPROP	vrpupdv	View for updating property
APropertyView	VRPROP	vrpprpv	Property view
AUpLoadView	VRSERV	vrcuplv	Dialog box for generating the export files
ARealMainView	VRMAIN	vrmain	Main application view

Nonvisual Parts

Part Name	VBB File	File Stem	Description
NumDecOnlyKbdHandler	KBDHDR	kbdhdr	General-purpose keyboard handler
NumOnlyKbdHandler	KBDHDR	kbdhdr	General-purpose keyboard handler
UpperCaseKbdHandler	KBDHDR	kbdhdr	General-purpose keyboard handler
AMarketingInfo	VRPROP	vrpmrkt	Calculate property derived attributes
List_area	VRPROP	vrpcrtv	DACS part of LIST_AREA view
List_areaManager	VRPROP	vrpmngv	VDACS part of LIST_AREA view
Marketing_info	VRPROP	vrpsrcv	DACS part of MARKETING_INFO table
Marketing_infoManager	VRPROP	vrpsrrsv	DACS part of MARKETING_INFO table

Part Name	VBB File	File Stem	Description
Multidoc	VRPROP	vrpsrrsv	DACS part of MULTIDOC table
MultidocManager	VRPROP	vrpsrrsv	DACS part of MULTIDOC table
Property	VRPROP	vrpsrrsv	DACS part of PROPERTY table
PropertyManager	VRPROP	vrpsrrsv	DACS part of PROPERTY table
Property_address	VRPROP	vrpsrrsv	DACS part of PROPERTY_ADDRESS table
Property_addressManager	VRPROP	vrpsrrsv	DACS part of PROPERTY_ADDRESS table
Property_log	VRPROP	vrpsrrsv	DACS part of PROPERTY_LOG table
Property_logManager	VRPROP	vrpsrrsv	DACS part of PROPERTY_LOG table
Property_ad_log	VRPROP	vrpsrrsv	DACS part of PROP_AD_LOG view
Property_ad_logManager	VRPROP	vrpsrrsv	DACS part of PROP_AD_LOG view

E Source Listings

In this appendix we provide the source code for the BuildClause member function of APropertySearchParameterView (see Figure 138 on page 358). We also give the source code for the FlatFile class (see Figure 139 on page 358 and Figure 140 on page 359).

BuildClause member function

```
/*********************************************************************/
/*                                                                 */
/*    Declaration of the BuildClause member function               */
/*                                                                 */
/*    Description:                                                  */
/*          This method builds an SQL clause from entry controls.   */
/*          The inputs are selected according to the status of      */
/*          APropertySearchParameterView check boxes.               */
/*                                                                 */
/*********************************************************************/
public:
        Boolean APropertySearchParameterView::BuildClause();
```

Figure 138. BuildClause Member Function: Declaration

Flat File Class

```
/*********************************************************************
 * FILE NAME: FLATFILE.h                                            *
 *                                                                  *
 * DESCRIPTION:                                                     *
 *   Constant declarations for class:                               *
 *     FlatFile- This part handles a file                           *
 * ---------------------------------------------------------------- *
 * Warning: This file was generated by the VisualAge C++            *
 * Visual Builder.                                                  *
 * Modifications to this source file will be lost when the part     *
 * is regenerated.                                                  *
 *********************************************************************/
#ifndef _ICCONST_
#include <icconst.h>
#endif
#ifndef _IVBDEFS_
#include <ivbdefs.h>
#endif
#ifndef WND_FlatFile
#define WND_FlatFile  VBBASEWINDOWID
#endif
```

Figure 139. Flat File Class: H File

```
/*************** FILE NAME: FLATFILE.hpp ***************************
 *                                                              *
 * DESCRIPTION:                                                 *
 *   Declaration of the class:                                  *
 *     FlatFile- This part handles a file                       *
 * ------------------------------------------------------------ *
 * Warning: This file was generated by the VisualAge C++        *
 * Visual Builder.                                              *
 * Modifications to this source file will be lost when the part *
 * is regenerated.                                              *
 ****************************************************************/
#ifndef _FLATFILE_
#define _FLATFILE_
class FlatFile;
#ifndef _ISTDNTFY_
#include <istdntfy.hpp>
#endif
#include "istring.hpp"
#include "fstream.h"
#include "FLATFILE.h"



/*--------------------------------------------------------------*/
/* Align classes on four-byte boundary.                         */
/*--------------------------------------------------------------*/
#pragma pack(4)
//****************************************************************
// Class definition for FlatFile
//****************************************************************
class FlatFile : public IStandardNotifier {
public:
    //------------------------------------------------------------
    // Constructors / destructors
    //------------------------------------------------------------
```

Figure 140. (Part 1 of 2) Flat File Class: HPP File

```
    FlatFile();
    virtual  ~FlatFile();
    //-----------------------------------------------------------------
    // public member functions
    //-----------------------------------------------------------------
    virtual FlatFile & initializePart();
    // public member data
    //-----------------------------------------------------------------
    static const INotificationId readyId;
protected:
    //-----------------------------------------------------------------
    // protected member functions
    //-----------------------------------------------------------------
    virtual Boolean makeConnections();
private:
#include "flatfile.hpv"
};    //FlatFile



/*----------------------------------------------------------------*/
/* Resume compiler default packing.                               */
/*----------------------------------------------------------------*/
#pragma pack()
#endif
```

Figure 140. (Part 2 of 2) Flat File Class: HPP File

```
/******************** FILE NAME: FLATFILE.cpp ************************
 *                                                                 *
 * DESCRIPTION:                                                    *
 *   Class implementation of the class:                           *
 *      FlatFile- This part handles a file                        *
 * --------------------------------------------------------------- *
 * Warning: This file was generated by the VisualAge C++          *
 * Visual Builder.                                                 *
 * Modifications to this source file will be lost when the part    *
 * regenerated.                                                    *
 ******************************************************************/
#ifndef _INOTIFEV_
#include <inotifev.hpp>#endif


#ifndef _IOBSERVR_
#include <iobservr.hpp>#endif


#ifndef _ISTDNTFY_
#include <istdntfy.hpp>
#endif
#ifndef _FLATFILE_
#include "FLATFILE.HPP"
#endif
#ifndef _IVBDEFS_
#include <ivbdefs.h>
#endif
#ifndef _ITRACE_
#include <itrace.hpp>
#endif


#pragma export (FlatFile::readyId)
const INotificationId FlatFile::readyId = "FlatFile::readyId";
//-----------------------------------------------------------------
// FlatFile :: FlatFile
//-----------------------------------------------------------------
```

Figure 141. (Part 1 of 2) Flat File Class: CPP File

```
#pragma export (FlatFile::FlatFile())
FlatFile::FlatFile()
{
}     //end constructor
//----------------------------------------------------------------------------
// FlatFile :: ~FlatFile
//----------------------------------------------------------------------------
#pragma export (FlatFile::~FlatFile())
FlatFile::~FlatFile()

{

}
//----------------------------------------------------------------------------
// FlatFile :: initializePart
//----------------------------------------------------------------------------
#pragma export (FlatFile::initializePart())
FlatFile & FlatFile::initializePart()
{
   makeConnections();
   notifyObservers(INotificationEvent(readyId, *this));
   return *this;
}



//----------------------------------------------------------------------
// FlatFile :: makeConnections
//----------------------------------------------------------------------
#pragma export (FlatFile::makeConnections())
Boolean FlatFile::makeConnections()
{
   this->enableNotification();
   return true;
}


#include "flatfile.cpv"
```

Figure 141. (Part 2 of 2) Flat File Class: CPP File

```
// Default Part Code Generation begins here...
public:
  FlatFile& close();
  FlatFile& open( IString newFileName );
  FlatFile& readLine();
  FlatFile& readFile();
  FlatFile& setCurrentLine(const IString& aNewLine);
  FlatFile& writeLine(IString aLine);
  FlatFile& setFileName(const IString& aFileName);
  IString fileName() const;
  IString currentLine() const;
  static INotificationId currentLineId;
  static INotificationId endOfFileId;
  static INotificationId openedId;
private:
  IString iFileName;
  IString iCurrentLine;
  fstream aFile;
  Boolean eofReached;
  Boolean aFileIsOpen;
// Default Part Code Generation ends here.
```

Figure 142. Flat File Class: HPV File

```
// Default Part Code Generation begins here...
INotificationId FlatFile::openedId = "FlatFile::opened";
INotificationId FlatFile::endOfFileId = "FlatFile::endOfFile";
INotificationId FlatFile::currentLineId = "FlatFile::currentLine";


IString FlatFile::fileName() const
{
   IFUNCTRACE_DEVELOP();
   return iFileName;
}


FlatFile& FlatFile::setFileName(const IString& aFileName)
{
   IFUNCTRACE_DEVELOP();
   if (iFileName != aFileName)
   {
      iFileName = aFileName;
   }
   return *this;
}
IString FlatFile::currentLine() const
{
   IFUNCTRACE_DEVELOP();
  return iCurrentLine;
}
FlatFile& FlatFile::setCurrentLine(const IString& aNewLine)
{
   IFUNCTRACE_DEVELOP();
   iCurrentLine = aNewLine;
   ITRACE_DEVELOP( "NewLine ->" + iCurrentLine );
   notifyObservers(INotificationEvent(FlatFile::currentLineId, *this))
;
   return *this;
}
FlatFile& FlatFile::readLine()
{
   IFUNCTRACE_DEVELOP();
```

Figure 143. (Part 1 of 3) Flat File Class: CPV File

```
        IString strNewLine = IString::lineFrom( aFile );
        ITRACE_DEVELOP( "Line -> " + strNewLine  );
        if( aFile.fail() )
        {
         eofReached = true;
         notifyObservers(INotificationEvent(FlatFile::endOfFileId, *this));;
        }
        else
        {
         setCurrentLine( strNewLine );
        }
        return *this;
}


FlatFile& FlatFile::readFile()
{
    IFUNCTRACE_DEVELOP();
    while( eofReached == false )
    {
        readLine();
    } /* endwhile */
    return *this;
}
// be aware that this function writes at the end of file only
FlatFile& FlatFile::writeLine(IString aLine)
{
    IFUNCTRACE_DEVELOP();
    ITRACE_DEVELOP( "Writing -> " + aLine );
    // save read pointer
    long mark = aFile.tellg();
    // write line ( always to end of file )
    aLine = aLine + "\n";
    aFile << aLine;
    // restore read pointer
    aFile.seekg( mark );
    return *this;
}
```

Figure 143. (Part 2 of 3) Flat File Class: CPV File

```
{
   IFUNCTRACE_DEVELOP();
   if( aFileIsOpen )
   {
      close();
   } /* endif */
   ITRACE_DEVELOP( "Opening-> " + newFileName );
   // open file for read and append
   aFile.open( newFileName, ios::in | ios::app );
   if( aFile.fail() == 0 )
   {
      eofReached = false;
      aFileIsOpen = true;
      iFileName = newFileName;
      // reset file position to beginning of file
      aFile.seekg( 0, ios::beg );
      notifyObservers(INotificationEvent(FlatFile::openedId, *this));
   } /* endif */
   else
   {
      IAccessError exc = IAccessError( "Could not open file: " +
                                       iFileName );
      ITHROW( exc );
   }
   return *this;
}
FlatFile& FlatFile::close()
{
   IFUNCTRACE_DEVELOP();
   if( aFileIsOpen )
   {
      aFile.close();
      aFileIsOpen = false;
      iFileName = " ";
   } /* endif */
   return *this;
}


// Feature source code generation begins here...


// Feature source code generation ends here.
```

Figure 143. (Part 3 of 3) Flat File Class: CPV File

Glossary

This glossary defines terms and abbreviations that are used in this book. If you do not find the term you are looking for, refer to the *IBM Dictionary of Computing*, New York:McGraw-Hill, 1994.

This glossary includes terms and definitions from the *American National Standard Dictionary for Information Systems*, ANSI X3.172-1990, copyright 1990 by the American National Standards Institute (ANSI). Copies may be purchased from the American National Standards Institute, 1430 Broadway, New York, New York 10018.

A

abstract class. A class that provides common behavior across a set of subclasses but is not itself designed to have instances that work. An abstract class represents a concept; classes derived from it represent implementations of the concept. For example, IControl is the abstract base class for control view windows; the ICanvas and IListBox classes are controls derived from IControl. An abstract class must have at least one pure virtual function.

See also *base class*.

access. A property of a class that determines whether a class member is accessible in an expression or declaration.

action. A specification of a function that a part can perform. The Visual Builder uses action specifications to generate connections between parts. Actions are resolved to member function calls in the generated code.

Compare to *attribute* and *event*.

argument. A data element, or value, included as part of a member function call. Arguments provide additional information that the called member function can use to perform the requested operation.

attribute. A specification of a property of a part. For example, a customer part could have a name attribute and an address attribute. An attribute can itself be a part with its own behavior and attributes.

The Visual Builder uses attribute specifications to generate code to get and set part properties.

Compare to *action* and *event*.

attribute-to-action connection. A connection that starts an action whenever an attribute's value changes. It is similar to an event-to-action connection because the attribute's event ID is used to notify the action when the value of the attribute changes.

See also *connection*. Compare to *event-to-action connection*.

attribute-to-attribute connection. A connection from an attribute of one part to an attribute of another part. When one attribute is updated, the other attribute is updated automatically.

See also *connection*.

attribute-to-member function connection. A connection from an attribute of a part to a member function. When the attribute undergoes a state change, the member function is called.

See also *connection*.

B

base class. A class from which other classes or parts are derived. A base class may itself be derived from another base class.

See also *abstract class*.

behavior. The set of external characteristics that an object exhibits.

C

caller. An object that sends a member function call to another object.

Contrast with *receiver*.

category. In the Composition Editor, a selectable grouping of parts represented by an icon in the leftmost column. Selecting a category displays the parts belonging to that category in the next column.

See also *parts palette*.

class. An aggregate that can contain functions, types, and user-defined operators, in addition to data. Classes can be defined hierarchically, allowing one class to be an expansion of another, and can restrict access to its members.

Class Editor. The editor used to specify the names of files that Visual Builder writes to when the user generates default code. This editor can also be used to do the following:

- ❏ Enter a description of the part
- ❏ Specify a different .vbb file in which to store the part
- ❏ See the name of the part's base class
- ❏ Modify the part's default constructor
- ❏ Enter additional constructor and destructor code
- ❏ Specify a .lib file for the part
- ❏ Specify a resource DLL and ID to assign an icon to the part
- ❏ Specify other files to be included when the application is built.

Compare to *Composition Editor* and *Part Interface Editor*.

class hierarchy. A tree-like structure showing relationships among object classes. It places one abstract class at the top (a base class) and one or more layers of less abstract classes below it.

class library. A collection of classes.

class member function. See *member function*.

client area object. An intermediate window between a frame window (IFrameWindow) and its controls and other child windows.

client object. An object that requests services from other objects.

collection. A set of features in which each feature is an object.

Common User Access (CUA). An IBM architecture for designing graphical user interfaces by use of a set of standard components and terminology.

composite part. A part that is composed of a part and one or more subparts. A composite part can contain visual parts, nonvisual parts, or both.

See also *nonvisual part, part, subpart,* and *visual part*.

Composition Editor. A view that is used to build a graphical user interface and to make connections between parts.

Compare to *Class Editor* and *Part Interface Editor*.

concrete class. A subclass of an abstract class that is a specialization of the abstract class.

connection. A formal, explicit relationship between parts. Making connections is the basic technique for building any visual application because that defines the way in which parts communicate with one another. The visual builder generates the code that then implements these connections.

See also *attribute-to-action connection, attribute-to-attribute connection, attribute-to-member function connection, custom logic connection, event-to-action connection, event-to-attribute connection,* and *event-to-member function connection,* and *parameter connection.*

const. An attribute of a data object that declares that the object cannot be changed.

construction from parts. A software development technology in which applications are assembled from existing and reusable software components, known as parts.

constructor. A special class member function that has the same name as the class and is used to construct and possibly initialize class objects.

CUA. See *Common User Access.*

cursored emphasis. The appellation of a choice when the selection cursor is on that choice.

custom logic connection. A connection that causes customized C or C++ code to be run. This connection can be triggered either when an attribute's value changes or an event occurs.

D

data abstraction. A data type with a private representation and a public set of operations. The C++ language uses the concept of classes to implement data abstraction.

data member. Private data that belongs to a given object and is hidden from direct access by all other objects. Data members can only be accessed by the member functions of the defining class and its subclasses.

data model. A combination of the base classes and parts shipped with the product and the classes and parts a user saves and creates. They are saved in a file named vbbase.vbb.

data object. A storage area used to hold a value.

declaration. A description that makes an external object or function available to a function or a block.

DEF file. See *module definition file.*

derivation. The creation of a new or abstract class from an existing or base class.

destructor. A special class member function that has the same name as the class and is used to destroy class objects.

DLL. See *dynamic link library.*

dynamic link library (DLL). In OS/2, a library containing data and code objects that can be used by programs or applications during loading or at run time. Although they are not part of the program's executable (.exe) file, they are sometimes required for an .exe file to run properly.

E

encapsulation. The hiding of a software object's internal representation. The object provides an interface that queries and manipulates the data without exposing its underlying structure.

event. A specification of a notification from a part.

Compare to *action, attribute,* and *part event.*

event-to-action connection. A connection that causes an action to be performed when an event occurs.

See also *connection.*

event-to-attribute connection. A connection that changes the value of an attribute when a certain event occurs.

See also *connection*.

event-to-member function connection. A connection from an event of a part to a member function. When the connected event occurs, the member function is executed.

See also *connection*.

expansion area. The section of a multicell canvas between the current cell grid and the outer edge of the canvas. Visually, this area is bounded by the rightmost column gridline and the bottommost row gridline.

F

feature. (1) A major component of a software product that can be installed separately. (2) In Visual Builder, an action, attribute, or event that is available from a part's part interface and that other parts can connect to.

full attribute. An attribute that has all of the behaviors and characteristics that an attribute can have: a data member, a get member function, a set member function, and an event identifier.

free-form surface. The large open area of the Composition Editor window. The free-form surface holds the visual parts contained in the views a user builds and representations of the nonvisual parts (models) that an application includes.

G

graphical user interface (GUI). A type of interface that enables users to communicate with a program by manipulating graphical features, rather than by entering commands. Typically, a graphical user interface includes a combination of graphics, pointing devices, menu bars and other menus, overlapping windows, and icons.

GUI. See *graphical user interface*.

H

handles. Small squares that appear on the corners of a selected visual part in the visual builder. Handles are used to resize parts.

Compare to *primary selection*.

header file. A file that contains system-defined control information that precedes user data.

I

inheritance. (1) A mechanism by which an object class can use the attributes, relationships, and member functions defined in more abstract classes related to it (its base classes). (2) An object-oriented programming technique that allows one to use existing classes as bases for creating other classes.

instance. Synonym for *object*, a particular instantiation of a data type.

L

legacy code. Existing code that a user might have. Legacy applications often have character-based, nongraphical user interfaces; usually they are written in a non-object-oriented language, such as C or COBOL.

loaded. The state of the mouse pointer between the time one selects a part from the parts palette and deposits the part on the free-form surface.

M

main part. The part that users see when they start an application. This is the part from which the main() function C++ code for the application is generated.

The main part is a special kind of composite part.

See also *part* and *subpart*.

member. (1) A data object in a structure or a union. (2) In C++, classes and structures can also contain functions and types as members.

member function. An operator or function that is declared as a member of a class. A member function has access to the private and protected data members and member functions of objects of its class.

member function call. A communication from one object to another that requests the receiving object to execute a member function.

A member function call consists of a member function name that indicates the requested member function and the arguments to be used in executing the member function. The member function call always returns some object to the requesting object as the result of performing the member function.

Synonym for *message*.

member function name. The component of a member function call that specifies the requested operation.

message. A request from one object that the receiving object implement a member function. Because data is encapsulated and not directly accessible, a message is the only way to send data from one object to another. Each message specifies the name of the receiving object, the member function to be implemented, and any arguments the member function needs for implementation.

Synonym for *member function call*.

model. A nonvisual part that represents the state and behavior of an object, such as a customer or an account.

Contrast with *view*.

module definition file. A file that describes the code segments within a load module.

Synonym for *DEF file*.

N

nested class. A class defined within the scope of another class.

nonvisual part. A part that has no visual representation at run time. A nonvisual part typically represents some real-world object that exists in the business environment.

Compare to *model*. Contrast with *view* and *visual part*.

no-event attribute. An attribute that does not have an event identifier.

no-set attribute. An attribute that does not have a set member function.

notebook part. A visual part that resembles a bound notebook containing pages separated into sections by tabbed divider pages. A user can turn the pages of a notebook or select the tabs to move from one section to another.

O

object. (1) A computer representation of something that a user can work with to perform a task. An object can appear as text or an icon. (2) A collection of data and member functions that operate on that data, which together represent a logical entity in the system. In object-oriented programming, objects are grouped into classes that share common data definitions and member functions. Each object in the class is said to be an instance of the class. (3) An instance of an object class consisting of attributes, a data structure, and operational member functions. It can represent a person, place, thing, event, or concept. Each instance has the same properties, attributes, and member functions as other instances of the object class, though it has unique values assigned to its attributes.

object class. A template for defining the attributes and member functions of an object. An object class can contain other object classes. An individual representation of an object class is called an object.

object factory. A nonvisual part capable of dynamically creating new instances of a specified part. For example, during the execution of an application, an object factory can create instances of a new class to collect the data being generated.

object-oriented programming. A programming approach based on the concepts of data abstraction and inheritance. Unlike procedural programming techniques, object-oriented programming concentrates on those data objects that constitute the problem and how they are manipulated, not on how something is accomplished.

observer. An object that receives notification from a notifier object.

operation. A member function or service that can be requested of an object.

overloading. An object-oriented programming technique that allows redefinition of functions and most standard C++ operators when the functions and operators are used with class types.

P

palette. See *parts palette*.

parameter connection. A connection that satisfies a parameter of an action or member function by supplying either an attribute's value or the return value of an action, member function, or custom logic. The parameter is always the source of the connection.

See also *connection*.

parent class. The class from which another part or class inherits data, member functions, or both.

part. A self-contained software object with a standardized public interface, consisting of a set of external features that allow the part to interact with other parts. A part is implemented as a class that supports the INotifier protocol and has a part interface defined.

The parts on the palette can be used as templates to create instances or objects.

part event. A representation of a change that occurs to a part. The events on a part's interface enable other interested parts to receive notification when something about the part changes. For example, a push button generates an event signaling that it has been clicked, which might cause another part to display a window.

part event ID. The name of a part static-data member used to identify the notification that is being signaled.

part interface. A set of external features that allows a part to interact with other parts. A part's interface is made up of three characteristics: attributes, actions, and events.

Part Interface Editor. An editor that the application developer uses to create and modify attributes, actions, and events, which together make up the interface of a part.

Compare to *Class Editor* and *Composition Editor*.

parts palette. A palette control that holds a collection of visual and nonvisual parts used in building additional parts for an application. The parts palette is organized into *categories*. Application developers can add parts to the palette for use in defining applications or other parts.

preferred features. A subset of the part's features that appear in a pop-up connection menu. Generally, they are the features used most often.

primary selection. In the Composition Editor, the part used as a base for an action that affects several parts. For example, an alignment tool will align all selected parts with the primary selection. Primary selection is indicated by closed (solid) selection handles, whereas the other selected parts have open selection handles.

See also *selection handles*.

promote features. Make features of a subpart available to be used for making connections. This applies to subparts that are to be included in other parts, for example, a subpart consisting of three push buttons on a canvas. If this example subpart is placed in a frame window, the features of the push buttons would have to be promoted to make them available from within the frame window.

private. Pertaining to a class member that is accessible only to member functions and friends of that class.

process. A program running under OS/2, along with the resources associated with it (memory, threads, file system resources, and so on).

program. (1) One or more files containing a set of instructions conforming to a particular programming language syntax. (2) A self-contained, executable module. Multiple copies of the same program can be run in different processes.

protected. Pertaining to a class member that is only accessible to member functions and friends of that class, or to member functions and friends of classes derived from that class.

prototype. A function declaration or definition that includes both the return type of the function and the types of its arguments.

primitive part. A basic building block of other parts. A primitive part can be relatively complex in terms of the function it provides.

process. A collection of code, data, and other system resources, including at least one thread of execution, that performs a data processing task.

property. A unique characteristic of a part.

pure virtual function. A virtual function that has a function definition of = 0;.

R

receiver. The object that receives a member function call.

Contrast with *caller*.

resource file. A file that contains data used by an application, such as text strings and icons.

S

selection handles. In the Composition Editor, small squares that appear on the corners of a selected visual part. Selection handles are used to resize parts.

See also *primary selection*.

server. A computer that provides services to multiple users or workstations in a network; for example, a file server, a print server, or a mail server.

service. A specific behavior that an object is responsible for exhibiting.

settings view. A view of a part that provides a way to display and set the attributes and options associated with the part.

sticky. In the Composition Editor, the mode that enables an application developer to add multiple parts of the same class (for example, three push buttons) without going back and forth between the parts palette and the free-form surface.

structure. A construct that contains an ordered group of data objects. Unlike an array, the data objects within a structure can have varied data types.

subpart. A part that is used to create another part.

See also *nonvisual part, part,* and *visual part*.

superclass. See *abstract class* and *base class*.

T

tear-off attribute. An attribute that an application developer has exposed to work with as though it were a stand-alone part.

template. A family of classes or functions with variable types.

thread. A unit of execution within a process.

toolbar. The strip of icons along the top of the free-form surface. The toolbar contains tools to help an application developer construct composite parts.

U

UI. See *user interface*.

unloaded. The state of the mouse pointer before a user selects a part from the parts palette and after the user deposits a part on the free-form surface. In addition, a user can unload the mouse pointer by pressing the Esc key.

user interface (UI). (1) The hardware, software, or both that enables a user to interact with a computer. (2) The term *user interface* normally refers to the visual presentation and its underlying software with which a user interacts.

V

variable. (1) A storage place within an object for a data feature. The data feature is an object, such as number or date, stored as an attribute of the containing object. (2) A part that receives an identity at run time. A variable by itself contains no data or program logic; it must be connected such that it receives run-time identity from a part elsewhere in the application.

view. (1) A visual part, such as a window, push button, or entry field. (2) A visual representation that can display and change the underlying model objects of an application. Views are both the end result of developing an application and the basic unit of composition of user interfaces.

Compare to *visual part*. Contrast with *model*.

virtual function. A function of a class that is declared with the keyword virtual. The implementation that is executed when a program makes a call to a virtual function depends on the type of the object for which it is called. This is determined at run time.

visual part. A part that has a visual representation at run time. Visual parts, such as windows, push buttons, and entry fields, make up the user interface of an application.

Compare to *view*. Contrast with *nonvisual part*.

visual programming tool. A tool that provides a means for specifying programs graphically. Application programmers write applications by manipulating graphical representations of components.

W

white space. Space characters, tab characters, form-feed characters, and new-line characters.

window. (1) A rectangular area of the screen with visible boundaries in which information is displayed. Windows can overlap on the screen, giving it the appearance of one window being on top of another. (2) In the Composition Editor, a part that can be used as a container for other visual parts, such as push buttons.

List of Abbreviations

APA	all points addressable
CAD	computer-aided design
CORBA	Common Object Request Broker Architecture
CRC	class-responsibility-collaborator
DDE	dynamic data exchange
DLL	dynamic link library
DSOM	Distributed System Object Model
DTS	Direct-to-SOM
FAT	File Allocation Table
GUI	graphical user interface
HPFS	high-performance file system
IBM	International Business Machines Corporation
IDE	integrated development environment
IDL	interface definition language
ITSO	International Technical Support Organization
LAN	local area network
LPEX	Live Parsing EXtensible editor
MMPM/2	Multimedia Presentation Manager/2
NLS	National Language Support
OMG	Object Management Group
OMT	object modeling technique
OOA	object-oriented analysis
OOD	object-oriented design
OOSE	object-oriented software engineering
PM	Presentation Manager
RDD	responsibility-driven design
SOM	System Object Model
SQL	Structured Query Language
UPM	user profile management
VBB	Visual Builder binary
VBE	Visual Builder export
VMT	visual modeling technique
WWW	World Wide Web

Index

A

abstraction 8, 65, 83
ABTICONS.DLL file 179, 181, 198
accelerator key 314
access specifier 260, 263
actor 69–74
application
    analysis 5, 13, 14, 15, 61, 62, 63, 67, 69,
        77, 82, 83, 89, 92
    design 5, 12–15, 62, 82–90, 108, 227,
        235, 245, 267
    implementation 12–15, 43, 63, 64, 81–
        83, 87, 89, 90, 100, 105, 215, 267
    problem domain 12, 13, 14, 63, 65, 69,
        74, 87
    requirement specification 64, 68, 73, 94,
        318
    tuning 19, 46, 85
association
    multiplicity 91
attribute
    derived 90, 91, 214, 215, 354
    tearing off 244, 310, 316, 317, 318

B

BIND 142
Boolean part, See IVBBooleanPart
browser
    database 47, 50, 332
    interacting with Visual Builder 332
    QuickBrowse 47, 50, 332
business object 213, 214
business part xxxi, 16, 92, 105

C

canvas
    minimum size 149, 150
    See also IMultiCellCanvas, ISetCanvas,
        ICanvas
category
    Buttons 168, 193, 202
    Composers 152, 159, 161, 168
    Data entry 151, 162, 165, 168, 181
    Frame extensions 174, 232, 254
    Lists 140, 152, 184, 186
    Models 238, 244, 253, 272
    Other 229, 238, 247, 253, 320
CD-ROM xxxiii, 143, 144, 146, 342
check box 189
class
    abstract class 39
    ancestor/base class 9, 10
    attribute 7, 8, 9
    delete 282
    derived class 9, 49
    instance 8, 11, 36, 96, 213
    method 28, 36, 90, 93
Class Editor 35, 57, 154, 155, 172, 175, 178,
    182, 188, 192, 196, 199, 202, 205, 208, 211,
    217, 251, 258, 282, 333, 334
class interface part
    and notification framework 214
    See also IDate, ITime
class-responsibility-collaborator card, See
    CRC card
client/server 83
code generation file 35, 36, 155, 172, 175,
    178, 182, 188, 196, 199, 202, 205, 208, 211,
    333
code trace 40, 54, 259
coding xxix, xxxii, 11, 20, 62, 85
collaborator 12, 75, 76, 86, 236
collection combination list box, See
    ICollectionViewComboBox
collection list box, See ICollectionViewList-
    Box
combination list box, See IComboBox
compiler
    code optimization 42
    locales support 42
    memory management 41, 42, 51
    precompiled headers 42
composite part 27, 28, 32, 34, 57, 106, 141,
    144, 172, 175, 243, 250, 318
Composition Editor
    code generation 35
    creating a nonvisual part 278, 279
    free-form surface 16, 32
    palette 32, 140, 141, 147, 151, 186, 232,
        238, 272, 368
    toolbar 32
CONFIG.SYS file 54, 111, 119, 121, 125,
    180, 319
connection
    attribute-to-attribute 29, 214, 220, 236,
        238, 240, 244, 254, 256, 264, 269, 318,
        326, 329

G

generalization 9
graphic push button 200
graphical user interface, See GUI
group box, See IGroupBox
GUI prototype 64, 70, 84, 90

H

handler
    IHandler 221, 225
    IKeyboardHandler 222
    UpperCaseKbdHandler 214, 222, 223, 224
    using 221, 225
help
    context-sensitive help 38, 172, 238, 248, 318, 319
    general help 314
High Performance File System, See HPFS
HPFS 107, 132

I

ICanvas 148, 159, 183, 325, 337
ICC, See compiler
ICheckBox 189
ICLUI 121, 122
ICollectionViewComboBox 189, 191
ICollectionViewListBox 140, 190, 191
IComboBox 147, 151, 152, 162
icon 179
IContainerColumn 185
ICONV 42
ICSBRS, See browser
ICSDATA, See Data Access Builder
ICSPERF, See Performance Analyzer
IC_TRACE_DEVELOP 121
IDatastore 90, 137, 139, 142, 203
IDate 249, 250, 306
IDE, See WorkFrame/2
IDSConnectCanvas 137
IEEE POSIX P1003.2 42
IEntryField 147, 151, 162, 168, 170, 189, 190, 194, 204, 207, 324, 325, 327
IFrameWindow 138, 148, 172, 183, 189, 200, 263, 264, 330
IGraphicPushButton 200
IGroupBox 168, 170
IHelpWindow

IIConControl 179
IInfoArea 172, 174, 177, 195, 202, 209
ILINK 45, 46
IMenu 232, 233, 270, 314
IMenuItem 232, 270, 314
IMenuSeparator 232, 314
IMessageBox
    message severity 293
    showing an exception 259, 329
    tracing the program flow 292
IMMDigitalVideo 230, 266
IMMPlayerPanel 166, 167, 168, 231
implementation phase 15, 16, 215, 267
import file, See VBE file
IMultiCellCanvas 147, 148, 153, 179, 183, 209
IMultiLineEdit 165
info area, See IInfoArea
inheritance 8, 9, 15, 17, 25, 47, 48, 57, 80, 85, 123, 124, 128
INoteBook 157
INotifier 324, 326
installing the application 341
instance, See class and part instance
integrated development environment, See WorkFrame/2
Internet xxxiii
INumericSpinButton 162
IObserver 324, 325, 326, 337
IPersistentObject 135
IPF compiler 318
IPOManager 136
IProfile 206, 299, 306
IPushButton 168, 189, 337
ISetCanvas 150, 160, 189, 209
IStandardNotifier 214, 324, 331
IStaticText 151, 161, 167, 170, 181, 198, 202, 204, 209, 211, 325
IStringGenerator 191
iterative technique 13, 90, 93
ITime 249, 250
ITitle 254, 264
IVBBooleanPart
    enabling control 260, 284
    used with IMessageBox 295, 296
IVBContainerControl 182, 189
IVBFactory
    create method of 272
    creating part dynamically 272, 287
IVBFileDialog 228
IVBFlyText
    bubble help 247, 316
    using info area 238, 247, 248
IVBLongPart 260
IVBStringPart 260, 286

IViewPort 159
IVSequence 291
IWF_DEFAULT_PROJECT 111

K

key identifier 133, 269
key identifier, See data identifier under Data
　Access Builder part
keyboard handler, See handler

L

language 3–7, 10, 15, 21, 32, 36, 40, 41, 43,
　85
legacy code 85, 214, 334
LIBPATH 125, 179
linker, See ILINK
LOCALDEF 42
long part, See IVBLongPart
LPEX editor 40, 218

M

menu, See IMenu, IMenuItem, IMenu-
　Separator
module definition, See DEF file
multicell canvas, See IMultiCellCanvas
multimedia, See IMMDigitalVideo
multiple line edit control, See IMultiLine-
　Edit

N

naming convention 124, 144, 333
nonvisual part
　connecting to a visual part 233
notification framework
　dispatchNotificationEvent method 327,
　　339
　enableNotification method 326
　handleNotificationFor method 326, 338
　notification event 324, 338, 339
　notifier 214, 323, 324, 326, 329, 330,
　　331, 336
　notifyObservers method 220, 282, 327,
　　330, 331, 336, 337

observer 220, 323, 324, 325, 326, 327,
　329, 330, 337, 339
notifier, See IStandardNotifier
numeric spin button, See INumericSpin-
　Button

O

object
　attribute 6, 8
　business object 92, 213, 214
　design 15, 83, 84, 89
　finding 73
　function 6–8, 10
　interface 6–8, 10, 224, 324, 331, 332,
　　335
　semantic object 15
　technical object 213
Object Modeling Technique, See OMT
object-oriented analysis, See OOA
object-oriented design, See OOD
object-oriented method, See OMT, OOSE,
　RDD, VMT
Object-Oriented Software Engineering, See
　OOSE
observer, See IObserver
OMT
　class dictionary 74, 75, 84, 353
　dynamic model 12, 227
　notation 343
　static model 12
OOA
　building use case 68
　class dictionary 84
　deliverable 63, 82, 84
　user interface prototype 64, 70, 71, 84,
　　90
OOD
　deliverable 84
　object design 15, 83, 84, 89
　system design 15, 83–85
OOSE
　use case 13
Open Class Library
　Application Support Class Library 39
　Collection Class Library 32, 39
　Data Access Builder Class Library 39
　Standard Class Libraries 40, 250
　User Interface Class Library 32, 38, 118

P

part
  abstract class 324, 326
  as observer 220, 323–329, 330, 337, 339
  asString method 190, 249, 250
  attribute 214, 220, 225, 316
  browsing 301
  clone 272
  constructor 35, 141, 272
  dictionary 353
  feature source code 217, 334
  generating source code 27, 36, 217, 250, 260, 334
  import 136, 224, 323, 332, 333, 335
  initialization 325, 326, 330
  instance 243, 251, 271–276, 287, 291, 302, 311, 315, 328
  interface 28, 29, 30, 32, 36, 224, 324, 331, 332, 335
  method 215–220, 250–261, 263, 267, 269, 272, 319, 332, 333
  naming convention 124, 144, 333
  prefix 250, 264, 286, 326
  promoting a feature 34, 154, 156, 171, 204, 244, 246, 247, 265, 318, 337
  saving 282, 334
  tabbing and depth order 152, 153, 231
Part Interface Editor
  creating actions 33
  creating attributes 33, 216
  creating events 34
  promoting features 34
  selecting preferred features 32, 35
  user-defined files 217, 251, 258, 260, 263, 282, 287
pattern 55, 65, 72
Performance Analyzer 19, 54
persistent data 92, 108
persistent object, See IPersistentObject
PM 27, 38, 53, 95, 221, 228, 318
polymorphism 10, 85
pop-up menu 232
portability 37, 38, 42, 107
Presentation Manager, See PM
primitive part 27, 106
problem domain 12, 13, 14, 63, 65, 69, 74, 87
profile
  system profile 305
  user profile 305
profile, See IProfile
proffer, See Performance Analyzer
project
  action 21

catalog 23, 24
composite 25
customization 20
element 20
inheritance 25
installation script 23
migration 27
source 22
target 20, 22
template 23
Project Smarts 23
promoted feature
public interface 338
push button, See IPushButton

R

RDD 12, 13
relationship
  use 271, 287
requirement specification 64, 68, 73, 94, 318
Responsibility-Driven Design, See RDD
reusability
  design consideration 235
  using variable part 236
REXX 21, 23, 24, 40, 41, 335
role 69–71

S

screen resolution 148, 149, 150, 179, 200
sequence, See IVSequence
set canvas, See ISetCanvas
SmartHouse 28, 30
SOM 36, 41, 43, 44, 47, 51, 128
source code xxxi, 20, 36, 40, 44, 47, 70, 93, 132, 191, 214, 215, 217, 330, 334, 357
specialization 9
SQL clause
  building 260
  in a parameter connection 267
  placeholder 260
SQLPREP 112, 114
standard canvas, See ICanvas
static model
  aggregation 15
  association 79, 80, 94, 102, 141, 156
  link 73, 77, 80, 81, 94–99, 102, 271, 283, 287
static text, See IStaticText
Sticky mark 151, 232

string generator, See IStringGenerator
string part, See IVBStringPart
subsystem 20, 23, 25, 47, 84, 85, 86, 90, 92,
   94, 108
System Object Model, See SOM

T

tabbing and depth order 152, 153, 231
tool box, See VBSAMPLES.VBB file
traceability 70, 89
transaction management 36, 213

U

use case 12, 68–71
User Interface Class Library

V

variable part
   and factory object 272
   tearing off an attribute 316
   using 243
VBBASE.VBB file 122, 259
VBDAX.VBB file 137, 146, 259
VBE file 136, 224, 335
VBMM.VBB file 146, 166, 230, 259
VBSAMPLE.VBB file 146, 259, 284, 286,
   301
viewport 159
views hierarchy 144
views, See visual part
Visual Builder concept 27
Visual Modeling Technique, See VMT
Visual part hierarchy 144
Visual Realty application 59, 66, 69, 74, 83,
   86, 88, 90, 91, 106, 125, 143, 206
VisualAge C++ 16, 89, 90
VisualAge Smalltalk 16
VMT
   roots 12
   visual programming 13

W

window
   modal 274, 277, 302, 304, 311, 315

modeless 289, 292
WorkFrame/2
   Build Smarts facility 26, 121
   concept 20
   integrated development
      environment 20
   MakeMake facility 20, 22, 26, 115
   Project Smarts facility 20, 23, 24, 110,
      115, 116
World Wide Web xxvii
wrapper 228, 300, 301

X

X/Open portability 42

LICENSE AGREEMENT AND LIMITED WARRANTY

READ THE FOLLOWING TERMS AND CONDITIONS CAREFULLY BEFORE OPENING THIS DISK PACKAGE. THIS LEGAL DOCUMENT IS AN AGREEMENT BETWEEN YOU AND PRENTICE-HALL, INC. (THE "COMPANY"). BY OPENING THIS SEALED DISK PACKAGE, YOU ARE AGREEING TO BE BOUND BY THESE TERMS AND CONDITIONS. IF YOU DO NOT AGREE WITH THESE TERMS AND CONDITIONS, DO NOT OPEN THE DISK PACKAGE. PROMPTLY RETURN THE UNOPENED DISK PACKAGE AND ALL ACCOMPANYING ITEMS TO THE PLACE YOU OBTAINED THEM FOR A FULL REFUND OF ANY SUMS YOU HAVE PAID.

1.   **GRANT OF LICENSE:** In consideration of your payment of the license fee, which is part of the price you paid for this product, and your agreement to abide by the terms and conditions of this Agreement, the Company grants to you a nonexclusive right to use and display the copy of the enclosed software program (hereinafter the "SOFTWARE") on a single computer (i.e., with a single CPU) at a single location so long as you comply with the terms of this Agreement. The Company reserves all rights not expressly granted to you under this Agreement.

2.   **OWNERSHIP OF SOFTWARE:** You own only the magnetic or physical media (the enclosed disks) on which the SOFTWARE is recorded or fixed, but the Company retains all the rights, title, and ownership to the SOFTWARE recorded on the original disk copy(ies) and all subsequent copies of the SOFT-WARE, regardless of the form or media on which the original or other copies may exist. This license is not a sale of the original SOFTWARE or any copy to you.

3.   **COPY RESTRICTIONS:** This SOFTWARE and the accompanying printed materials and user manual (the "Documentation") are the subject of copyright. You may not copy the Documentation or the SOFTWARE, except that you may make a single copy of the SOFTWARE for backup or archival purposes only. You may be held legally responsible for any copying or copyright infringement which is caused or encouraged by your failure to abide by the terms of this restriction.

4.   **USE RESTRICTIONS:** You may not network the SOFTWARE or otherwise use it on more than one computer or computer terminal at the same time. You may physically transfer the SOFTWARE from one computer to another provided that the SOFTWARE is used on only one computer at a time. You may not distribute copies of the SOFTWARE or Documentation to others. You may not reverse engineer, disassemble, decompile, modify, adapt, translate, or create derivative works based on the SOFTWARE or the Documentation without the prior written consent of the Company.

5.   **TRANSFER RESTRICTIONS:** The enclosed SOFTWARE is licensed only to you and may not be transferred to any one else without the prior written consent of the Company. Any unauthorized transfer of the SOFTWARE shall result in the immediate termination of this Agreement.

6.   **TERMINATION:** This license is effective until terminated. This license will terminate automatically without notice from the Company and become null and void if you fail to comply with any provisions or limitations of this license. Upon termination, you shall destroy the Documentation and all copies of the SOFTWARE. All provisions of this Agreement as to warranties, limitation of liability, remedies or damages, and our ownership rights shall survive termination.

7.   **MISCELLANEOUS:** This Agreement shall be construed in accordance with the laws of the United States of America and the State of New York and shall benefit the Company, its affiliates, and assignees.

8.   **LIMITED WARRANTY AND DISCLAIMER OF WARRANTY:** The Company warrants that the SOFTWARE, when properly used in accordance with the Documentation, will operate in substantial conformity with the description of the SOFTWARE set forth in the Documentation. The Company does not warrant that the SOFTWARE will meet your requirements or that the operation of the SOFTWARE will be

uninterrupted or error-free. The Company warrants that the media on which the SOFTWARE is delivered shall be free from defects in materials and workmanship under normal use for a period of thirty (30) days from the date of your purchase. Your only remedy and the Company's only obligation under these limited warranties is, at the Company's option, return of the warranted item for a refund of any amounts paid by you or replacement of the item. Any replacement of SOFTWARE or media under the warranties shall not extend the original warranty period. The limited warranty set forth above shall not apply to any SOFTWARE which the Company determines in good faith has been subject to misuse, neglect, improper installation, repair, alteration, or damage by you. EXCEPT FOR THE EXPRESSED WARRANTIES SET FORTH ABOVE, THE COMPANY DISCLAIMS ALL WARRANTIES, EXPRESS OR IMPLIED, INCLUDING WITHOUT LIMITATION, THE IMPLIED WARRANTIES OF MERCHANTABILITY AND FITNESS FOR A PAR-TICULAR PURPOSE. EXCEPT FOR THE EXPRESS WARRANTY SET FORTH ABOVE, THE COM-PANY DOES NOT WARRANT, GUARANTEE, OR MAKE ANY REPRESENTATION REGARDING THE USE OR THE RESULTS OF THE USE OF THE SOFTWARE IN TERMS OF ITS CORRECTNESS, ACCURACY, RELIABILITY, CURRENTNESS, OR OTHERWISE.

IN NO EVENT, SHALL THE COMPANY OR ITS EMPLOYEES, AGENTS, SUPPLIERS, OR CONTRACTORS BE LIABLE FOR ANY INCIDENTAL, INDIRECT, SPECIAL, OR CONSEQUEN-TIAL DAMAGES ARISING OUT OF OR IN CONNECTION WITH THE LICENSE GRANTED UNDER THIS AGREEMENT, OR FOR LOSS OF USE, LOSS OF DATA, LOSS OF INCOME OR PROFIT, OR OTHER LOSSES, SUSTAINED AS A RESULT OF INJURY TO ANY PERSON, OR LOSS OF OR DAMAGE TO PROPERTY, OR CLAIMS OF THIRD PARTIES, EVEN IF THE COMPANY OR AN AUTHORIZED REPRESENTATIVE OF THE COMPANY HAS BEEN ADVISED OF THE POSSIBIL-ITY OF SUCH DAMAGES. IN NO EVENT SHALL LIABILITY OF THE COMPANY FOR DAMAGES WITH RESPECT TO THE SOFTWARE EXCEED THE AMOUNTS ACTUALLY PAID BY YOU, IF ANY, FOR THE SOFTWARE.

SOME JURISDICTIONS DO NOT ALLOW THE LIMITATION OF IMPLIED WARRAN-TIES OR LIABILITY FOR INCIDENTAL, INDIRECT, SPECIAL, OR CONSEQUENTIAL DAMAGES, SO THE ABOVE LIMITATIONS MAY NOT ALWAYS APPLY. THE WARRANTIES IN THIS AGREE-MENT GIVE YOU SPECIFIC LEGAL RIGHTS AND YOU MAY ALSO HAVE OTHER RIGHTS WHICH VARY IN ACCORDANCE WITH LOCAL LAW.

ACKNOWLEDGMENT

YOU ACKNOWLEDGE THAT YOU HAVE READ THIS AGREEMENT, UNDERSTAND IT, AND AGREE TO BE BOUND BY ITS TERMS AND CONDITIONS. YOU ALSO AGREE THAT THIS AGREEMENT IS THE COMPLETE AND EXCLUSIVE STATEMENT OF THE AGREEMENT BETWEEN YOU AND THE COMPANY AND SUPERSEDES ALL PROPOSALS OR PRIOR AGREE-MENTS, ORAL, OR WRITTEN, AND ANY OTHER COMMUNICATIONS BETWEEN YOU AND THE COMPANY OR ANY REPRESENTATIVE OF THE COMPANY RELATING TO THE SUBJECT MAT-TER OF THIS AGREEMENT.

Should you have any questions concerning this Agreement or if you wish to contact the Company for any reason, please contact in writing at the address below or call the at the telephone number provided.

PTR Customer Service
Prentice Hall PTR
One Lake Street
Upper Saddle River, New Jersey 07458
Telephone: 201-236-7105

IBM EVALUATION AGREEMENT

This is a no charge Evaluation License ("License") between you and International Business Machines Corporation ("IBM") for the evaluation of IBM's software and related documentation. ("Program")

IBM grants you a non-exclusive, non-transferable license to the Program only to enable you to evaluate the potential usefulness of the Program to you. You may not use the Program for any other purpose and you may not distribute any part of it, either alone or with any of your software products.

IBM retains ownership of the Program and any copies you make of it. You may use the Program on one (1) machine only.

You may not decompile, disassemble or otherwise attempt to translate or seek to gain access to the Program's source code.

The term of your License will be from the date of first installation of the Program, and will terminate 60 days later, unless otherwise specified. THE PROGRAM WILL STOP FUNCTIONING WHEN THE LICENSE TERM EXPIRES. You should therefore take precautions to avoid any loss of data that might result. You must destroy and/or delete all copies you have made of the Program within ten (10) days of the expiry of your License.

If you are interested in continuing to use the Program after the end of your License, you must place an order for a full license to the Program and pay the applicable license fee. In that event, your use of the Program will be governed by the provisions of the applicable IBM license for the Program.

IBM accepts no liability for damages you may suffer as a result of your use of the Program. In no event will IBM be liable for any indirect, special or consequential damages, even if IBM has been advised of the possibility of their occurrence.

YOU UNDERSTAND THAT THE PROGRAM IS BEING PROVIDED TO YOU "AS IS", WITHOUT ANY WARRANTIES (EXPRESS OR IMPLIED) WHATSOEVER, INCLUDING BUT NOT LIMITED TO ANY IMPLIED WARRANTIES OF MERCHANTABILITY, QUALITY, PERFORMANCE OR FITNESS FOR ANY PARTICULAR PURPOSE. Some jurisdictions do not allow the exclusion or limitation of warranties or consequential or incidental damages, so the above may not apply to you.

IBM may terminate your License at any time if you are in breach of any of its terms.

This License will be governed by and interpreted in accordance with the laws of the State of New York.

This License is the only understanding and agreement we have for your use of the Program. It supersedes all other communications, understandings or agreements we may have had prior to this License.

Software Requirements

- OS/2 V2.11 or higher (OS/2 Warp recommended)
- To use Data Access Builder, DB2/2 V1.2 or higher
  (DB2V2 trial version provided on the CDROM)

Hardware Requirements

- Processor: 386 minimum (486 or higher strongly recommended)
  (for 386 machines, a 387 coprocessor is highly recommended
  for floating-point operations)
- Display: VGA minimum (SVGA recommended)
- RAM: C development – 8M minimum, 12M recommended
  C++ development – 12M minimum, 16M recommended
  visual C++ development – 16M minimum, 24M recommended
- Disk Space: 91MB for compiler and tools
  102MB for samples and online information
  30MB for swap space (minimum)

Software Installation

- Start OS/2
- Open an OS/2 session
- Switch to CD-ROM drive
- Type Install
- Press ENTER